Praise for *The Full Catastrophe*

For those who are willing to learn, to grow, to look at themselves and change where necessary, astrology can be extremely valuable, even in its simplified, sun-sign form. I'd like to say that those amazing coincidences between Karen's life and the readings I gave are entirely proof of astrology's veracity.

—**Jonathan Cainer**, Astrologer, *Daily Mail*

Captivating and often profound, Karen E. Lee's *The Full Catastrophe* eloquently expresses the complex journey of her marriage to a larger-than-life, charming, yet violent man who dies before she's ready to let him go. Wise and full of gorgeous detail, this is a brave, self-aware, and compulsively readable memoir. In it, Lee has done something rare: she's told her story with an unflinching eye to her own accountability and with a depth of hard-earned wisdom.

—**Lauren Carter**, author of *Swarm*

The Full Catastrophe conveys the story of a person who overcame serious adversity of an invisible kind, and was not only able to recover but also to gain from the ordeal. Through the lines of this book the authentic voice emerges of the unutterable suffering, of the resilience, and of the inspirational transformation. A unique document of the indomitable human spirit.

—**Renos K. Papadopoulos**, PhD, Jungian Analyst,
Professor, University of Essex, The Tavistock Clinic, London

A beautifully written, frank, thought-provoking portrayal of a difficult, and at times harrowing, journey through uncertainty, fear, and abuse. This honest and courageous self-reflection will lead readers to rethink and reexamine many of their assumptions and beliefs about their own life stories.

—**Dr. N. Ogden**, PhD, Professor, Department of Psychology,
Mount Royal University, Calgary, Canada

Karen E. Lee's *The Full Catastrophe* is at once insightful, heartbreaking, and personal. It is as sad as it is important to read. Lee gives full attention to the cold and shadowed world of domestic abuse—a world affecting successful, well-educated professionals. It is a world that is often well hidden. As a physician, Lee's account is a reminder of the firmest possible kind that I must be diligent to look for and be open to the reality of domestic abuse—no matter how unlikely or obscured. Abuse must be discussed openly if we are ever to find it out and eradicate it. I hope to be a better physician for having read Lee's work.

—**Dr. Brendan JW Miles MD, MPA, CCFP**,
Family Physician, Clinical Lecturer,
University of Calgary, Faculty of Medicine

Karen E. Lee has laid bare the isolating reality of living in an abusive relationship. Her experience of feeling conflicted about wanting a loving connection with Duncan while at the same time recognizing the unhealthy nature of her relationship is a common experience for women in abusive relationships. This book also sheds light on 'upscale domestic violence'—an insidious, misunderstood, and often not talked about situation that happens to women who appear to have financial and social resources but in fact are often more isolated because of the desire to be private and 'bear their shame in silence.' I applaud and am grateful to Lee for writing this book and sharing her experience. It will help other women experiencing domestic violence and will help all of us to support victims of domestic violence—whatever their socioeconomic background.

—**Andrea Silverstone**, Executive Director, Peer Support
Services for Abused Women (PSSAW), Calgary, Alberta

The Full Catastrophe

The Full
Catastrophe

a memoir

Karen Lee

SHE WRITES PRESS

Published 2016
Printed in the United States of America
ISBN: 978-1-63152-024-2
Library of Congress Control Number: 2015956576

For information, address:
She Writes Press
1563 Solano Ave #546
Berkeley, CA 94707

She Writes Press is a division of SparkPoint Studio, LLC.

Contents

The Funeral

I stood up from my pew and walked to the podium of the large chapel at Tickford Abbey, just north of where we lived in Buckinghamshire County, England. Dreamlike, I heard my voice carry out over the heads of the people who'd come to my husband, Duncan's, funeral.

"Stop all the clocks, cut off the telephone,
Prevent the dog from barking with a juicy bone,"

Duncan and I had heard this poem in the movie *Four Weddings and a Funeral*, and for some reason it had resonated for him. He'd asked me to recite this poem if he ever died. Because he never really believed he would ever die.

Duncan had been on the faculty of Brookton University, one of the UK's highest-rated universities, so I'd dressed carefully, putting on a black, businesslike, wool crepe suit, the starkness of which was somewhat relieved by my black blouse dotted with small embroidered pink flowers. I had to look appropriate, solemn. Sometimes that was difficult because, at fifty, I was really too old for the freckles, gifts from my Irish ancestors, sprinkled all over my face. The steeliness people thought they saw in me was in direct contrast to how fragile I felt most of the time. Usually I wore a huge smile, one that Duncan had always told me could light up a room. But not this morning.

From the front of the chapel, I could see that all the pews were occupied. The area to the rear of the chapel, visible through glass panels, was standing room only, filled with those who had come too late to get a seat. At the front sat my mother, my youngest son, Jamie,

1

Duncan's son, Greg, and Duncan's best friend, Bob, all of whom had flown in from Canada as soon as they'd heard about Duncan.

Four days before, a driver from the university had taken me to Heathrow to meet my mother. My father, in his need to protect himself, had found a way to justify not coming. As we drove up the M1, I screamed out to her, "What am I going to do now?"

My mother reached out with stiff arms to embrace me, whispering, "Oh, Karen."

When we drove into my street, we looked in amazement at the roof of Duncan's and my house. Lined up along the peak were at least one hundred crows, just sitting, waiting. None were visible on any other house.

Sitting in the front pew next to my family were Duncan's university department head, Frederick, and his wife, both friends and colleagues. As his brother had travelled to see him from Canada earlier in the summer, he didn't make the return trip for the funeral.

I continued to read.

"Silence the pianos and with muffled drum
Bring out the coffin, let the mourners come."

The dark, polished wood coffin sat on a stand, closed, the lid covering the shadow of the man Duncan had become from the cancer. The day after he died, I picked it out at the funeral home where his body had been taken. The small matching casket was waiting for his ashes.

The coffin was covered with an extravagant arrangement of lilies and chrysanthemums sent by his brother in Toronto. Next to the flowers sat two framed photos of Duncan, both taken only one year before when we'd gone to Lebanon, the land of his mother's parents, to celebrate his fifty-eighth birthday. It was, after all, the side of himself that he felt proudest of and most closely resembled. I'd taken one photo as he sat on a camel in Palmyra, Syria, and the other as he stood next to ruins in Byblos, Lebanon. Smartly dressed in white trousers, a black shirt, and a jacket, he looked handsome and robust.

"Let aeroplanes circle moaning overhead

Scribbling on the sky the message 'He Is Dead'."

My practiced public speaking voice sounded weak and thin. My hands trembling ever so slightly, I continued reading. I had to do for him what he could no longer do for himself.

o o o

Tickford Abbey—in the village of Tickford, to the north of Brookton—is both a Benedictine convent and a small community of Catholic brothers. The original house was built in 1605. Though the chapel is much newer, it was built of the same golden sandstone.

Over to the right of the coffin sat the monks and brothers of the monastery, men Duncan had become close to. The Abbey had become a place of refuge for him in the last ten months of his life. Brother Joseph had explained to me that they never held funerals at the monastery for anyone except a member of the order, but for Duncan—well, he affected people that way.

"Put crepe bows round the white necks of the public doves,

Let the traffic policemen wear black cotton gloves."

Duncan had occupied space in life—physical space, psychological space, emotional space. With his double-breasted suits, Borsalino fedora, and polished Florentine shoes, he looked like a cross between a high-priced lawyer and a mobster. He only needed the raspy voice and Italian subtitles. When he was in the room you didn't notice anyone else. People would meet the two of us and only remember him. In New York City for seven days, we saw eight Broadway plays. He could get front row tickets to *Cats*, front table seats to *Sinatra*, and be mistaken for Burt Reynolds all in one day. He was a madman, a Renaissance man, and the most sincere man I had ever met. Now he took up such a small amount of space, lying beneath the lid of his coffin.

"He was my North, my South, my East and West,

My working week and my Sunday rest,"

I glanced down at the program brochure I'd prepared for the service as I continued reading the poem. The picture of Duncan taken at Byblos was on the cover, the poem by Auden on the inside. On the last page was a message from a gravestone beside St. Mary's Church in Crawley Church End, the village where we lived. The graveyard was only a short walk from our house and Duncan had spent time there when he was sick. He even considered being buried there.

One day I asked him, "What if I return to Canada to live after this is all over—would you still want to be buried here?"

"No," he replied, "I'd want to be in Canada too, in your family's plot in Ontario. I have no place like that, where all my family is buried together."

Duncan had envied that about me—that I know my family and want to be with them in life and in death.

While I kept his ashes with me for six years, I eventually took him home to Gananoque, on the shores of the Thousand Islands, to be buried with my father, my grandmother, grandfather, great-grand-parents, and other ancestors from Ireland—at least one representative from every generation since the first of my family got off the boat in the 1850s.

"My noon, my midnight, my talk, my song;
I thought that love would last forever: I was wrong."

o o o

One week before the funeral, Duncan closed his eyes for the last time. The afternoon before, he was taken to intensive care, unable to move, burning up with pain, exhausted and emaciated from diarrhea and constant vomiting. The doctors circled round to carry out some procedure that I didn't understand, installing a central line.

"Is it the end?" I whispered to the doctor who'd been called, as he rushed in with his motorcycle helmet still in his hand.

"No, he's nowhere near the end."

I didn't see how that could be true. I put the stuffed bear that Jamie, my youngest son, had sent, into my husband's hands. He reached up, wordless, and caressed the side of my breast.

I left the room, walked down the stairs of the clinic, and out the front door into the sunshine. It was a perfect July day, hot and cloud-less, unusual for England. The song, "You Get What You Give," by the New Radicals, popular that summer, rang through my mind as I walked along Marylebone Road to the train station. The flow-ers blooming alongside Park Crescent at the end of Portland Place seemed more colorful than they should, the sky more blue. I felt giddy and tearful, no longer grounded, safe, and secure. But I was not going to be able to just drift off into space. Duncan was still here.

Why was I leaving the clinic so early? I had no one to go home to, no one waiting for me. As I pondered this, a message came into my mind as clearly as if someone had actually spoken it: *You can go now.*

Was the message for Duncan, telling him he was free to leave this earth, or for me?

I walked to Euston Station, took the train home, and went to bed. The phone rang on my bedside table the next morning at 6:00 a.m. It was someone from the clinic. I didn't catch the name.

"You should come."

"Has something happened? Is he gone?"

"You need to come."

I got up without hesitation, dressed quickly, and drove to the train station. It took me almost two hours to park, buy my ticket, ride the train all the way back to Euston Station, and walk to the clinic. When I arrived, I was taken to a small waiting room I'd never seen before. I was told that Duncan was downstairs in a special room.

The surgeon who'd had the motorcycle helmet the day before came into the room and sat down. "Your husband is on life support."

I was confused. This same doctor had told me just the day before that Duncan was nowhere near dying. Also, after his first surgery I had signed a Do Not Resuscitate Order.

"Did Duncan ask for life support so I would have time to say good-bye?" I asked.

The doctor didn't really answer my question, only responded, "I'll have a nurse take you into the room as soon as the priest leaves."

As though in a fog, I was led down a short hallway and into a room set up with machines that monitored Duncan's heartbeat and breathing. His face was covered with an oxygen mask.

"He's not in any pain," the nurse said. "He can't hear you or respond to you, either."

That's not true, I thought. When my Nana was near the end, the nurses cautioned us to be careful of what we said. Hearing is the last sense to go. I walked over to the side of Duncan's bed away from the machines, leaned over and said very clearly into his ear, "Duncan, it's Karen. If you can hear me, blink two times."

He blinked two times. He couldn't move or talk, but he could hear me. The nurse busied herself with the machines and then said she was about to turn them off. I had a few moments and Duncan would be gone.

I couldn't help him or stop the inevitable, but I could be with him. Leaning in closer, I whispered into his ear, "Don't be afraid." I told him the truth—that I loved him—and then a lie, "I'll be all right."

I stood by the side of the bed while the the nurse shut down the machines. As she did so, a bell rang and Duncan's eyes turned toward the sound. Then his piercing black eyes returned to stare at me. His alarm lifted goose bumps on my skin as his eyes closed for the last time.

The nurse took Duncan's mask off and said, "I'll leave you with him for a few minutes."

When she was gone, I again moved up close to his head, sat bewildered, and then yelled, "You said you would never leave me!"

Silence. There were no tears then, just stunned disbelief. When I returned to the waiting room, three friends had gathered there, expecting to visit Duncan.

"He's gone," was all I could say.

❀ ❀ ❀

His death had to be registered with the City of Westminster. July 20, 1999, was another hot, vibrant day, so I walked the short distance up Marylebone Road. The registrar understood that I had just come from Duncan's bedside, and her gentle voice reflected her concern.

She gave me the application form. After filling out name, address, and occupation, there was a section for cause of death. I copied "Ruptured oesophagus and Carcinomatosis Stomach" from the death certificate, and left the office with a large brown envelope containing five beautiful, stamped, vellum copies of the death registration.

I took the train, then drove home, having turned down a friend's offer to stay at her house that night. I had to spend the night in our home, in our bed. I made phone calls to the funeral home and to friends and family members letting them know the end had come.

Throughout our years together, Duncan would phone me at least three times a day. Sometimes more. My sons and I used to joke that Duncan should have had a phone receiver grafted to the side of his head. Even while he was in the hospital, we would talk on the phone when I wasn't visiting.

When the phone rang that first evening of widowhood, I picked up the receiver. There was a deep, thick, empty feeling in the receiver as I repeated, "Hello? Hello?" Nothing. I hung up. The phone rang a couple of minutes later. Again the phone sounded hollow and empty. I held the receiver nervously and whispered, "Duncan? Duncan?" Nothing. I hung up. He never phoned again. Over the months to follow, the kitchen echoed with the lack of ringing.

 ° ° °

I stood there looking over the chapel, the outer edges growing murky. My feet floated above the floor. I gripped the solid edge of the wooden podium and choked out the poem's last lines.

"The stars are not wanted now: put out every one,

Pack up the moon and dismantle the sun,

Pour away the ocean and sweep up the wood;

For nothing now can ever come to any good."

I could hear comments, whispers, and questions as I finished and stood there, listening to "Shine On You Crazy Diamond," the Pink Floyd song that Duncan had chosen. People started to file out of the chapel to stand, uncertain, on the flagstone outside.

"She looks surprisingly well."

"She sounds angry," said one of the monks, a critical edge to his voice.

"Well, she is. Her husband just died."

As I followed the crowd outside, their words echoed through my head. *Angry? You have no idea.*

I sat in the chauffeur-driven limousine with my family while Duncan was carried out to the hearse to be driven to the crematorium. An entourage of about fifty cars wound its way through the small country roads from Tickford to Milton Keynes. I had come to love the green English countryside. The roads were edged with bent wood fences and blackberry brambles that wound precariously around thatched cottages that refused to stay neatly in rows. I sat in the limousine, amazed at the spectacle. Duncan would have approved of all this pomp and circumstance for his farewell.

The Farewell

The hearse stopped at the side of the crematorium. Attendants carried the coffin into the small chapel and placed it on a platform in front of a set of double doors. I sat in the first row with my family and close friends, staring at the coffin, trying to picture Duncan contained inside. The chapel was filled with those who had followed from the funeral.

Duncan's friend Bob stepped to the podium at the front of the chapel. I had seen him writing the eulogy the night before at our home. Bob was staying at the house along with my mother, Greg, and Jamie. He was a good writer and a sincere friend so I trusted he could capture Duncan's qualities, both good and bad.

"To give warm praise, this is the purpose of a eulogy," Bob began. "And now, along with all that has been said and thought, it is my great honor to have been asked by Karen, Greg, and Jamie to eulogize Duncan Edward Streeter, Dr. Duncan Streeter—my friend, Duncan."

As I sat there listening, I drifted back to February 1981, when I'd first met Duncan. My marriage to my first husband, Joe, my boys' father, had recently fallen apart after years of insults, lies, and bullying. Well, not fallen—sort of imploded. For five years I'd been in anguish, watching him try to rid himself of us. The marriage counselor said we had the worst marriage she had ever seen. At the end, Joe repeatedly bashed my head into the living room wall. I screamed at him to leave the house and he did, for the last time. His attack left me with a concussion and dislocated shoulder, and it all happened in front of our sons, three and five years old.

After several months of struggling with no child support and a job that barely paid all our expenses, a good friend suggested I come along to a group session she was attending on rebirthing. Rebirthers in Calgary held a potluck dinner once a month for those who wanted to learn what it was about their birth that made them the way they were. Rebirthing originated in California, home of fashionable therapies. It seemed perfect for my quest to create a new life for my boys and myself; I thought it might help me figure out why I'd married a man who was so selfish and angry that he would turn to violence.

The rebirthing coach asked us to lie on our backs on the floor with our eyes closed and do deep breathing. This meditative practice was meant to guide you back to the point of your birth, to help you to tap into the memories stored in your body. You could then correct the birth experience and stop harboring resentment. Or so they said.

Afterward, the workshop leader talked about the benefits of rebirthing, and then we waited for the potluck meal to begin. As I stood by the table of baked goods, casseroles, and organic salads, a strikingly handsome older man—he looked as though he was in his early forties—approached me and asked, "What did you bring?"

"Bread I bought at the bakery—no time to cook, I'm afraid. And you?"

"The dolmades are mine."

"You made them?"

"No, I bought them from a Lebanese restaurant. I'm half-Lebanese," he explained. "Try one." He held out a small green leaf-wrapped bundle between slim, finely formed fingers.

That first evening I learned about Duncan's Lebanese mother, his father, who was of Scottish descent, and his six-year-old son. He told me how he'd hoped to spare his son his own fate—his parents divorcing when he was young—but hadn't succeeded.

Duncan's eyes were black as a moonless night—not dark brown but black, with barely any distinction between the iris and the pupil.

His hair was thick and dark, waved in soft kinks. He had a round-ish face and a black moustache. His body was square, and he had short, shapely legs. Many years later, I recognized the influence of his mother's Lebanese heritage when we visited Lebanon and then Syria. In Palmyra, a man on the street began to speak to him in Arabic. Dressed in a white, full-length thobe, Duncan looked like he belonged there—it was no wonder the man thought he was a local. The same thing happened when he was in Bahrain on business. Though a bit embarrassed that he couldn't speak the language, he was proud that his heritage was so obvious he was taken for a native.

o o o

Bob continued with the eulogy. "Duncan welcomed demands upon his loyalty, his knowledge and, yes, his wisdom. He came to Brookton University full of hope, expecting to work with world-class colleagues, determined to meet the expectations of his director and especially his esteemed colleague, Frederick Klassen. And he rose. He 'arrived' at Brookton."

I noted Bob's compliments as I sat on the hard pew of the chapel, safe between my mother and youngest son, hearing the sounds of Duncan's colleagues clearing their throats, sniffling into tissues. Then I returned to my memories.

The first night we met, I told Duncan, "I separated from my husband only two months ago."

"I separated from my wife six months ago" Duncan replied. "You know, you can look on it as a gift." He handed me his business card. "Call me and I can lend you some books. They've really helped me."

Was that a line? It was much too early to think about dating, but Duncan seemed so much older than I was. Maybe he did just think of me as someone he could help. Why not? We both worked in down-town Calgary for oil companies—I could call him and we could meet for lunch.

Bob continued, "Duncan would not settle for a declining conva-lescence. He charged forward into the depths of darkness—trying again and again to pierce the armor of death. He loved life. He loved Karen with a burning passion; he loved Greg with a patient hope that a father has for a son who has great potential. Wise, incisive, generous, warm, full of praise. How easy it is to give Duncan warm praise! Thank you, Duncan."

Bob finished his thoughtful admiration of Duncan, his friend, and stepped away from the podium.

My mind concentrated on the chapel and the colleagues, friends, and family who had gathered for this last good-bye, as the doors behind the podium opened and the coffin moved on a conveyor belt into the space behind the doors. The doors shut. Tears formed in my eyes and ran down my cheeks. It was true, then. He was gone, to be reduced to ashes.

o o o

The sandwiches and tea were served in our garden. I was glad I'd had the small pond dug at the edge of the stone patio at the beginning of the summer. I'd always wanted a pond. The yellow marsh marigolds and purple water irises were at their peak. The flowering almond tree we'd planted was no longer in bloom, but the leaves were full and dark green. The arbor in the corner of the garden was hung with baskets of pink fuschias and partially covered by clematis and night-flowering jasmine. I often came out in the evenings to sit on the wooden bench in its shadow.

The dark pink star lilies Duncan and I had planted the previous autumn were in bloom, and I'd filled the pots on the patio with pale pink, yellow, and mauve annuals. He'd never liked to spend much time outdoors, and had only agreed to help me plant the lilies in hopes that I would appreciate his effort to mend the rips in our marriage. I had appreciated the help, but there'd been too many tears for even the most beautiful flowers to heal.

I sat on my garden patio and talked and drank tea with a couple Duncan had known from their graduate days at Case Western in Cleveland. They thanked me for spending so much time with them, but, in fact, I couldn't bear doing a round of well-meaning small talk with all the guests. I felt the weight of loss crushing me, and the need to grasp at air so I wouldn't faint. I was hiding in plain sight.

After the last guest left, I laid the small dark casket, ashes inside, on the fireplace hearth, along with the two framed pictures from the funeral, and surrounded them all with bouquets of flowers. A shrine.

At last, it was over. Finished. The lid closed on that part of my life. I was free.

Of course, at the time, I didn't realize that chains are not broken that easily. The handcuffs were not gone. I couldn't see then that it would take years before I could walk away a free woman, released from what Duncan and I started all those years ago.

The Beginning

*I*n Calgary, Canada, seventeen and a half years before his funeral, I phoned Duncan after our first meeting to arrange a lunch date. Before we could meet, however, he called me and asked me out for a Friday night movie and a meal, dinner at his townhouse.

That Friday, he cooked chicken with an almond coating and a side of spaghetti with tomato sauce. I later found out it was one of the few dishes he could make, but that night I was impressed. Over dinner, he explained he was already seeing someone but was angry because she was in Montreal with another man. I wilted at the thought that I might be just a revenge date. Duncan told me that a friend of his, also divorced, wanted a "main squeeze" and the freedom to see other women, so that was what he wanted too. "I was married a long time and now I want to have some fun."

I can't say that Duncan forced himself on me, exactly. But it was clear he wanted sex, with little romance. He chided me for my hesitancy, my naiveté. That should have been the first warning sign, but I was still so numb from all the years of criticism and public put-downs from Joe, I just tucked it away, both noting it and ignoring it.

"I'm a very intense person," he said as I dressed the next morning. I was not really sure what he meant—then.

I have already said that Duncan was handsome; he was twice mistaken for Burt Reynolds. He ate Middle Eastern food, the names of which I could barely pronounce. And he told me he was bisexual. I was too inexperienced to see what the implication of that even

14

was, so to me, it didn't pose a problem. In the summer he wore tight T-shirts, shorts, and small neckerchiefs tied at the side of his neck. He was attractive, intelligent, and transparent in a way I had never encountered before. He had a PhD in organizational psychology, an executive position at an oil company, and a love of opera, especially Caruso or Maria Callas singing Puccini, Donizetti, or Verdi. On Saturdays he did tai chi and on Sunday nights attended a poetry and drama group.

After my husband Joe left, it was clear I couldn't pay the mortgage on our house on my own. The boys and I moved to a fourplex I could just barely afford, hoping that in time he would start to pay the child support he'd promised. I had to sell my reliable Datsun because I couldn't afford the hundred-dollar monthly payment, so I drove a gigantic old clunker, named Miss Piggy by her previous owner, a single mother who'd moved from Calgary to Toronto after meeting the man of her dreams.

Each morning began in the same way. Miss Piggy would only start after I opened the hood, took off the large air filter, and used a screw driver to hold the carburetor open while I ran to start the ignition— with my sons, by now four and six, squirming in the back seat. When my mechanical efforts didn't work, I had to bundle the boys into a cross-town bus that connected with another bus in the center of Calgary, then walk them over to the day care, from which my oldest son went to school—a detour that ensured I was late for work most days. After our separation, Joe almost immediately started dating a woman whose children were at the same day care center, so our boys saw their dad when he dropped off the other woman's children in the mornings. For many months, it was the only time they did see him.

In some ways, it was a relief to meet Duncan. The lukewarm sexual response I'd had to the father of my children left me wondering if I was just naturally frigid. Unresponsive. Was it any wonder he went to others? But when he did, I froze more. It had never occurred to me that I could be different with another man. Someone who wore black shirts with black ties, a riverboat gambler, Bat Masterson and

Palladin all rolled into one. Duncan. My lover, my savior, my erotic fascination. Who, the more I got to know him, excited my imagination. Who rang me late at night for phone sex. Despite telling me he just wanted fun and casual dating relationships, Duncan wanted me by his side, to be his muse, to share his life, to be what he wanted in a woman.

And, in some ways, he brought out the best in me. One night after we'd attended a lecture given by two personal development gurus, Duncan turned to me to ask, "Well, what did you think?"

I gave my opinion of the talk and threw some comments out for him to consider. "I get that these men are a bit avant-garde, but does that make them relationship experts? They dress alike in matching black outfits and say they have an open relationship, yet they have to be present before either of them can have a sexual relationship with someone of the opposite sex. I don't get it."

I was shocked as I listened to myself talk. In my marriage to Joe, I'd never been asked my opinion, except about what we should eat for dinner or what color we should paint the living room.

"Wow, I didn't know you could think like that," Duncan said admiringly.

Shocked, I mumbled, "Neither did I."

❍ ❍ ❍

In very short order, he loomed too large in my life. I did feel swamped with my life, my work, and my children and I needed help—but not necessarily Duncan's kind of help. Usually he wanted to educate me, rescue me, have sex with me, and dress me in black sequined outfits, but sometimes he surprised me. One evening he phoned just as I walked in from work. "Can I come over? I have something for you."

He showed up at my door with the perfect gift for a mother of two with a full-time job: a portable dishwasher.

Despite his stated desire to have fun as a single man, Duncan told me his fantasies of marrying again, to someone young enough to have at least six children. On his bedroom wall was a reproduction antique portrait of a man who married at age sixty and had ten children. This didn't appeal to me, and yet after that I looked into having my tubal sterilization reversed. My doctor said it wasn't possible, and I was grateful for that—but unhappy that I was letting Duncan and my doctor dictate what I already knew: two children were enough for me. Why couldn't I just say that?

One evening I was at home, my boys asleep in their beds. I wanted to be alone, so I'd taken my phone off the hook. Reading in bed, I heard a knock at my window. I opened the curtain. It was Duncan. He had tried to phone but couldn't reach me. I let him in.

My friends' reactions were definitive.

"Why would you just be at his beck and call?"

"Why does he have access to you whenever he wants?"

"What if you had a visitor there already?"

"Get rid of him."

o o o

About six months into our relationship, we drove to Lake Louise for the day. I was feeling very hemmed in by Duncan and wanted to either end the relationship or at least cool things off.

"I don't want to continue seeing you. I don't think I'm ready for a relationship." I mumbled my words fearfully, nervous that Duncan wouldn't listen to me. We walked on in the snow.

He darkened. "No, wait. I understand. I'm ready to commit. I want to be with you."

My stomach churned. I didn't want to be spoken for, committed, or controlled less than a year out of my marriage to Joe. But I answered, "Oh, all right then."

I didn't realize until many years later, after we'd moved to England, that my reactions were not based on logic or rational thinking. I was afraid—afraid that I was always wrong, guilty even, if I wanted what was best for me. This feeling was so much a part of me that it was simply my normal state; I was full of a frantic desire to do what someone else wanted me to do so I wouldn't be "wrong."

I'd always tried to be a good girl—valedictorian of my high school class, anxious to remain stain-free so I could go to communion at Sunday Mass, a person who did the things I was asked to do by my parents, teachers, and priest. I argued with people who wanted to rule my life, but I always gave in. So on the outside I looked strong, sometimes even difficult—but the truth was, I was easily led. Like my mother, I knew my own mind, but had no strength to oppose those who were more forceful than I was, and this had led me to make some bad decisions in the past. Now, with Duncan, I had the feeling that I was going to do the wrong thing again.

Despite all my misgivings about Duncan, I knew I fulfilled his fantasies and I liked that. Taller than him, slim and dark-haired, I could look stunning in a skin-tight red satin gown, standing quietly at the side of a crowded party with a glass of champagne in my hand. An attractive image was part of my shield against the world.

I wanted to be like my father's mother. A professional woman, she wore mink and diamonds, drank vodka martinis, and smoked cigarettes in jeweled cigarette holders held by fingers dipped in scarlet nail polish. So different from my mother, whose sense of hurt and defeat were summed up in a story she told me many times about meeting an old school acquaintance when I was a baby. This woman looked into my carriage admiringly and asked, "How did *you* ever have such a good-looking baby?" I could see Mom shrink every time she repeated this story.

It didn't seem to matter that she'd been such a talented figure skater that she was offered a place in the Ice Capades. "Too far from home," she explained. Her goal was marriage, a nice home and children. When she found out after my birth that she could have no more children, she and my father adopted my sister and brother to give her the perfect family she desired.

Duncan joked that people would see us and assume there could only be two reasons I was with him: his money or his large manhood—and they knew he didn't have a secret fortune. Of course, this comment reflected badly both on his sense of self-worth and his understanding of my values. However, there was some truth to his statement. I was very vulnerable as a single mother, struggling, a geological technician not earning enough to give my boys the life they deserved, and Duncan's executive salary offered a solution to my money problems.

Putting up boundaries with Duncan was difficult. He phoned me at work one day and I picked up the phone quickly, in the middle of scanning a document.

"Sorry, Duncan, I don't have time to talk."

He raised his voice in complaint. I apologized again and hung up. He phoned again, and continued to argue. I hung the phone up. He rang again, yelling this time. I left the phone off the hook. The phone protested. You can't take company phones off the hook. I picked up the receiver and immediately hung it up. He rang again, and again, and again. I ran to the washroom. Three telephone messages were on my desk when I returned. The phone rang again. Defeated, I sat down. With tears running down my face, I spoke with him, whispering, my back to my colleagues. He stopped complaining when he got what he wanted. Another warning sign that I ignored.

Duncan had started therapy when his marriage broke up to help him sort through his feelings. His ex-wife Vera attended several sessions as well. When I felt I needed someone to talk with, Duncan recommended Megan, the same therapist he and his wife had gone to. During my appointment with her, she warned me that Duncan had caused his wife's main problem—her alcoholism—or had at least contributed to it. I stiffened, rejecting this. My father was an alcoholic and I was not prepared to accept that other family members could have been responsible for his problem, so I dismissed her words.

Was I avoiding the truth?

o o o

Duncan had an incredible energy and appetite for life. I had never met anyone who wanted me like he did. I liked the feeling that someone needed me in his life so badly he would risk baring his faults to me, as Duncan did when he behaved in a demanding way, and soon I craved that feeling. He was passionate about life and, when he got what he wanted, romantic and attentive.

He was a smoldering-eyed, take-charge bad boy, but I sensed an even darker side as he dressed me up and showed me off. I was caught in a web of sexual and intellectual attraction. I tried to ignore the drawers and bags full of *Playboy* and *Hustler*, though I did ask him to keep them out of sight when my sons visited his home.

The first summer I knew him, we took a short vacation to the States. We stopped in a town in northern Washington State that had one main street, dusty sidewalks, a single gas station, a tired-looking general store—and an adult store. We parked the car and he turned to me.

"I'm going in. If you don't feel comfortable, you can wait in the car."

I followed him inside, relieved that no one looked my way when we entered. I tried not to look at the covers of the magazines. Tried not to breathe. There was a tawdriness in the air that I didn't want to have inside me. Duncan moved around the shelves and studied the magazines displayed on the walls. He spied a door at the back of the store and seemed to know where it led. He lowered his voice and said he wanted to watch films in the back cubicles.

A short hallway was lined with a row of doorways, each covered by a curtain. He brushed one aside to reveal a tiny room. I looked twice at the soiled cushion before I sat down very slowly, trying to rest the least possible amount of my bottom on it while he put quarters into a machine. Through a glass window he watched video clips. When the film stopped mid-action, he had to feed more quarters into the machine. When he'd seen enough, we left the shop, and I could breathe again.   ❍ ❍ ❍

From the time we met, Duncan dropped hints into our conversations. He'd done some swinging. He'd put an ad in a swinger's magazine. Nowadays, when people want to have different kinds of sexual adventures, they look on the Internet, but back then they purchased local magazines in porn shops. Through these magazine ads, Duncan had met at least two women who'd become his swinging partners—not girlfriends—and he'd done this while still married. He said he'd gone out when his wife was too drunk to talk. He rationalized that he'd been lonely and needed human contact, but hadn't wanted to end his marriage. Sexual exploration had been his solution. But if that were the real reason for the sexual adventures, why did he want to continue exploring now that he was with me? I could see myself slipping down a slope, falling into the mud below where my shoes were getting stuck so I couldn't get back up.

A conference Duncan was attending in New York City gave him the opportunity he wanted to introduce me to the swinging scene. He arranged my flight from Calgary to New York, met me at JFK Airport with red roses, and whisked me off to Broadway that evening to see Raul Julia starring in *Nine*. He got front-row seats for *Evita*, as well as tickets to *Dream Girls*, and made a reservation in SoHo for us to hear live jazz. At a tiny, expensive restaurant, I tapped my spoon on the hard caramel topping of crème brûlée for the first time. For a girl who'd grown up in the country, this was exotic.

One evening we met up with an old friend of Duncan's, a management consultant who worked in New York for the same oil company as he did. Giorgio was handsome and charming—and flamboyantly gay. Duncan asked if he would take us to a well-known gay nightclub. Giorgio looked astonished and whispered to him, "You can't take Karen there." Duncan looked disappointed that we wouldn't be going.

Back at the brownstone bed and breakfast just off Central Park, where we were staying, Duncan said he wanted to go to a swinger's club called Plato's Retreat. I had never heard of it and had no idea it was famous. We walked along West 34th, a street lined with warehouses, and went into a door that was painted black with a large "509" in gold on the outside. The club had a dance floor, sauna rooms, and a swimming pool with waterfalls. I later learned that during its heyday, in the '70s, Plato's Retreat was considered the world's most infamous sex club, popular with celebrities, porn stars, and well-to-do couples looking for a quick fix for their stalled libidos. There were separate rooms for people wanting to find others to hook up with. A couple asked Duncan and I to party and Duncan turned them down. I breathed a sigh of relief. In another room, a man started to put his hand on my back. Duncan told him to stop and, turning to me, said, "Can we leave?"

I relaxed. Duncan liked the fantasy of this club, not the reality. But an image flashed through my mind as we left the club. Dangerously, I was floating along like flotsam in a stream, letting someone else decide what I was going to do, when I already knew what I felt.

When we were back in the brownstone B&B, Duncan observed me closely and said, in a very serious tone, "You're so normal."

o o o

When we returned home to Calgary, Duncan still wanted to find couples that would swing with us. Each time he contacted someone and they refused, I counted myself lucky that I had escaped.

I was caught like a fish. Suspended on a line over the water of everything my family, church, and upbringing had taught me to avoid. Dangling in the murkiness of my own confusion about who I was and what was driving me. Years of not being seen or protected in my family and the hopelessness of my first marriage cemented what was already part of me: an overwhelming sadness at feeling that I always do the wrong thing.

Farther Down the Rabbit Hole

*O*ne year after Duncan and I met, in February 1983, my sons and I moved into his modern townhouse condominium with a corner fireplace and mezzanine over the living room. We positioned my burgundy velvet love seats on either side of his stone fireplace. My restored and refinished oak table, given to me by my great uncle, took up the center of his dining area, flanked by my antique pressed-back chairs. We moved Duncan's table with the loose legs and peeling paint out into the garage. I persuaded him to take down his pictures of suffering, Christ-like faces, give them back to his ex-wife, and put up some of my colorful, inspiring paintings instead. I wanted my sons to be surrounded by good art. My furniture and his space came together, but there were some large wrinkles to iron out.

When we moved in, Duncan agreed to get rid of his pornography. He loaded garbage bag after garbage bag into the trunk of his car and drove them to a dumpster in an industrial site to dispose of them. He asked if I was comfortable with him keeping one pocketbook-sized magazine, and I said I was. He kept it in the drawer of his night table where I found it after he passed away fifteen years later.

The day after we moved in together was Valentine's Day. As soon as my boys went to bed that night, I decorated the fireplace with candles and chocolate hearts. I waited and waited. Duncan came home at about 11:00 p.m.

"Where have you been?" I asked, disappointment in my voice.

"I told you we had Marilyn Ferguson as guest speaker today at work. She asked me to go to dinner with her." Duncan couldn't resist the lure of famous people.

"It's Valentine's Day." Hurt and angry, I stomped off, then stopped on the stairs and turned back to say, "I'm going to bed."

What had I done by moving in with Duncan? I'd already moved twice since the end of my marriage. I didn't want to disrupt my boys again. I needed help.

o o o

I went to see Megan, the therapist, again. I explained to her that I felt trapped. I was afraid of Duncan's anger and persistence. I told her about him wanting to swap with another couple and that Duncan wanted to continue looking for someone to do this with. I never wanted to do it, but I'd made myself dependent on him. I was afraid that if I opened any discussion with him, it would turn into a shouting match—something for which he had unlimited energy.

"Tell Duncan you're going to leave if he insists on the sexual experimentation," Megan was quick to advise me.

Like an automaton, I could do this if she said I should.

That night, after dinner and with the children gone to bed, I told him. To my utter surprise, he replied, "Of course we won't if you don't want to. You're more important to me than sexual adventures."

Perhaps I could relax. Maybe everything would be all right after all. But I was still uneasy, and even a bit let down by his response. If he'd disagreed, I'd have had a good excuse to leave.

o o o

Who was this man with his unhealthy appetites and need for control? I needed to know and understand Duncan. Otherwise, how was I going to feel good about my choice of him as a partner?

From the time I met him, Duncan told me about his history: his parents' divorce, his own divorce, his ethnic origins, his hopes and dreams. He was born at Western Hospital in Toronto. His mother, Hazel, was a short, dark-haired beauty, the daughter of a Lebanese mother and a Syrian father. She cooked traditional dishes that Duncan liked, beans and rice, tabouleh, kibbeh, and kofta—and had married a man, Duncan's father, who could not provide for her in the way she wanted. While still married, Hazel had a boyfriend who helped her cash in savings bonds and a life insurance policy.

"Where are you going?" Hazel asked her husband one night as he went to the door to leave their apartment.

"Out to get a Coke," he said, but he walked out and never came home again. Duncan wouldn't see his father from the time he was six years old until he was twenty-one.

At six years old, because Duncan was intelligent, his mother felt he was mature enough to leave in charge of his little brother Davey when she wanted to go out. One night, as their uncle approached on the sidewalk underneath their apartment, he saw Davey at the window screaming, something red and sticky matting his hair and running down his face. Duncan had put catsup on his brother as a joke.

Their mother was not pleased to be called from the local bar to come home and deal with her sons. When she got there, she did as she always did when the boys misbehaved: called a woman they all called Aunt Cubie to come over and deliver a punishment. She sat at the kitchen table, smoking a cigarette, while Aunt Cubie took the two young boys to the bathroom.

"Take your pants down," she said. "Kneel on this broomstick. I'll tell you when to get up."

They were familiar with this punishment, and tried to find ways to relieve the pain. If they leaned forward to support some of their weight on the edge of the tub, the stick wouldn't dig into their tender skin quite so much. Duncan never knew who Aunt Cubie was, whether she was really his aunt or not, but it was clear she didn't like little boys.

Hazel had plans for her boys, but not the income to make those plans happen. She sent Duncan for piano lessons, but at home he could only practice on a cardboard foldout of a keyboard. To earn pocket money, he collected wire hangers for dry cleaning stores at one cent per hanger. Christmas came out of a box from the Star Newspaper Christmas fund. The priest put their name on the list. After school one day, Duncan and Davey came around the corner onto the street where they lived and saw the chrome and plastic chairs from their kitchen, the dresser and tables from their living room, and their dishes stacked in boxes on the sidewalk. This was not the first time they'd had to move at short notice. Their mother hadn't paid the rent, again.

Every Sunday, Duncan's mother would send him off to see Jim, his Scout leader. She wanted a break and turned a blind eye to the type of relationship that could develop between a handsome young boy and an older man. Jim played records of the great operas, but especially Caruso and Maria Callas. When he was only thirteen, Duncan went to New York with Jim for a weekend away to see the opera. Their relationship had very quickly become sexual, and it lasted from the time he was twelve until he was seventeen. Duncan rationalized that this was something completely separate from his real life, his normal life—school, sports, dating. He didn't realize that, at twelve, he didn't have the ability to distinguish what was harmful.

Years later, Davey discovered their father working at a local bar. Davey met with him a couple of times and then, one evening, he and Duncan walked into the bar together. "I want to introduce you to someone," Davey said to their father. Duncan Sr. looked at his oldest son blankly.

Duncan and his father tried to make up for those lost years by sharing stories. It was only then that the two brothers found out that their father had phoned many times wanting to see his two boys, after he left the family home. Their mother, Hazel, would tell him, "Come at 3:00 p.m. and pick them up," but then have them out the door and gone by the time he arrived.

Sometimes, their father said, he had hung around their school-yard in order to catch a glimpse of them, but eventually he stopped.

These many years later, he had a new life, a new wife, and a new child, Duncan and Davey's half-sister. They had little in common, but Duncan and his father maintained a relationship with one another for the rest of the older man's life.

Though Duncan had an IQ of 140, he failed two grades in high school. He had no bedroom, so studying had to be done in the kitchen, where there was constant disruption. One night, for example, his mother's boyfriend, the Boxer, came into the kitchen smelling of beer. "What are you doing here at the table?" he snarled. "Taking up room? You think you're so smart?" He grabbed Duncan around the neck and started to choke him while Hazel screamed. Davey pushed the Boxer off, and the two teenage boys ran out of the apartment. They knew they couldn't go back until the Boxer collapsed in the only bedroom in the apartment.

The priests in the parish watched out for Duncan, and because of his potential, gave him a scholarship to St. Michael's College, a private high school, and permission to study in the school library at night. He finally graduated from St. Mike's and was accepted at university. By this time, Duncan's mother had remarried and she and her new husband threw a big party for Duncan to prove what a good mother she'd been. At twenty-one, Duncan left his home in Toronto to go to university in Windsor. He won scholarships, majored in psychology, and dated nuns and priests. Classmates joked that he would "fuck anything with a crack in it."

After graduating with a master's degree in clinical psychology, he immediately moved west to start lecturing at a university in Saskatchewan, where he won an award for being the best lecturer in the psychology department. He married Vera, a farm girl from north of Saskatoon, and they moved to Cleveland, Ohio, so Duncan could do a PhD in organizational psychology. After several years of consulting in the States, plus a brief stay in Vancouver where their son Greg was born, Duncan and his wife moved to Calgary so he could work for a major oil company.

Gregory started school while Vera stayed home. The plan was for her to return to work, so they hired a Vietnamese houseboy to cook and do the housework. He only lasted a few months. Bao approached Duncan one evening and said he was quitting. He told him that Vera drank a twenty-six-ounce bottle of vodka every day and by early afternoon was too drunk to speak.

Vera's drinking was not a new problem. Duncan would often phone home when he was going to leave work to ask his wife to meet him so they could dine out. For some time, he'd noticed that, more and more when he phoned, she slurred her words, and that by the time she arrived by taxi to join Duncan at a restaurant, she'd be so drunk she couldn't carry on a conversation. Duncan's credit cards were maxed out—mostly for alcohol.

Duncan began spending most weekends at the office and seeing other women. One evening, during an argument, he hit Vera in the face. With blood streaming down her cheeks, she ran to the closet to escape. At the hospital she was treated for minor injuries. Their marriage had reached a crisis. Duncan urged Vera to get treatment for her drinking, and they both went to Megan for counseling.

By this time, there were two myths operating: one that Duncan was responsible for his wife's drinking, and, two that despite her drinking, Vera was still a good mother. Vera ended their marriage and went into a month-long treatment program while Greg stayed with Duncan in a small apartment. When she finished her program, Vera rented a townhouse, and Greg went to live with her.

Six months after his marriage to Vera ended, I met Duncan at that rebirthing potluck party.

The Nightmare Really Begins

*B*lending two families was bound to have its challenges. Greg, who was six, was the same age as my oldest son. He visited his father every other weekend, and every Wednesday they went to Cub Scouts together. Vera seemed settled into her new life, though she often called Duncan to pick up cigarettes for her or to ask for more money for Greg, despite the generous child support Duncan was already paying. She also continued to do Duncan's laundry.

"Why don't you send her your laundry too? She's not working," Duncan explained. "And she could use the money."

I felt very uneasy about this whole arrangement. He and his wife were divorced, but she still did his laundry—a wifely chore. I was the new woman in his life, in his home, and I wanted to take on the household tasks. The idea of having Duncan's ex-wife do my laundry, and that of my sons, was embarrassing. Duncan, however, assured me that she was a very practical woman and would simply appreciate the extra income. I was working full time, and this would relieve me of one task, while she would benefit. To him this was a logical, not an emotional, arrangement. I agreed to this for a while, but after my lovely white summer sundress came back pink, I told him I would do my own laundry—and his.

Once we moved in together, I enrolled my boys at a local school, sent them to a lovely woman for before and after-school care, and tried to settle into my new normal: life with Duncan.

"AAAAAAHHHHHHHHHH ooooooooo!" I leaped out of bed early one Saturday morning after hearing a scream from my oldest son. Upon entering the boys' room, I saw that blood was running from his foot, and his large toenail was almost severed. Greg had pulled a heavy wooden box out from under the bed with such force that it had rammed into Adam's foot.

"I didn't mean to," Greg said.

Two weeks later—"AAAAAAAAHHH HHHHHH ooooooooo!" This time the scream was from my younger son, down in the play-room. Greg had hit him in the head with a truck. Again he stated, "I didn't mean to."

"He didn't mean to," Duncan echoed, defending his son.

"I don't care if he meant to or not, he has to take responsibility for what he's done."

"Okay, I'm taking Greg back to his mother."

"No. *You* are responsible for Greg while he's with you. He's your son too. Taking him home to his mother can't be a punishment."

I was afraid that Greg felt envious now that my sons lived with his father. While our life was a bit upside down at the moment—the boys and I in a new home, getting adjusted to a new life—so was Greg's. Two young boys, almost his age, were now living with his father and he wasn't. They now had the room that had been his. Was this why he was acting out so much, both when he was with us and at school?

Meanwhile, I had all the usual things to deal with when you have two young children: getting them to and from school, arranging for care for them while I was at work, making lunches, organizing birth-day parties, helping them build model rockets, skirting the Legos lying all over the floor, buying them shirts and trousers that fit when they seemed to grow faster than the clothing could keep up with, managing their involvement in soccer, swim lessons, and art camp. It was a huge juggling act just to keep up with the normal things of life, and now I had to extend my time, energy, and planning to include one more child. Entering into my relationship with Duncan, I had naively expected Vera to look after Greg in the same way I looked after my boys, but I quickly learned that our ideas about parenting differed drastically.

"Vera said that when Greg acts up, she locks him in the laundry room for an hour or so," Duncan told me one day. "She read about this method in a child development book."

Even while barely seven years old, when he came to visit us, Greg would disappear on his bike. One day I went out into the neighborhood to search for him, and found him a couple of blocks away. "If you want to leave our yard, you have to ask us first and tell us where you are going," I said firmly. "You can't just wander off. I want you to come home now and play at the house."

He complied, and from that point on, asked permission to ride his bike off our property. But I had the uneasy feeling that when he was at home with his mother he simply went wherever he wanted whenever he wanted.

It was clear that Duncan loved his son, but he didn't pay too much attention to the details. In addition, he believed that Vera was a good mother, so he didn't question anything she said about how she dealt with Greg. Alarm bells were going off in my head about what kind of care and supervision he got when he was with his mother, but as the new woman in Duncan and Greg's lives, I knew it was not really my role to interfere with his upbringing.

In the meantime, my boys' father, Joe, didn't just want to get out of paying the child support he'd agreed to (and was legally obligated to pay) but he'd made it clear he wanted no responsibility at all—no part in our boys' lives. He only picked them up to see them when he was going to visit his parents. When speaking to him changed nothing, I made appointments for the two of us to go to counseling. I explained to the therapist how much our boys wanted to see their father. In response, Joe just sat silent, offering neither excuse nor explanation for his lack of involvement.

This particular counselor was part of a team of family therapists. She left the room to consult with her team behind a one-way mirror, then returned to give their feedback to Joe, "My team said to tell you that you're a bastard."

"That's right, I am," Joe said, smirking, "and I don't intend to change."

I have no idea why he even agreed to come to the sessions. Calgary Family Service, Catholic Family Service, Jewish Family Service—we tried them all, and no one could get through to him. One counselor suggested that when there is a disagreement between parents about who should do what regarding their children, they often traded off responsibilities. "However," the counselor said, "in your case, Karen can't do any more. She already does everything."

"Yes," Joe responded in a smug tone, "she does."

In order to escape paying his court-ordered child support, Joe left Calgary to bum around through Mexico and Belize in a VW camper van. He didn't return for over eighteen months, and when he did the boys barely recognized him. But at least on his return he began to pick them up for visits on a more regular basis than he had in the past. After a couple of months, however, he said he was too busy with his social life to continue with the visits, and, although he lived in Calgary, he fell back into the pattern of only seeing them when he visited his parents.

So my boys would have some sense of normalcy and continuity, I'd maintained a relationship with my ex-in-laws. In addition to shielding them from the truth about their son's assault on me, I didn't tell them about their son's deliberate, cold, and callous behavior toward their beloved grandchildren. They loved our boys and I felt they weren't responsible for their son's behavior.

I spoke frequently with Joe's father on the telephone as he tried to come to terms with our separation. It was clear that when Joe spoke with his parents he told them I had ended the marriage and blamed me for being too difficult to deal with. He told them I wanted to keep the boys from him. Who were they going to believe? Not the daughter-in-law they held responsible for the marriage breakdown. His father blew up in anger at me many times. No matter how much

I reassured them that I would continue to honor their relationship with the boys, Joe's parents were distrustful of me. Despite our differences, however, I kept my promise to keep them in our lives.

My own parents were far away—2,200 miles away, to be exact. Within a week or so of Joe's violent departure from our family, I phoned them for support, and my father was clearly taken aback by my tears and fragility. When I told him that I didn't know if I could cope, he replied that I was strong and would manage. I didn't complain; I just hung up the phone and whispered to myself, "I think you're wrong." The message from my father was as clear as it had been throughout my life: I would have to manage without help from them. By now I knew what to expect, but I couldn't help but continue to hope—especially now when I felt so unprotected.

We only saw my parents every couple of years, and then only if we made the long journey back east. They never asked for the boys to visit. They were long-distance grandparents in many ways, emotionally as well as physically. We received a big box every Christmas loaded with clothes, treats, and whatever the latest toys were, for all three boys; my mother made sure to include Greg in all that she sent. She liked shopping. But my parents were not warm and cuddly like Joe's parents. They had never been able to relate intimately to me and they were the same with their grandchildren.

o o o

About six months after we moved in together, Duncan picked me up after work, grinning widely. As he drove, he shoved some brochures onto my lap and asked me to take a look at them. There were palm trees and deep turquoise waves on the covers.

"What do you think?" he asked. "I want to go on a vacation to Hawaii, just the two of us."

Duncan already had a plan—he made things happen, just as he had when we went to New York. I was stunned, excited. I so wanted to travel. "That would be wonderful," was all I could say. Luckily he had chosen a vacation destination that I really liked.

"I'll go tomorrow, book our flights to Honolulu, and reserve a room for a few days in a Waikiki hotel. The travel agent said that Maui is the most beautiful island, so we can take a small plane from Honolulu to get there. Look, here's a brochure for Sugar Beach Resort, Maui. That's where she recommended we stay."

Only two weeks after making the reservations, I dropped my boys off at their grandparents' and we flew to Hawaii. When we got off the plane, women with long dark hair and flowered dresses circled our necks with plumeria leis. We could look down from our hotel room near Waikiki beach and see the ocean. We ate at a beach restaurant where I ordered blue drinks with little umbrellas and breathed in perfumed air. We went to a nearby nightclub to hear Don Ho. And after a few days, we flew to Maui and stayed at Sugar Beach Resort in north Kihei, where our apartment balcony doors opened onto the ocean. Most evenings we left them open so we could hear the surf roll in and allow the warm, moist air of the island flow in around us.

I loved exploring Maui. We bundled up in toques and jackets and drove to the top of Haleakala, the extinct volcano that dominates the island, to see the sunrise. We ate fresh grilled ahi at Longhi's Restaurant in Lahaina, and after touring the galleries on Front Street, bought a signed print by Margaret Keane. We drove to Little Beach, a clothing-optional beach on the other side of a spit of lava north of Big Beach. After climbing up and over the black rock, we stepped onto a perfect beach with honey-colored sand, stripped off our clothes, and swam in the warm, clear, turquoise waters of the ocean.

The following day, we took a boat tour out to Molokini to snorkel in the waters of the submerged volcano crater, where angel fish, several varieties of butterfly fish, wrasse, and even the humuhumunukunukuapua'a, Hawaii's state fish, gathered in the thousands. The water was alive with color—yellow, greens, reds, and oranges. I stayed in the water suspended over what felt like a magical world until the last minute, snorkeling until it was time to board the boat and go. Duncan stayed on board and talked with the crew, frightened by the depth of the water.

I could almost convince myself that this was real—a perfect holiday, a perfect relationship, a happy life, with only a minor local earthquake to jolt our otherwise flawless week on this island paradise. After a brief trip to a small shopping mall, Duncan brought a ring box to me and asked me to open it. The ring had a red stone surrounded by sparkling diamontes, set in silver. I looked up and thanked him for the gift, but I could tell by the look on his face that he was disappointed. He'd wanted me to be fooled, to think that it was really diamonds and a ruby. Weeks later, when a woman in Walmart complimented me on my fabulous ruby ring, I turned away, embarrassed that she thought it was the real thing when I knew it was only an illusion.

o o o

Two years later, we invited our boys into the living room of our house and presented each of them with a gift card: "Good for one trip to Maui." That December, we took them out of school for three weeks and flew to Honolulu, where we stayed a couple of days in Waikiki before flying to Maui to stay, once again, at Sugar Beach.

In Hawaii, we showed our boys all the sights Duncan and I had loved on our first trip, drove them to the top of Haleakala, took a boat over to Lanai, the pineapple island, snorkeled, and searched for sea urchins in tide pools. During this second trip, my love for Maui grew even more. At one point in the trip, I jokingly said to my boys, "The first one of you that makes a million dollars has to buy me a condo on Maui!"

I was not to know until many, many years later how important this trip, this request, and this island would be to my ultimate happiness.

The Noose Tightens

 I have no clear memory of Duncan asking me to marry him or me deciding I would, but I do remember us going to a gem dealer and picking out a diamond for my engagement ring. I had to decide what design the ring would be, so I looked in jewelry store window after jewelry store window looking for just the right setting. When I showed off my beautiful ring at work, I felt I was finally legitimizing living with Duncan.

I shared my decision to marry Duncan with Megan, my therapist. A few days after my announcement, she called and asked me to lunch. I knew it was a highly unusual thing for a therapist to do, but I agreed.

Over salad, Megan urged me to leave Duncan. "It might be all right now," she said, "but it will get worse when you're married. He's violent."

She had first seen Duncan shortly after his separation from Vera, so she must have known things about him I didn't, but she couldn't tell me specifics, only warn me. Still, despite her clear message, I left that lunch undeterred. As with the other warning signs, I couldn't take it in or act on it.

o o o

While we were making plans to be married, we bought a new home, large enough so all three of our sons could finally have their own bedrooms. There was a fireplace in the family room adjoining the kitchen, a cathedral ceiling over the living room and dining room, a large backyard, and a huge master bedroom. Ideal for a family of five.

We decided to hold the wedding and reception in our new home and set the date for December 21, 1984, almost two years after we'd moved in together.

Would I have agreed to marry Duncan if I wasn't both needy and vulnerable? At that point in time, I didn't fully appreciate my tendency toward emotional numbness, a sort of non-drug-induced avoidance of reality. Because I certainly had hints of the reality I was entering into. I had been warned.

When my marriage to Joe ended, instead of being angry with him for his behavior toward me and the boys, I felt guilty and broken-hearted. I saw the demise of the relationship as *my* failure to make the marriage work. I couldn't accept that it was not all up to me. When Joe assaulted me, he did more than punch my face. He changed me emotionally. Up until that point in time, I thought we might try marriage counseling again, repair our relationship, make everything all right. I still loved him. But when he beat me, everything changed. It colored all the choices I made in the years to come. My understanding of life was off-kilter; I was seeing the world from an angle that distorted my judgment.

I was plunging again, headlong over the precipice. I would not recover from this decision—my decision to marry Duncan—for many years, and before it was over, much more pain and fear would rule my life.

o o o

While I was ignoring the conscious warnings not to marry Duncan, my dreams tried to shake me into paying attention to impending danger. They were showing me things I wouldn't face, but knew deep down.

In April 1984, about eight months before our wedding, I had a significant dream. *A woman is talking with an evil man. She neatly splits his head down the center with a meat cleaver. He puts the two parts of his head together so he can look normal. He's alive and smiling but every once in a while his head falls apart revealing the inside.*

When I woke, I tried to see the connection between the dream and how I felt about Duncan. There were two sides to him: the sincere, intelligent, supportive companion, and the man who would not stop screaming at the world and me. But I didn't take seriously enough the dream's message.

In the summer of 1984, six months before we married, *a man in my dream tells me I should leave Duncan and that he will help me do it.* But even in the dream I was ambivalent, torn, and still anxious about Duncan. Though his pushiness made him appear strong, there was a part of me that knew he needed me.

One weekend, Vera asked if my boys wanted to come over and play with Greg. I was still a bit unsure about her disciplinary methods but Greg had stopped his overt attacks on my boys, so when Adam and Jamie wanted to go, I allowed them. When Duncan and I went to pick them up at the end of the afternoon, it was clear something was wrong. Vera was slurring her words. The boys said she had fallen down in the middle of an intersection when they all crossed the road in front of traffic. I sat in her living room, horrified by what I was hearing, fully convinced she'd been drinking. When we left, I told Duncan my boys would not be allowed to visit again.

Duncan talked with Vera many times over the following months. She insisted that she had a strange kind of PMS that made her woozy, dizzy even, and that she was going to a highly respected feminist physician to deal with this problem. She assured him that she was not drinking but when Duncan picked Greg up for the weekends and dropped him back off with her he witnessed more and more episodes of Vera slurring her words. Still she continued to proffer incoherent and unbelievable explanations for her behavior.

Greg's actions became more erratic as well. One day his school phoned to say that he was making strange animal noises in class and climbing up onto his desk to make the other children laugh. He was often put out into the hallway as a punishment. Vera said that sugar and food dyes were making Greg act this way and we were not to give him sugar when he visited us. But when he went away with us on a two-week vacation, he calmed down and behaved himself after the initial two or three days. One day when he was visiting, he mentioned that there was often no food in his house and that the day before, his mother had sent him to the local corner store to get bread and cheese for supper. He was only seven years old.

In Duncan's discussions with Vera about what was happening with Greg, she repeatedly insisted that she was ill, not drinking, and under a doctor's care. Duncan was so focused on her and whether or not she was drinking, that he glossed over concern for Greg.

After several months of this, I said to him in frustration, "I don't care why Vera's doing what she is, or whether she's drinking or not. The main concern is Greg. She's not looking after him properly."

Duncan looked at me and suddenly seemed to get it. He phoned his ex-wife's home and Greg answered.

"Put your mother on the phone, Greg."

After a few seconds, Greg returned to the phone, "She can't come, Dad. I can't wake her up."

It was seven in the evening. Duncan turned to me with a worried look. My children were visiting their grandparents, so we drove over together to find out what was happening. I waited in the car while Duncan went in. He came back a couple of minutes later. "She's asleep. I looked into the fridge and there's only an onion in it. Greg doesn't want to leave her."

"Greg doesn't get to make this decision, Duncan. You can't leave him there."

Duncan returned to the townhouse. When he came back to the car, he had Greg in his arms, squirming to get away, screaming and yelling that he wanted to go back to his mother. Duncan put his son into the back of the car and we drove home.

We put Greg to bed and Duncan phoned Vera's brother, Al, who lived near Edmonton. I overheard him trying to explain the situation to him. "No, she says she's sick, not drinking, but I don't know, actually. She seems passed out. I have Greg here with me . . . You can come down tomorrow? Take her back with you? That's great."

Al drove down the following day in a covered truck, found out that Vera was about to be evicted for non-payment of rent, and loaded all her things into the truck. He called an ambulance to pick her up. Then he drove back up north to his home.

After spending time in the detox ward and then the inpatient psych ward of the general hospital, Vera was finally released to a women's halfway house, where she would live for the next two years, returning to the hospital often for more treatment. Initially Vera wanted Greg to go back and forth, living with her based on her sobriety, but finally I put my foot down.

"Duncan, this is no way for Greg to live," I told him. "We can provide a more stable home for him and he can visit her on weekends when she's not drinking."

Duncan applied for, and received, full custody of his son, though Vera never stopped fighting him for control of Greg's life.

o o o

The invitations had been sent out, all the arrangements made for the wedding. The night before the ceremony, I sat up in bed at about three in the morning, with one thought: *Marrying Duncan is the stupidest thing I have ever done.*

I fell back to sleep and went right into a dream:

I walk into my parents' first apartment, the one they lived in when I was born. There is someone in the bedroom, hiding under the covers. I pull back the sheet and underneath it is me, about seven years old. I tell her sadly that she will have two major heartaches in her life: Dad's alcoholism and the breakdown of her marriage to Joe. "But," I tell her, "you'll make it."

It was as though my dream was telling me that I was helpless to prevent the things that would happen in my life, but deep within me I knew that, eventually, things would work out all right. I woke the next morning to prepare for the wedding, still unable to turn away from my commitment to marry Duncan.

I'd asked my best friend Bev to be my matron of honor. We'd met when our first husbands started doing work projects together and then extended the relationship to social events. As both our marriages deteriorated, she and I had often met for lunch to share stories and give each other support. Now she was married for a second time and I was about to marry Duncan. She arranged for us to spend the morning before the wedding at her hairdresser's so we could each have our hair upswept in suitably elegant styles. But I was disappointed that none of my other women friends had thought to do anything special. No girls' night out, no shower. I invited them all to join me for a pre-wedding lunch after the hairdressing appointment, then sat and listened, hurt and embarrassed, as they each, one after another, described marriage as a trap they would never go into again. They didn't have to be specific. They weren't happy for me.

o o o

I had sewn my wedding dress, a slim-fitting white taffeta gown with a simple neckline, and picked out a headpiece of white stephanotis. We'd arranged for a caterer to prepare a buffet of Lebanese food, including baba ganoush, dolmas, hummus, pita, and tabouleh. I'd baked our wedding cake and had it decorated at a local bakery, and tied padded satin hearts that I'd sewn onto the upright bars of the stair railing of our new home. As I went through all the wedding preparations, I heard the cage clicking shut, but I couldn't stop it.

About an hour before the guests arrived, I stood in the kitchen in my white dress, talking to my parents. About a month before, they had called to say they wouldn't be coming—they wouldn't travel in the winter. Besides, my father already considered us married because we were living together, so why go to the effort to come to the wedding? Now they'd phoned to wish us well. When I replaced the receiver, I swept my arm over the countertop in a rush of hurt and anger, tears hitting the papers and pens clattering to the floor. But I had to get myself under control, calm myself down. The ceremony would start soon.

When it was time to start the procession, Adam and Greg, by this time eight years old, descended the staircase, scattering flower petals. Jamie, age six, carried a pillow with our rings on top, wedding bands custom-made to match my engagement ring. I followed, coming down the steps to stand next to Duncan, who was formally dressed in a tuxedo, bow tie, white shirt, and black patent shoes. The guests, including my sister Bonnie and her husband, who were now living about ninety miles away in Red Deer, watched from either side of the staircase. Everything was perfect. A few songs and verses later, those rings of gold were on our fingers. Duncan, handsome Duncan, was by my side, supporting me, caring for me, providing stability for my sons. At last I felt I had chased away my doubts and fears.

o o o

A few days after the wedding, I started to cough. It was a cough I couldn't shake, no matter what I did. The doctor said, "It's tracheitis, not quite bronchitis, and normally I would put you in hospital, but you could be at risk of further infection there. You're not infectious, so go home and stay in bed."

I felt as though I had a huge weight on my chest. I could barely lift my head off the pillow, hardly catch a breath. I couldn't go downstairs to make supper. Duncan seemed irritated with me. He came into our bedroom and said that he and Greg were going out for dinner and to a movie. I tried to tell him to take my sons too, but he was already on his way down the stairs to leave the house. Adam and Jamie came and sat on the bed with me. I lifted myself up and put on my dressing gown. I held the stair rail tightly, stepping slowly as I made my way down, coughing continuously. *At least I'm not infectious*, I reassured myself. I went into the kitchen, opened a can of chicken noodle soup, and heated it up for my sons. Sitting at the kitchen table, I held my head in my hands until they finished their soup, then crawled back upstairs and into bed, where tears ran down my face until I fell into a deep sleep.

o o o

My feeling of distance from my mother and father intensified after they made their decision not to attend our wedding. Though my aunt and I were close, she didn't come either, since my mother, her sister, wasn't making the trip. Her very presence at my wedding would have been seen by my mother as a criticism for her own lack of effort to attend. I hadn't expected my father to come—in all the years I'd lived away from my home province of Ontario, he'd never come to visit me—but my mother occasionally made the effort, so I was crushed by her unwillingness to do so for this major life event.

About a month after the wedding, I had a dream:

Duncan and I look at each other with sadness and realization. I say to him, "You know, don't you?"

"Yes," he admits.

I explain that we have to part. That he is too strong. That I am being crushed and swept aside and that every day is a struggle. He tells me that this happened once before with someone else. He says he needs someone more aggressive, brusque, and matter-of-fact, someone who won't get squashed.

But it was only a dream. At this point in our relationship, Duncan and I were never this honest with each other. I was on my own. Unsupported by my parents, and with my friends seemingly dismayed at my choice of Duncan as a husband, I had to deal with him myself, and hope I was strong enough.

Our Life Together

Duncan began to teach a night course for corporate executives on "change in organizations" and soon caught the interest of the human resources manager of a large oil company. As a result, he was offered a long-term freelance project. I encouraged him to quit his full-time job with the oil company he'd been working for and jump at this opportunity to become an independent consultant, to do work that was meaningful and exciting to him.

Among the positives in my relationship with Duncan had been his support for me finding my path in life, professionally. I had recognized for some time that I was not happy in my job, mapping oil finds for an upstream oil company, but I'd had to stay in order to support my sons.

About three years into our relationship, Duncan said to me, "Let's sit down and figure out if you can quit your job and explore what it is you're good at and what you really want to do. You could take a part-time job and also study."

As a result, I started working at the Y Women's Resource Centre. I enjoyed my work there so much I realized that being a counseling therapist was my path in life. In my spare time, I began to take graduate-level psychology courses at the local university.

Though he was a management consultant, Duncan's first love was psychology. In his early thirties, he'd wanted to do a PhD focusing on the work of Carl Jung but then switched to organizational psychology. When I initially had dinner at Duncan's home, he described the Myers-Briggs Type Indicator (MBTI), based on Jung's personality types. The MBTI questionnaire helps you determine if you're an Introvert or Extravert, Intuitive or Sensing, and a Thinking/Logical or Feeling type. The first time Duncan explained it to me, I knew immediately what I was: an introverted intuitive type with feeling (INFJ). He made the mistake of thinking I was a different type because of the job I had at the oil company, but I knew all along I wasn't doing work that really suited me. Duncan was an extraverted intuitive type with feeling (ENFP), and though his type had similarities to mine, the difference between introvert me and extravert him was enormous. Duncan needed to interact all the time. I needed time and space by myself. We tried at various times to use these differences as a way to solve the problems in our relationship, but it didn't work. Our "type" differences were only the underpinnings for all the understandings about life we'd learned in our original families, the lenses through which we experienced our separate worlds.

I had an affinity for the MBTI and found it interesting and valuable in understanding people's tendencies and values. After a time, Duncan began to see ways in which we could work together professionally. He invited friends and colleagues to our home to demonstrate the MBTI so we could practice giving workshops together. Ironically, working together was something we did well, despite our chaotic home life.

More and more, Duncan included me in presentations he was asked to give, workshops he was paid to deliver. Eventually, we went to a lawyer to establish our independent consulting business as a legal partnership. As we worked together designing and presenting workshops for the oil company Duncan had a contract with, we also started to attract new clients: a nurses' association, a local brewery, city councils going through transitions. In addition, I started a long-distance graduate program in clinical psychology at the Fielding Institute based in California. Over and above research papers I wrote at home, I traveled around the States attending workshops and discussion groups and devouring the lecture material.

I was finally doing something that challenged me intellectually and was developing my skills and knowledge—but it was a double-edged sword. As much as this professional path excited me, I was digging myself deeper and deeper into dependence on Duncan. Now we were not only life partners, we were business partners as well. With each new project, my personal life and my income were more and more linked to him.

Despite our stimulating intellectual projects, holidays, skiing and bicycling with the family, Duncan's support for my education, and a satisfying physical relationship, Megan had been right. Duncan pumped up the volume once we were married. He ranted, raved, yelled, insulted, wouldn't listen to reason, no matter where we were. During one grocery shopping expedition, I stood open mouthed when he became so angry he started grabbing cans and boxes blindly off the shelves and throwing them into the cart. I saw people turn away from our aisle, avoiding the screaming monster Duncan had become. With my heart pounding from fear, I whispered to him, "Please, Duncan, please stop. Other people are trying to shop. We can discuss things outside." But my request only enraged him more. I stood aside until he slowed down and finally stood next to the cart. Then, shaking, I removed the things from the cart that we didn't need. He followed me to the check out and then out the door to the car. What was the issue? I can't remember. I likely just disagreed with him about something, anything. Why didn't I walk out of the store? Because I had taken on the responsibility to manage him.

One afternoon I was visiting a friend, the mother of Jamie's best friend. We were chatting and having a lovely afternoon when I got a frantic call from Duncan.

"Come home this minute. There's water shooting all over the kitchen."

"Why, what happened?"

"I tried to change the washer in the kitchen faucet."

"Did you shut off the water first?"

"No, the plumber is doing it now. He's here. It's a mess. The water shot up like a fountain and gouged a hole in the ceiling above the sink. There's water everywhere."

"Well, what can I do?" I asked, trying to keep the annoyance out of my voice.

"I just want you here. Come home."

"It sounds as though you have the situation covered. I'll come home when I'm finished."

"No, come home now!" he shrieked.

I wondered if the whole incident had been created to make sure I came home when he insisted. I hung up the phone, determined to make the point that I would not be bullied. But I couldn't stop glancing at the clock as I tried to finish my visit. I could feel anxiety creeping into my stomach as I stayed longer. After saying good-bye to Shari, I drove home to find that he was right: the kitchen was a mess. We spent the next two months getting the ceiling and floor completely replaced. Luckily, Duncan was so absorbed by the mess he'd caused, he just muttered angrily as I came in the door.

o o o

In June 1985, I wrote in my journal that I'd reached a reluctant conclusion, the same one I'd reached many months previously—that my marriage to Duncan was a mistake. That same morning, Duncan and I flew to Chicago for an MBTI conference. Duncan made such an angry fuss on the plane, arguing and yelling at me, that the stewardess came over and asked me if I wanted to change seats. I did. Just as the plane was preparing for landing, she came to me again and asked if I wanted information about women's shelters in Chicago. Surprised, I just muttered, "No, thank you."

She recognized what I could not. To me, Duncan's behavior was just another all-too-familiar occurrence. I couldn't allow myself to relate to the stewardess' concern, so I couldn't accept her offer. But that night I entered into my journal, "I am always afraid of him."

After returning home from Chicago, the endless arguments, threats, and fault finding continued, day after day, week after week, month after month. During one disagreement, Duncan screamed, "I'm firing you from our business."

I looked at him from halfway up the stairs, restrained myself from replying in kind, and quietly responded, "I own the business too. I am also the boss. You can't fire me."

For some mysterious reason, that reached him, and he even started to laugh. "Ha, I'm trying to fire the boss."

I was still shaking with anger as he walked away, chuckling.

After another argument, another time of not being able to reach him with words, I ran to the door, got onto my bicycle, and rode down the street, away from the house. Tears were pouring down my face as I raced to nowhere. All of a sudden, I saw a car out of the corner of my eye. It screeched to a halt in front of me. Duncan had come after me.

"Go home!" he yelled.

I didn't want to go home, but I couldn't get around him. Humiliated, feeling like a misbehaving child, I went home. Where else was I going to go?

The arguments didn't just affect me. During one particularly loud disagreement, while Duncan screeched, my oldest son, Adam, by this time about eleven years old, tried to save us. He ran into our bedroom and picked up the phone.

When I came into the room, Adam was asking the operator to connect him with the nearest police station. I panicked at what he was doing—calling attention to the craziness of our home. I didn't want anyone to know. I grabbed the phone out of his hand and he grabbed it back.

"Let me deal with him, Adam!" I yelled. "We're not going to phone anyone!"

Adam tried again to ask an operator to help him. This time, when I grabbed the phone from his hand, he ran into his own bedroom. Duncan followed him, still in a rage, and as I peeked around the corner of the door into my son's room, I saw Duncan grab Adam's forearm as though to restrain him. I stood there shocked, immobile with disgust at Duncan's behavior and with shame that I let my fear stop me from helping my son. It was only a few seconds before Duncan came back out again, but the damage was done—not physically, but to Adam's sense of safety. His father had already let him down, and now Duncan. And I wasn't protecting him either.

o o o

Now that we had a freelance consulting business together, Duncan often introduced me to well-known people in management and psychology. After a guest lecture in the elegant glass penthouse dining room at the Palliser Hotel, Will Schutz, up from California to promote his latest book, looked across the luncheon table at me with seven pairs of eyes on him and said, "You look like a high-priced hooker."

Duncan said nothing as he heard this man insult me, his wife and business partner. I sat as still as I could, wishing I were not there. Schutz's comment had come out of nowhere. I could feel myself blush as I looked down at my salad. Why would someone say such a thing? *He's just kidding*, I told myself—the same thing I used to say when Joe would criticize me in public.

I excused myself from the table and went to the ladies' room. As I studied my reflection in the massive mirror, I observed a woman I barely related to anymore—someone flawlessly dressed in a navy tailored suit, white blouse, and black stiletto-heeled pumps. I had no quick comebacks to deal with this sort of situation. Instead, I hid my hurt and embarrassment behind artfully applied makeup and perfectly arranged hair. I refreshed my lipstick and wondered, *Can this man see that I have sold myself out?*

o o o

On the surface it would have looked to anyone like Duncan and I were living the high life. We had moved from our affordable home in the suburbs to a larger, older house in a newly gentrified part of Calgary. The houses on our new street were pre–First World War, the time of a major building boom in Calgary, and close enough to the inner city to be prime choices for refurbishment. We were surrounded by young, wealthy geologists who were knocking down walls and installing spa bathrooms.

We carpeted the first floor in a rich blue-green, setting off a decorator-inspired black-and-white color scheme. At a sale of Chinese imports we bought shiny black end tables, a gold leaf side cabinet, and a six-panel gold and green painting of egrets flying over a lake. These complimented our black faux–Art Deco couch and the antique French china cabinet with tulipwood inlay and beveled glass doors. Our limited edition Margaret Keane print, which we'd bought during our first trip to Maui, hung on the wall above the sofa. The focus of the dining room was a new thick glass table with a granite base that could seat eight. The third-floor family room had a soaring ceiling, a stone fireplace, and wall-to-wall windows that overlooked the city skyline.

But behind the scenes, in addition to his anger problem, Duncan was unconcerned about the reality of money. He didn't even want to look at our bank account, and whenever I wanted to talk about our finances, he claimed I would never have to worry—that he would provide and live up to his duty. But he was not practical. Saturday afternoons were spent shopping for 100 percent cotton sheets, matching towel sets, crystal glassware, CDs, books, and double-breasted suits and shirts with coordinating ties. If he wanted it, he bought it.

"Let's go out for dinner," Duncan said one Thursday as he came in the door from work.

"Duncan, we've already spent four hundred dollars this week eating out. I can make something for us here at home."

As usual, he was quick to yell. "DO YOU HAVE TO ARGUE WITH ME ALL THE TIME?"

You didn't say "no" to Duncan—so we went out and spent another hundred dollars at Earl's, a popular upscale eatery with its own pizza oven and booths large enough for a family of five.

In contrast to my time living alone, when I'd counted every penny,

I was now nervously watching the credit card balance creep up and up. But we couldn't resolve any of my financial concerns. If I raised any serious issues with Duncan, we ended up in horrible arguments.

In addition to money worries, threats were standard fare. One day, during a particularly loud argument, Duncan screamed, "I am going to change the locks and throw you and your kids out onto the street."

As I heard this, I could see, back through time, young Duncan's family's chrome and plastic chairs standing on the cold sidewalk in front of their apartment building. The deep pain and anger he still felt as a result of his childhood seeped into every aspect of the life we were trying to build.

During the next fight, he picked up a kitchen chair and broke it into pieces over the center island in the kitchen. After that, he crumpled stainless steel saucepans into the side of the same cupboard with such force that they were dented beyond repair. I tried to take some comfort in the proud proclamation he'd made to me more than once—"I've never hit you"—but it didn't take much imagination to picture my skull hitting the edge of the counter.

I yelled back, especially when we were first together. I needed to feel powerful, and it's so easy to confuse noise and anger with strength. Staying quiet in the wake of his fearsome loudness made me feel as though I had no space in the relationship. So I argued, defended, threatened, and threw my diamond ring on the floor so many times I was surprised it survived. "Stop, stop, just please stop, you fucking asshole!" I'd sob in frustration. I frightened myself with my violent language. I was sick and tired of my passivity, but engaging in endless arguments didn't solve any problems with Duncan.

What would a fly on the wall have seen during that time? Duncan, entering the house after having been away for a four-day business trip. Me, excited about him coming home. Rushing to the front door to kiss him, help him with his briefcase, tell him news of what had transpired while he'd been away. Then, standing at the kitchen counter boiling water for tea. Taking the cups out of the cupboard. Setting out the milk and sugar in matching china, while upstairs he unpacks his suitcase from the trip.

Duncan calling out from the top of the stairs, "Where is my black pullover?"

"Not sure!" I yell up to him.

"KAREN, WHERE IS MY BLACK PULLOVER?"

"Duncan, I don't know."

Him rushing down the stairs. "WHERE is my black pullover?"

"Do you have to have it right now? I'm trying to make the tea."

"CAN'T YOU COOPERATE with me for one minute?"

Me just staring at him.

"YOU CUNT, WHERE IS MY BLACK PULLOVER?"

I heard this particularly odious insult so often it was almost as though I was immune to its effect. But I wasn't. I was shut down, not letting myself be aware of the wounds that were being inflicted. I had to endure. If I'd paid attention, I couldn't have coped at all.

Eventually, the tedious repetitiveness of our pointless arguments, and my ongoing failure to get him to listen to me, made me suspect that he actually enjoyed our arguing. He seemed undisturbed by our bouts. He would joke that, with his Lebanese background and my Irish heritage, we were naturals at fighting. It was natural for him, an inherited skill. He reveled in it. But to me it wasn't a joke.

Following such confrontations, I would end up with a sore throat and be hoarse for days, feeling a complete sense of failure. It was as though I was punch drunk. Hit in the head so many times I couldn't think straight. I would go to my corner, patch myself up, continue in therapy, buy new outfits, try to fool myself into thinking that it would all turn out all right, and step back into the ring to go another round.

Over the years, I yelled less and tried to deal with Duncan using education and negotiation. It was as though educating him became part of my job. What choice did I have? I thought it was a much better approach than yelling. Maybe he would actually learn and something would change.

During one of Duncan's blowups, he bellowed from the living room, "Who messed up my Sunday paper?"

Not only did Duncan have a need to assign blame, he also had to be able to read the newspaper in the condition in which it entered our house.

I steeled myself and went into the living room, rehearsing in my head how to explain to him that his reaction was unjustified. After a two-hour discussion, he reluctantly conceded that perhaps the newspaper that came to our door was not technically his and thus could be read by anyone in the house. "But if someone reads it before me, they have to put the sections back together properly, so I can read it front to back," he insisted.

"No, Duncan, they don't," I said wearily.

I was still spending far too much of my valuable time dealing with Duncan's issues—time I could be using for my own pursuits. But if I didn't try to change him, I would be leaving him on his own to insult, scream, bully, holler, rant, and rave. Wasn't he still my responsibility?

◦ ◦ ◦

When we found out there was a Jungian analyst in Calgary, an in-depth therapist who explored the unconscious through dreams, who was taking on clients, both Duncan and I made appointments to see her. I wanted help with my marriage but also wanted to explore my past and my motivations in greater depth. We both decided to enter individual therapy with her, despite a Jungian rule that ana-lysts shouldn't see both partners of a marriage. Juliet didn't seem to think this was a problem, but now Duncan and I were once again both going to the same therapist. In the back of my mind, I had the fleeting thought that perhaps sharing a therapist with Duncan was not good for me.

Juliet was a slightly chubby, mumsy woman who oozed comfort from her very pores. So different from my angular, cool mother. Soon Duncan was referring to her lovingly as Mary Poppins. As I filled journal after journal with my dreams and thoughts, my analysis with

Juliet became increasingly important to me. It was a validation that the way I saw the world was real and worthwhile and that an exploration of this could lead me to a greater understanding of my own path in life. Carl Jung believed we are guided by the part of the psyche he called the Self to the truest, most authentic wholeness of our personality. The Self sends us messages through dreams, intuitions, and synchronicities to point us toward individuation, our true essence, and away from the inauthentic life we may have constructed to deal with past wounds.

Juliet said that I was like a tortoise—a soft, fragile being carrying around a huge, heavy, armor-plated shell to protect myself from life. When things got difficult, I pulled inside, like the tortoise. When people saw me they didn't see *me,* they saw my protective coating, my shield, my uniform—which meant that people at times perceived me as cold, unapproachable, and stiff.

After a few sessions with Juliet, I began to suspect that Duncan hadn't really married me, Karen the person, but rather a body upon which he could project his fantasies—fantasies of a beautiful, sexually appealing woman he could escort on glamorous evenings out. Who would dote on his every word and dress in the clothing he bought—mainly black and covered with sequins. He needed me to be a certain way for him, and if I wasn't, I was in trouble. Yet there was no consistency to his demands, his needs, his criticisms, his dissatisfaction, so there was no way I could stay out of trouble.

I hoped that in-depth therapy would help Duncan deal with his impatience and anger. However, Juliet either didn't see the damage that Duncan was doing to my sons and me or, because she was there to be as supportive to him as she was to me, she wouldn't acknowledge it.

Despite therapy, my feelings of impotence and rage were reaching a dangerous level. I admitted to my family doctor that I had hurt the side of my hand banging the wall in frustration, in the midst of yet another argument. An X-ray showed a crack in one of the bones. I hadn't hurt Duncan. Instead, I was hurting myself.

I didn't trust or respect Duncan but was held by fear, dependence, a feeling of responsibility, and, possibly, an attraction to dangerous macho-ness. Many women think they want a more feminist man, but I suspect I was pre-programmed to be attracted to square-jawed, take-control men in black tuxedos who drink martinis—shaken, not stirred.

I brought frightening disaster dreams to Juliet. Dreams that should have indicated how damaging my home life was to me. Dreams of storms and floods, people dying, men clinging to the out-sides of buildings blown horizontal by the wind, people driven mad, others in hospital. Dreams of Duncan lying on a floor while I hit him with large, heavy vases, but in the end I run away, afraid of his power. Dreams in which I felt desperately helpless.

In my waking life, I kidded myself into thinking I was dealing with the difficulties of our marriage by the very fact that I was pour-ing my life out to a therapist.

o o o

After about two years, Duncan started going to a different therapist, Zachary, at Juliet's referral. She felt he would benefit from going to a male analyst. Again, I held out hope that things would improve. Deep down, I felt that now there was someone out there who would understand what Duncan was doing and what I was going through. And save me.

Duncan had a master's degree in clinical psychology. He was going to an analyst. He believed in the art of analysis—but as an interest-ing intellectual pursuit. He didn't translate any of it into behavioral change. Duncan said that he was exploring his anger with Zachary. He explained that he couldn't remember anything he said or did when he became extremely angry because he went into a "blind rage"—like when someone drinks way too much and blacks out. This gave me a different coping technique. When Duncan went into his rages, I'd phone his analyst to "talk him down." Sometimes I phoned from the house, but if Duncan was between me and the phone, I dared not try to get by him. I would go down the street to the nearest pay phone and call Zachary.

If Duncan was driving the car when he went into his rage, he would often pull over and get out, screaming and yelling on the sidewalk. When that happened, I would drive the car farther up the block and wait until he walked over, got into the car, and sat fuming in the passenger seat. Then I'd drive us home.

Years later, Natalie, my next-door neighbor and dear friend, told me stories from that time.

I usually went to bed before Duncan, so I didn't witness any of what occurred. She was a university professor. One night she was working late in her home office, visible from our kitchen window. Duncan could see Natalie at her desk in her office. When he phoned and she didn't answer—she was trying to get caught up with marking term papers—he called again, and then again and finally she answered. When she did he tore into her, saying he needed to talk, he could see that she was home, and that she was being rude by not answering—at two in the morning. In addition, when Duncan stood outside our house and yelled obscenities at me, she and her husband would call their kids indoors. I consoled myself with the thought that my boys only heard some of the fighting. But I heard it all—and so, I guess, did the whole neighborhood.

° ° °

I felt bombarded on all sides—I was trying to raise my boys, study to be a psychologist, and deal with my marriage. And the pressures didn't just come from Duncan. On one side, we continued to deal with Vera's addiction and instability; on the other side, we were still dealing with my ex-husband Joe's callousness and irresponsibility.

The summer of 1986 was a big year in Canada: the year of the World's Fair in Vancouver. Adam and Greg were ten, Jamie eight. Duncan and I planned our three-week summer vacation for August to include going to Vancouver for a few days to attend the Expo. We arranged a B&B months in advance because the city was going to be inundated with visitors. We also reserved a cottage on Pender Island for two weeks for the rest of the vacation, to include side trips to Victoria and Salt Spring Island.

Early in June that same summer, Jamie came home from a visit with his father. He was so excited, he was jumping up and down. "Dad's going to take us to Expo '86 in Vancouver!"

"Oh," I said, trying not to show my skepticism.

I waited several weeks to see if Joe would call to arrange the trip Jamie was expecting, and then I called him. "The boys are really excited that you're planning to take them to Vancouver."

"Oh," he said lightly, "if I go, I'll just call at the last minute and pick them up."

"But we're going to be away for three weeks in August."

"Well, if they can't go when I'm ready, I'll just go without them."

"Joe, they're children. They can't understand that."

He mumbled something irritably and then hung up.

At the end of July, the week we were to leave for the coast, I phoned Joe to beg, please, please, could he see the boys before we left on vacation? He hadn't seen them for at least six weeks.

"No, I'm busy," he replied.

"Can't you just take them out for an hour? They don't care where— take them to McDonald's. They just want to see you."

"No, I don't have time."

The night before we left for the coast, we dropped our pet cat at Adam and Jamie's grandparents' so they could look after her while we went on vacation. The boys' grandpa hugged and kissed them both, grabbing them up in his arms.

"Wait a minute," he said and ran back into the house.

He came out a few minutes later. Joe was there, visiting his parents, and his dad had tried to get him to come out and see his boys. He refused. My father-in-law looked at me sadly and a bit shame-faced and said that Joe knew Adam had a cold and didn't want to get infected. He lifted Adam up again and said to me, "How could a man be afraid of hugging his own son?"

How, indeed?

Several weeks after we returned from our own trip to the world's fair, the boys saw their father for the first time in nearly three months. Jamie returned home, angry and yelling, tears coming down his face. "Dad *did* go to Expo '86, and he told us about all the rides he went on."

We'd been home in Calgary when Joe went, but he'd never called the boys to invite them to go along with him.

I could deal—barely, but I could—with Joe's past assaults on me, both physical and emotional. But I sobbed in despair at the unfairness of him abusing our sons in this way and my frustration at the actions of this man who I thought, once upon a time, I knew. Joe couldn't hurt me directly any more, but my sons' pain from broken promises—events that never materialized, soccer games never attended, birthday presents that never arrived, visits that never happened—was like a punch to my face all over again. And again, I thought it was my responsibility to make Joe live up to his role as a father.

My lawyer advised that I shouldn't let him see the boys at all until he agreed to a regular schedule they could count on. I was sick of trying to change Joe's attitude and actions toward our sons. I'd tried litigation, counseling, and negotiators. Nothing worked. So I took him to court, asking that he be compelled to visit them on a regular basis. The judge agreed. After that, Joe would usually pick them up every other weekend. But unbeknownst to me, he often left them for the entire time with his parents.

o o o

My analyst, Juliet, listened to my endless complaints about Joe until finally, during one session, she said, "Maybe you envy your ex-husband's irresponsibility."

I choked down my tears, and my stomach clenched as I felt the tension rise. With that one quick comment, she reinforced my feelings of guilt, my doubts and fears, my endless questioning of myself, my mothering, and my motivations, rather than encouraging me to face and really do something about what my sons and I were enduring.

❍ ❍ ❍

After Vera left the halfway house and started living in her own apartment, problems continued. She told Greg that his father made so much money he should be able to have anything he wanted. She implied that Duncan and I were being selfish when we said that Greg would have the same type of bicycle, clothes, and skateboard as my sons. Selfish when we said that he could not have shoes that cost $175. I couldn't blame Greg for his constant demands when it was his mother instigating the havoc, but as all the boys were more or less the same age and going to the same school, it was important to raise them with fairness.

Greg had a quirky sense of humor that took delight in things like fake sawn-off body parts. A talented artist, he also loved playing guitar, so we signed him up for lessons to learn to play Spanish guitar properly. By the time he was fifteen or sixteen, he'd often have his friends over to hang out in the family room and practice music. After growing his hair for a while, Greg put dreadlocks in it. The next day Duncan walked into the house wearing a full-length Bob Marley rasta wig. The boys and I howled with laughter until tears were running down all our cheeks.

If Duncan had only been consistently horrible or wonderful, it would have been a lot easier.

❍ ❍ ❍

On a Sunday night while Greg was visiting his mother for the weekend, the phone rang. Duncan answered. It was Greg.

"I'm not coming home," he told his father.

"Oh, so you'll stay there tonight, go to school tomorrow from your mom's apartment, then come home tomorrow after school?"

"No, I'm going to live here now."

"No, Greg, you can't live with your mother full-time."

"Yes, I can. I'm fourteen now and Mom says I can live where I want. I'm not coming home." Greg hung up the phone.

Duncan had heard Vera in the background coaching her son as to what to say. He phoned back and got Vera on the phone.

"He wants to live with me. You treat him like a second-class citizen. You put *her* sons before your own."

Duncan phoned the police, who told him to bring his custody papers and they would meet him at Greg's mother's apartment building. About an hour and a half later, Duncan and Greg returned home together.

Even after this, Vera did not give up on her campaign to influence her son and have him live with her.

o o o

I'd wanted a home for my sons different from the one I'd grown up in. I'd wanted them to be able to express their opinions, laugh, cry, debate, disagree, free of the oppression I'd felt in my own family.

Every evening when I was growing up, my mother, father, sister, brother, and I sat around the antique oak table for supper. My mother liked to light a candle in the middle of the table and then say grace. It was a ritual I could count on. But we didn't talk during dinner. No discussion about anything important, interesting, or controversial. There was an unwritten rule that no one could laugh, cry, or relax. We never invited anyone for dinner. We would eat, then get up and do the dishes. After that, I would go to my room to do my homework. My parents treated my homework time as sacrosanct but for me, it was an escape from the rigidity of my family.

In our house, Duncan, the boys, and I would sit down nightly around the family dining table and loudly debate current events and politics. One evening, when Adam was about sixteen, he invited his girlfriend for supper. Tonya seemed a bit nervous about joining us.

"Tonya's family never talks at the dinner table," he told me. "She thinks we're fighting with one another."

But the memory of those lively dinner discussions is precious for me—they were some of the few occasions with Duncan during which there was genuinely no tension. It was the same at Christmas. As the turkey roasted, we played Trivial Pursuit, Duncan and I against our three sons. As they got older, amidst loud shoving and shouting the answers, they would win most of the time. Those were the times when I could see how it could be, should be, in a loving family.

False Front

With Duncan's enthusiastic support, and through my hard work, I completed my degree, then spent two years doing clinical training, followed by a hospital internship to become a chartered psychologist. I was learning more and more about myself through feedback about my work and how I came across to others. One day I turned to Ian, my internship supervisor, and said, "I'm such a bitch."

"Why would you ever say that about yourself?" he challenged me.

I was startled. That was how Joe and Duncan characterized me. They both wanted to point the finger at my faults - and I was so ready to hold myself responsible for their actions that I was not seeing accurately, not paying attention to the evidence.

Years before, a few months after Joe returned from his journey to Mexico and Belize, his girlfriend had phoned to say he had been picked up in Calgary for a road violation. The police put his name through a routine computer check and he was hauled off to jail for non-payment of child support. His girlfriend said that his parents, my ex-in-laws, were very upset. She didn't like Joe's attitude toward our sons either, but thought I should consider his parents' feelings. I went to court to ask that Joe be released. Despite that, he still didn't help to support our boys, or see them on a regular basis. I wasn't difficult. I was, in fact, too cooperative—a chump.

Twice now I had chosen irresponsible, childish men and then expected them to be mature. Instead of accepting how they really were, I'd tried to force them into being something they weren't, and they resented me for it. I ended up frustrated and they accused me of trying to control them. My sons ought to have had people in their lives who'd take responsibility for them and care about their feelings. But they weren't going to get those things from their father or Duncan.

In the midst of dealing with Joe, Duncan, and Vera, and worrying what effect all this was having on my sons, I was struggling to have a life—my own life. Sometimes it felt as though I was treading water, but sometimes I was making progress in the things that interested me. I became a founding member and president of the local Jung Society. I felt both a huge responsibility and excitement about managing the executive to form the new society.

In addition, around that same time, as a result of going to my analyst, Juliet, and working on my degree in psychology, I began to come to terms with some of my early family issues. I talked to some friends about my dad's alcoholism, only to discover that many of us had alcoholic fathers. As a result, I started a group for women who were daughters of alcoholics.

The first meeting was held in our home. Shortly after it began, Duncan came into the kitchen and sat down to join the group. He dominated the discussion and told the women the story of his abuse as a child. I didn't know what to do. If I interrupted Duncan, I risked a loud argument in front of these women. If I stayed silent, I was helping him preempt the meeting for his own purposes. I just kept my head down and hoped he wouldn't take long. After all the women had left, I told him he couldn't come to any future meetings. He seemed bewildered. He needed to tell his own story to as many people as he possibly could, and my group meeting had offered him a golden opportunity. My activities were there only to serve his needs.

❂ ❂ ❂

I realized early on that Adam, my oldest, with his constant questioning and confronting, was not going to last long in the conventional school system. Also, my two sons and Duncan's son were all naturally artistic. So when I read in the newspaper about a new school opening up, one based on the belief that all children learn best through the fine arts, I immediately enrolled Adam. Duncan decided to enroll Greg as well. After two years, Jamie also went to this wonderful school, which encouraged the children's creative talents and had teachers who listened to, cared for, and challenged the students.

In some ways Adam thrived in this environment, but he was often still confrontational—with me, the teachers, and the principal. He communicated his unhappiness in the only way he knew, by being argumentative. I wasn't allowed to say "no" as a child and was unassertive as an adult, so when Adam said "no," I was impatient and irritated with him. Why couldn't he just go along with things to make life a bit easier? But the truth was, the adults in his life had let him down, so why wouldn't he feel hurt and anger? I didn't want to feel impatient with my oldest son, but sometimes I couldn't stop myself. I should have simply loved and admired him for his determination to remain himself in the midst of a chaotic family—and to have the courage I never had—but at the time I couldn't see that.

Despite evidence to the contrary, I pretended my sons could be content even if I was miserable—even when I cried in frustration. I was only really happy when I took my sons out without Duncan, for hikes or bike rides, to ski in Banff, to hockey games, or out to restaurants for special dinners. Of course, I wanted us to be able to talk about what really mattered, but we avoided talking about the emotional atmosphere in our home.

The closest we ever got was when Adam confided one day, "I don't like Duncan. I know you do, but I don't."

I wanted to tell him that I felt the same way. But how could I? He was a child and shouldn't be burdened with my feelings of despair. So I tried to hold it all in, stuff it under my tortoise shell and carry on, endure.

I was living an illusion and my analyst supported that illusion. She assured me that the symbolism in my dreams indicated that my sons weren't being adversely affected by living with Duncan.

In retrospect, I think the fact that she was also Duncan's analyst colored her judgment. If I'd had support from her to either confront or leave him, he would have accused her of betraying him. Here I was again, going to a professional with mixed loyalties, one who was trying to be fair to both Duncan and me as we both went through the therapy process. I really needed someone that would help just me.

To promote the illusion I had created—that of a sophisticated, happy woman—I would slip on my black silk dress with the sequined pattern of a butterfly on the front, take up my limited edition gold case by Paloma Picasso, and carefully apply red lipstick. Then Duncan and I would head out to see the latest Thompson Highway play at Alberta Theatre Projects where I'd check my full-length black mink in the cloakroom.

Who was this woman who stored her confident red lipstick in her shiny eel-skin clutch purse? She was my tortoise shell, my false front, always there to fool the public. An elaborate front like on buildings in old western towns, designed to both protect and to show a more confident, more substantial and capable image to the world. She wore the power suit while I crept along behind, crouched in her shadow. I could barely connect with her. Robot-like, she and I were going to lunch with friends, working in my private practice office in a glass tower in the center of Calgary, taking my sons to art and swim lessons, and chatting with the other mothers at soccer games.

My work, in my own personal therapy, would be to connect to my small, hurt, unconfident self, hidden under the thick shell of appearance, bleeding with every new wound, and make her into an authentic person, the one I was really meant to be.

o o o

I didn't want to go through another divorce. Divorce was looked upon as a deep shame in my family, and a second one would be too much to bear. How could I tell my mother and grandmother I'd made another mistake?

I would listen as my mother talked of an old high school friend of hers, her contempt clear as she said, "All three of her children are divorced."

"What a relief, then, Mother," I replied in defense, "that only two of your children are divorced." My brother had brought shame too. And how quickly she'd forgotten that when I told her I wanted to divorce Joe, she'd supported my decision.

It seemed better to make the best of a bad situation—to try to change Duncan, take him to counseling, patch up the gaping holes in the reality of my marriage, than go through another divorce. One that Duncan would fight tooth and nail.

I went to therapy thinking I wanted to end the misery, but did I even know what a consistently happy existence was? Questioning, questioning. All of this and more went obsessively through my head. I wasn't addicted to drama in my life, as a friend had once suggested, but to the distractions that kept me numb. If I kept busy enough, engaged in therapy, bought a closet full of designer clothes, got a further degree, I could escape the reality of my life.

o o o

Before we moved to England in 1995, we'd traveled to Europe twice. The first time, Duncan, the boys, and I traded homes for two weeks with a family who lived in the countryside near Colchester, in the east part of England. I had long dreamed of going to England and every village and hedgerow brought back memories of reading *In Britain* magazine in my undergraduate days. After England, we flew Air France to Paris for a week. By the time we made this trip, Greg and Adam were fourteen, Jamie twelve. The boys snickered and glanced over to us when the stewardess asked if they wanted wine with their lunch. But while most of the trip was fun and exciting, Adam's surliness and unhappiness became more evident.

o o o

After nine years of struggling to get my ex-husband to spend time with his sons, and trying to deal with his callous disregard of them, there was a sudden about-face. Joe remarried.

A close mutual friend of Joe's and mine, Bernice, came out from Ontario to attend his wedding. As she and I sat having lunch the day after the wedding, she said, "I have to warn you. Your children are part of the deal."

"What do you mean?"

"Joe's new wife wants children and he won't agree. So, somehow, your sons are part of the marriage package with her."

I felt a cold chill inside me. Bernice was a very protective mother herself, and whatever she had heard from Joe and his new wife had upset her. Instead of getting the help and cooperation from Joe that I had so longed for, now I was afraid that he and his new wife would be rivals for my sons' affections.

Adam had become uncooperative and dismissive to me at home. He was such a bright and sensitive boy and I was worried about him. He'd been suspended from school once, and then expelled. He didn't like Duncan and didn't like being around him. I fully understood why and knew it was unfair to him. So when Joe and his new wife wanted him to live with them, I thought it would be good for Adam, who'd so longed for a relationship with his father. I fooled myself into thinking it would only be for a short time. I was wrong.

After he left our home, I woke up every night for a year. In the dark of the night, I'd head to our family room and sob until my head and chest ached with the pain of losing him and the guilt that I had failed my precious son. One thought sustained me: I couldn't get myself out, but at least Adam was out.

Anguish piled on top of frustration. When I phoned Adam's new high school advisor to make an appointment to talk about his school program, he told me he'd already met my son's parents. If I wanted to see him, I would have to produce custody papers. Which was the worst betrayal—Joe's fists against my face when my head hit the wall so many years ago, or the slap on the face I was getting now? Though

Duncan and I tried to talk with Joe and his wife about our sons, Joe was silent at such meetings. Instead, he turned again and again to his new wife as each question was discussed, each comment made, looking for her nods, waiting for her responses, taking no responsibility.

❀ ❀ ❀

Within three years, Duncan and I decided to visit Europe again, and this time buy Eurail tickets so we could see more countries. Jamie would come with us, Adam would go to visit his grandparents in the Czech Republic, and Greg—who, at seventeen, felt he was too old to tour Europe with us—would stay home. I didn't feel comfortable leaving a teenager alone in the house in Calgary for three weeks, but when I broached this with Duncan, he became angry, saying, "Why can't you just trust Greg to look after things?"

I didn't think we could count on a seventeen-year-old to hole up like a monk for three weeks, so we compromised: Duncan, Jamie, and I would go to Europe, and a friend would drop in periodically to check on Greg.

We flew to Amsterdam's Schiphol Airport and stayed in a hotel on one of the canals. From Amsterdam Centraal Station, we started our European train journey, traveling through Germany and Austria and on to Venice, Florence, and Rome. I strained my neck in the Sistine Chapel looking up to the finger of God enlivening Adam, while Jamie eased his video camera lens out of a space between the buttons on his shirt to shoot a quick, forbidden picture of Michelangelo's masterpiece. In the confessional at St. Peter's, the priest sent Duncan away, telling him to go home and marry me properly in the Catholic Church. We traveled south of Naples with a stop at Pompeii then stayed in the Hotel Settimo Cielo in Sorrento, perched high on a cliffside, overlooking Sorrento Bay, Vesuvius visible in the distance.

On a tourist map, Jamie recorded the number of McDonald's we ate in as we traveled through Europe. We hiked with packs on our backs, ran through train stations, ate agnolotti in Turin, drank strong coffee in Paris, and, after three weeks, arrived back in Amsterdam.

Despite minor glitches, we holidayed well together and thoroughly enjoyed Europe.

We returned home to Canada to find broken hand-blown glass, a hole smashed in the wall inside our front door, burn marks on the linoleum in the kitchen, and my university books wedged behind furniture. It took several days, but finally Lily, our cleaning lady, revealed stories of the teenagers who had partied and slept in our house while we were gone. The only reason the house was clean and tidy was because she had cleaned. She was not happy and neither were Duncan and I.

We called Greg in to talk with us and told him he was grounded. Duncan then added, "And you are not to drink for the next month."

"No, you can't do that. That's not fair," he yelled. "You're lucky. The house could have been trashed."

"Lucky? There shouldn't have been *any* damage."

"That's it, I'm going to live with my mother."

He walked out of the house. Only four months away from his eighteenth birthday, we felt that this time, we couldn't stop him. We'd gone from having a house full of teenagers to having only one son at home.

o o o

Duncan and I were in love with Europe, particularly England, and both of us said after our second trip that if an opportunity ever came for us to move there, we would. I suppose if you put something out to the Universe with enough intention, she will deliver, because about eighteen months after returning from Europe, Duncan read an ad in a Toronto paper. He always read the obits, and there was the ad, right beside the obituary column: Brookton University, north of London, needed a faculty member in a department that specialized in executive development. The ad was written as though they had Duncan in mind.

Duncan and I traveled to England in October 1994 so he could be interviewed and we could look around at housing and the countryside.

We were treated to pub dinners. I indulged in sticky toffee pudding and my favorite, spotted dick. He was offered the job. Because Adam and Greg were both eighteen and enrolled in Art College, they would stay in Calgary. For a few days after Duncan was invited to work for Brookton, Jamie considered staying in Calgary. I waited, anxious, careful not to say anything to sway him one way or the other. I felt he had the right to make his own decision. But when he came home after a weekend visit and said that he couldn't see himself living with his father, I exhaled with relief.

Unfortunately, by this point Duncan's disregard for the common-sense attitude that money coming in should exceed money going out, and my inability to rein in his spending habits, had brought us to bankruptcy. About six months before the job in England was to begin, we were reporting to government-appointed accountants and living on a strict budget. We had to keep detailed records of how much money we were bringing in and what we were spending it on. I was thankful that his new position in England would give us financial stability.

o o o

If there was ever a moment to separate from Duncan, this could have been it. For a few weeks, I debated whether I would remain in Calgary when Duncan left for England, and whether or not I would follow later. The stated reason to stay in Calgary was so I could finish a research project I was doing at a Calgary hospital and so Jamie could finish grade ten.

I looked at condo rentals for Jamie and me. I could almost taste freedom.

At first I didn't tell Duncan what I was contemplating. I needed to talk this decision through. So Duncan and I went to see his analyst, Zachary, together.

Early in the session, Zachary stated very matter-of-factly, "Duncan is a bully."

What, he knows?

Then he shocked me by asking, "But is it right to choose your son over your husband by remaining in Calgary?"

Once again, waves of that familiar feeling flowed over me, that overwhelming heaviness and guilt crushing my chest. I must be doing something wrong. Again. But was I? Shouldn't I choose a life for myself and my son that was not always overshadowed by Duncan's needs, demands, and bullying?

Zachary implied that I couldn't trust my own judgment. So I chose England and Duncan. After all, hadn't I dreamed of living in England since my university days? I finally had an opportunity to go. After selling our house and packing our possessions, Duncan, Jamie, and I moved to Buckingham, England in March 1995.

o o o

In the months before we moved to England, I was bombarded by many disturbing dreams, one more disturbing than the rest.

I hear my own voice begging me to wake up. I sat straight up in bed, shaking and crying as though I was coming up from out of a deep hole into the morning light. In the dream, *I am held captive in a concentration camp, while dark and evil forces want to hurt my son, Adam.*

I wasn't fearful that something bad was actually going to happen to Adam, so what was this about? Was the dream an attempt to wake me up to the reality of my life? By this time I was expert in ignoring obvious warning messages, so I let it go.

I'd gone to analysis to find out who I really was, what my own values were, to develop my inner self, my authentic self, but I still couldn't face the lie I was living. I didn't know yet that the different culture and completely different false front needed in the UK would startle me into the upheaval I truly needed. Living in England would provide a huge distraction from the difficulty of living with Duncan, but in addition, my experiences there would help me to dismantle— psychological brick by psychological brick—the protective shell I'd built around myself and help me deal with the truth.

The Beginning of the End

Ah, England. I'd wanted to live and work there since my undergraduate days and now here I was, about fifty miles northwest of London, an easy train journey into the city. But my excitement about moving here had left me unprepared for how strange it would be or how odd I would feel. My challenge was to get used to a country where I had to drive on the wrong side of the road and whose language was the same as mine though the words were different—I had to fill my motor with petrol, put my groceries into the boot of the car—and where the service in stores and restaurants was criticized by the English and visitors alike.

Only a few weeks after arriving, I felt so strange, I stopped the shopping trolley in the middle of Sainsbury's food store and burst into tears, shaking and unable to say what was wrong. Culture shock. Duncan came to me and put his arms around me until I stopped.

As an antidote to all the unfamiliarity, night after night I would run a bath of very hot water, get in, and read a murder mystery. Hide away. I cooked huge meals at our temporary rental home on campus. Roast beef with gravy and mashed potatoes with sticky toffee pudding for afters, or roast lamb with mint sauce and spotted dick for pudding. Comfort food.

Feeling vulnerable and ungrounded as I did, it was easy to get swept up in the glamour of the huge university community to which we now belonged. During the first month, we were invited to a reception at the university at which Princess Anne was the honored guest. In the summer, we went to Woburn Abbey to hear the Last Night of the Proms outdoor concert, wearing formal clothes and carrying a table and folding chairs, silver candelabra, baked salmon, small loaves of bread, and a bottle of sauvignon blanc for our gourmet picnic. We stood tingling from head to toe, singing—almost shouting—the traditional last song of the concert, "Jerusalem!"

Several months later, sitting in the dark on the grounds of Althorp, childhood home of Princess Diana, we thrilled to hear the stars of the Andrew Lloyd Webber musicals. A polite announcement said we should kindly refrain from erecting umbrellas as we would block the view of other patrons, so we sat with cold rain flowing down our faces, jackets heavy with water, laughing at the thought that we could never imagine doing this in Canada.

Like a hot air balloon escaping the ties that hold it to the ground, I was floating in that heady atmosphere. I was in a new performance, trying to sort out my role: "professional woman thrust into an English university community." I was used to my old false front role, "accomplished consultant dressed in designer suits," but this was different. I felt as though I were on a movie set in London's theaters, at Warwick castle, in a medieval pub. I walked the streets and roads in wonder, my feet perpetually six inches above the ground.

As we'd moved to England in March, Jamie joined his new school class only four months before the end of term so the school could assess his suitability for their university prep years. We lived out of town on the university campus for the first nine months before we bought a house, so either I would drive in to Buckingham to pick him up after school, or he would take a bus to our temporary home.

One day, Jamie seemed distressed as he opened the car door.

"I don't like coming home," he told me. "I'd rather stay at school. I can't stand it when you fight."

Changing countries had not changed things between Duncan and me, but Jamie didn't see Duncan as the problem in our home—he just hated the constant arguing. He didn't want to sort it out or assign blame. He simply wanted it to stop. I struggled between completely understanding him and feeling betrayed. *Wait a minute. I'm the victim here.* But was I? After all, I could theoretically choose to get away, but Jamie couldn't. Where would he go?

Adam and Greg, still living and attending Art College in Canada, flew over to visit us during the first summer we were there. Out at a restaurant, Adam watched as Duncan did his usual routine of complaining loudly to the waiter about the quality of his meal.

"Why are you chewing out the waiter when he has no control over your food?" Adam asked.

Adam had changed. He was older now, had new confidence, and seemed to have a different perspective on his stepfather. If I had challenged Duncan in the way Adam just had, I would have ended up a verbal punching bag, but when Adam spoke up and criticized Duncan, Duncan listened and stopped what he was doing. Living apart from us had been good for Adam, as I had hoped.

o o o

We bought a new house in a nearby town—a town so old it was listed in the Domesday Book—that was only a short walk from Jamie's new school. The house had been a show home. It was decorated with Laura Ashley wallpaper and matching draperies, and outfitted with hand-painted kitchen cabinets, top-of-the-line German appliances, gold bathroom fixtures, and a huge brick fireplace in the lounge. French doors led out to the back garden patio.

Duncan had been hired for a university department engaged in exciting and innovative work. He was lecturing MBA students and also facilitating workshops that challenged executives to look at how they impacted the corporate world in which they worked. Despite the lure of the work, many other faculty members had left that same department. Two of the faculty members who'd initially interviewed Duncan for his job later confessed that they had wondered, *Should we warn him about the problems in the department?* They decided not to, because they thought he was a strong man and might be able to solve the organizational issues. Duncan had inadvertently stepped into a hornet's nest.

The department was run by a woman named Sally. A tiny general of a woman, she had precisely cut blonde hair and preferred Ralph Lauren suits with matching bags and shoes. Although she was a freelance contract instructor and not an actual faculty member, she held the power in the team. Everyone in the department was more academically qualified than Sally, but Josie, the true head of the department, was scared of her. You either conformed to Sally's wishes or she threatened to quit. Everyone chose to ignore these dysfunctional personal dynamics because the department brought a huge amount of money into the university through its executive programs.

Sally used a human labeling system based on a Freudian-influenced theory of character armor devised in the 1920s. The five labels were designed to identify and give insight into an individual's psychological makeup, motivation, and behavior. She insisted that all facilitators use this system with participants in the executive development courses, despite obvious drawbacks with labeling people and accusations that her methods were cultish.

Duncan and I were introduced to the system even before he started to work with the department. He was easily labeled, but I was told I was a combination of four types. I guess I was harder to categorize. As I was not a permanent faculty member, it didn't occur to me that this would ever be a problem. The department needed to hire more qualified sessional facilitators for the executive courses it ran, so, at first Duncan's new colleagues were delighted that I was a chartered psychologist. But Sally felt threatened by anyone who was truly qualified.

While waiting for my tea during a break from a workshop session, I was approached by a course participant, "What type are you?"

"Actually, I've been told I'm a combination of four types."

"Oh, well, doesn't that prove it's all nonsense, then, if you can't be categorized?"

"No, I still think the system has merit in helping us to understand what might motivate someone in a social situation," I replied honestly.

Sally had been standing close enough to overhear my conversation. She approached me and asked me to meet with her alone in her room. "When someone asks you what type you are, I want you to stick to one answer."

"I can't do that," I said, shaking my head. "It would be a lie. Besides, you yourself were unable to categorize me."

"I don't care," she said, her jaw set. "I want you to do what I'm telling you now."

"Sally, I'm a psychologist, and I'm not going to act in an unprofessional manner by lying to anyone." I just couldn't do what she wanted.

Her mouth set in an unattractive way, much like a tiny dog that is about to snarl and bite your ankle. "All right, then, you're not going to be a facilitator for the program anymore."

I complained to Josie, but I was asking her to do the impossible: stand up to Sally. And of course, Sally denied she ever told me what to say about my type. Shortly after that, I got an official notice stating that I was no longer part of the team.

For so long, Duncan had wanted to be a part of an executive development department. Now, after just two years as faculty in the program, he just felt discouraged. If he stayed in the department led by Josie, he would have no choice—kowtow to Sally or risk ongoing confrontation. Presented with this issue, Frederick, the head of the Human Resources Department, decided that Duncan should move into Human Resources, removing him from the very reason we had moved to England.

o o o

Duncan was in a very tough situation at the university, but it was difficult to completely empathize with him when, at home, he continued to argue and hurl obscenities. Throughout the two years we had already spent in England, his criticisms, judgments, and threats had continued unabated. About the time he was dealing with his transition to the HR Department, he was standing in the kitchen, cursing me, calling me a cunt once again. Only this time, instead of yelling back at him to defend myself, I backed out of the kitchen, through the laundry room, and into the renovated garage we used as an office. Stumbling, I fell on the floor and drew my knees up to my chin, huddling in a fetal position. I squeezed my hands over my ears to try to block out the sound as Duncan continued to scream and rant.

After a minute or so I heard footsteps and realized he was peeking into the room to see what I was doing.

"Hurrumph" was his disgusted judgment as he turned away.

"What have I sunk to?" I whispered into the carpet.

o o o

I'd been in England two years with no therapist to talk with, so I decided to find a Jungian analyst in London. I assumed I would just pour my story out yet again. I knew the routine of being a good analysand and, so for my first appointment I brought a recent dream in which a voice said to me,

"I never dreamed I would hurt so much for so long."

But this woman was different from other therapists I'd been to—more forthright. No mincing of words.

"Get out of the marriage," she said. "Your husband is abusive and is not going to change. Get out. Then we can work on your issues."

Though a bit startled by her direct approach, I wanted to hear this. For so long I'd hoped Duncan and I would learn and grow together and heal ourselves, our past mistakes, our children, and our families. Now I was nearing the end of the road.

o o o

Many years later, I discovered an entry in my journal written at this time. I shivered as I read it:

I think Duncan was given two years notice on Friday. His contract at the university was supposed to be up in one more year. Normally it would be reviewed in November 1997 and either his contract would be renewed or he would have to leave in May '98. But the head of HR, Frederick, said Duncan hadn't had enough time to be fairly evaluated after leaving the troubled executive development department, so he won't be reviewed until Spring 1998. If he were then asked to leave, he would have a year's notice from that point.

Frederick is trying to be fair. Duncan has had a difficult time in that department, so he's being given this extra time to prove himself. Also, if things don't work out, Duncan will have the freedom to choose to go elsewhere in the UK. However, Frederick may also see Duncan as needing too much "hand-holding." While Frederick has offered Duncan a position in the main HR department, his style is that you should just get on with it. Duncan is pretty dependent—he only works up to his capacity if he's given a lot of support.

I ended this June, 1997, journal entry by writing, "After two years, what happens to us?"

I Wake Up

Starting analysis with a new therapist, one that was very straightforward about my position in my marriage, meant I could no longer shove things aside as I had been doing. Feeling guilty and sorry for myself, not asserting myself, enduring pain and frustration, thinking I always did the wrong thing—these behaviors had been my automatic fallback position throughout my life. Now was the time to pay attention to how I was living my life. And finally, something tipped the balance for me.

In October 1997, I prepared to meet Duncan for a weekend away in Brussels, where he'd been working on a consulting project. At Heathrow Airport, I found a space to park, took out a pen, and noted "Aisle F, Floor 2" on the parking ticket before rolling my suitcase to the airline check-in and boarding the plane.

Duncan was still with his executive group when I landed, so he sent a driver to take me to the Miravaux Hotel. In our room, I unpacked my suitcase, carefully placed my clothes into the dark wood cabinets, and hung a new outfit in the closet, then took the elevator down to the lobby bar where I would meet Duncan when he finished his day. I could feel the tension of the last workweek seep out the bottoms of my feet as I ordered a glass of sauvignon blanc.

Despite all our marriage difficulties, I marveled at my life. Only three years after we had made the choice to move to England, we were enjoying English music and drama, we'd solved our financial problems, and I was savoring the deliciousness of flying off to mainland Europe for a weekend break.

Duncan and I spent our weekend wandering the streets of Brussels, devouring hot waffles as ice cream and fruit syrup dripped down our chins, shopping for lace and tapestry cushions, and running our fingers over bronze Art Deco art.

An exhibit of drawings by Mucha took me back decades. I studied the original pencil sketches for "Monaco. Monte Carlo. Chemins de fers," a railway poster that had hung in my university residence room over twenty-five years before. Buying that poster at the time and putting it on the wall had signaled independence, separation from my family—freedom to express my own style.

When we flew back to London late Sunday evening, both of us were tired and looking forward to going home. I calmly retrieved the parking ticket from my bag. But the car was not in Lot 1 on floor 2, in aisle F.

Where is it? I felt a familiar tightening sensation in my chest as I anticipated Duncan's usual explosive reaction to my "carelessness." Where was our car?

Look again. I sped ahead to look for it in the next aisle. *Where is it?* My breath caught now as my throat tightened. *Don't panic. Don't panic. Don't—*

Duncan's look blackened. "Karen, where did you park it? What floor? What row?"

Again and again. "What floor? What row?" Each time louder. "What floor? What row? For fuck's sake, Karen, where did you park the car?"

I moved more quickly. Out of his reach. Fear started to build. *Please, Duncan, don't. No, no, not here, not here, not now. Where? Where is the car? Okay, calm down. Ask someone.*

"Excuse me, do you know where Parking Lot 1, floor 2, row F, is?" I asked a man nearby.

"It's here."

"It's here? See, Duncan, this *is* floor 2, row F."

But where is the car? Where is it? Oh my god, it's my fault.

Louder now, Duncan was yelling with that particular high note that meant he wouldn't stop. First I couldn't understand what I was hearing, and then I couldn't hear what he was saying. My ears felt full. Everything had gone black except a circular area right in front of me.

Don't panic. People are watching.

An elderly man turned to me and saw the tears beginning to roll down my face. He looked away, both attracted to and then embarrassed by someone making a fuss.

I asked someone else, who said, "Have you checked Parking Lot 1-A?"

No, we hadn't.

"Duncan, I think we have to go to another parking lot."

Several minutes later, there it was. Parking Lot 1-A, floor 2, row F. I was shaking so badly I collapsed in a heap on the boot of the car. Somewhere in the back of my head, I could hear a voice from long ago—a friend impatiently confronting me near the end of my marriage to Joe: "How can you let him talk to you that way?"

We drove up the M1 in the dark of night. I stared out the window, watching the cars in six lanes, moving quickly, more quickly than cars on a North American highway. I liked the way the road cut its way through the picturesque English countryside. Fields once joined as whole farms were now separated forever by this river of moving vehicles. I leaned into the door, staring at my face in the window. When Duncan turned the car into our driveway, I opened the door and got out before it came to a complete stop.

о о о

I knew then the meaning of the expression, "The penny dropped." Something had changed. Clicked into place. I could not go back to who I had been, but where was I going to go? What was I going to do? In January 1998, I picked up a magazine and read my horoscope for the year ahead. I was about to undergo a drastic change, possibly a loss, it said. My life would be turned completely upside down.

Our ugly dance could only end one way, couldn't it? With divorce?

Duncan became even more critical of me. He told me he was not going to "cater to my fucking neuroses." He tried to push me back into my box of submissive desperation, but something in me snapped further. He didn't understand that his old ways were not going to achieve what they had throughout our marriage.

This was a struggle I had to engage in if I was ever to break out of this half-life I'd created for myself. But I was also fearful. Awake now. Aware. I began to deliberately cover things up and hide things away if I thought they would anger him. I was heading down a new road and I would not be coming back. My smile—the one that Duncan had always said could light up a room—was now frozen on my face.

o o o

I woke up from a dream. *On the back of my head, underneath my hair, there is another face growing.* As I noted the dream in my journal, I remembered Janus, a god in ancient Roman religion and mythology. He was the god of beginnings and transitions, looking to the future and the past.

But even though I felt I was stepping across the threshold into my future, in reality we were still engaged in the same old pattern: the two of us arguing, Duncan running up the stairs and screaming that we were finished, Duncan retreating to the living room to sleep.

"I think you're unhappy," he finally said. "We should break up."

You would think this would have been the end, that I would have realized that no more could be done to salvage this wreck of a marriage. But that was not how it worked. I knew that Duncan had a bottomless pit of tolerance for pain, argument, and drama, but perhaps I did too—or perhaps I still had some hope.

"Well, before that," I suggested, "will you go with me to a marriage counselor?"

"That's just what you want, isn't it?" he shrieked.

A coldness and sense of isolation came over me, like I'd felt so long ago when I lived with my parents. My thick shell surrounded me but Duncan couldn't see it. I'd fought this feeling all my life, a feeling that was frightening and confusing yet familiar. Should I sink into the feeling now—face it, deal with it—rather than try once again to push back the ocean of loneliness with high fashion and light lunches?

Duncan was now on shifting sands in both areas of his life: his position at the university had substantially changed from the one he'd originally been hired for, and I was not quite so predictable anymore.

As for me, night and day, even when I would try to push it away, I couldn't forget the struggle I was engaged in. I had horrible dreams of men wanting to kill women and the women not believing it. One night I awoke from another vivid dream:

I'm holding a cat with a horrific injury on its leg. She is shaking with pain and fright. Others see her and don't think she is worth helping or worrying about, but I hold her and she rests her head on my arm in relief.

Was I getting a glimpse of the hurt, bleeding self I had hidden under my shell for so much of my life? This was what I had to face. If I could comfort that cat, I could save myself.

o o o

It still took one more incident before all the pieces snapped into place. But I was a different person when next Duncan attacked. It happened in February 1998, when we were to travel to Germany to work with an insurance company.

As we drove down the M1 on the way to the airport, Duncan asked me to phone the airline on my mobile to check the terminal number. As I tried to listen to the recorded message, he began to talk. I couldn't hear, so I waved my hand at him to be quiet.

He raised his voice. "Karen, you do this to me. You set things up so I'll yell and then you can blame me."

Huh? I could barely understand what he meant. Not content to blame me for *my* behavior, he also blamed me for his.

Duncan drove onto the side of the motorway, stopped the car, and threatened to get out. "I'm not going to Germany!"

With an eye on the hundreds of cars racing by only a couple of feet away, I was nearly whispering. "Duncan, I know you'd never let me go to Germany on my own, so why are you saying this?"

He was quieter now. "I find it hard to think about working with you when we've had an argument." He stayed in the car.

We slept in separate rooms in Bad Vilbel, Germany. Despite what was going on behind the scenes between us, as usual we did a professional job and the workshop was well received.

When we landed back at Heathrow, a steward was rude to me as I disembarked the plane. I was shocked but when I mentioned this to Duncan, he reacted with fury. Raising his voice, he attacked— "Karen, you're just so difficult"—and walked quickly on, ahead of me.

I was stunned and puzzled. I could feel my stomach tighten and began to feel sick. Hoping to avoid a further confrontation, I stood on the opposite side of the baggage carousel.

Duncan walked over to where I was standing as I grabbed my bag. "I don't feel like driving in the same car with you to go home."

I let out a big sigh. "Fine, who will use the car and who will take a cab?"

Obviously thinking better of this, he replied, "Well, we can drive together but not talk."

"Duncan, I can't do this anymore."

Sneering at me, he raised his voice. "Oh, yes, you can. *You love it.*"

While inside I was tight with hurt and anger, my exterior stayed calm. When I asked him for the parking ticket, he gave it to me. But he must have thought I was only posturing, because he said, "Let's go."

"No, Duncan, I'm not driving with you."

He followed along behind me while I looked for signs to the parking lot. "Okay," he said, "Let's drive together."

I couldn't blame him for ignoring what I'd just said. I'd given in to his threats so many times. I stopped, turned around, and faced him,

"You must not have heard me. I'm going to do what you wanted—go home separately."

I walked on ahead of him to the car, got in, drove home, and went to bed.

o o o

Sounds of knocking woke me at about two in the morning. There was no one at the front door so I went into the kitchen. Duncan was standing on the patio, knocking on the French doors that led into the breakfast area. He had come all the way from Heathrow by taxi and said he couldn't find a hotel room in Buckingham.

He followed me into the front hallway, where I turned, wiped my tear-stained face with the back of my hand, and quietly stated, "I want out." I looked down, pulled my wedding ring off my finger, reached over and put it into his suit pocket. Then I turned again and walked back up the stairs. He slept on the living room couch.

The following morning, Duncan came into our bedroom, carrying a suitcase from the front hallway closet. "Is this what you really want? Aren't you going to talk to me?"

I answered in a tiny voice that seemed as though it came from someone else. "I don't know what to say to you any more." My face was dry now.

Duncan was uncharacteristically quiet as he opened one of the drawers of his dresser, took out three folded shirts one by one, and carefully placed them into his suitcase. I suppose he was wondering how many days of clothing he would need. He looked at me and opened his mouth, then opened his sock drawer. I sensed that he'd turned around again but by then I'd turned away.

I wanted a divorce and I meant it—it was not a threat to bully him, or to get my own way. I was exhausted and wanted out. And this time he knew I meant it. Knew it in the fear-filled pit of his stomach and the lonely terror of his heart. A minute later I heard the zipper close on his case.

"I'm going to a hotel for a couple of days. We'll talk about this later."

I stood motionless in the bedroom and heard his feet hit the carpeted stairs. I listened as he paused to put on his shoes, as he opened the door and then closed it. Then I went into the bathroom and splashed my face with cool water, crawled back into our bed, and covered my head with the duvet. Tears crept out of my eyes, made their way down my face, and onto the pillow.

◦ ◦ ◦

Duncan came back home after a couple of nights in a local bed and breakfast. Begged me to give our marriage a chance. I was noncommittal. If I were going to end this, I needed to buy time and get realistic about how I was going to support both myself and my son.

A couple of weeks later, still in February, I heard from a university in Mexico where I'd applied to do a presentation paper for a conference. They said my topic was too management-oriented and they really wanted something that would fit in with their psychological curriculum. I wasn't invited to the conference and felt devastated. Here I was, a psychologist who'd only fallen into management work because of Duncan, being rejected from a conference because my approach was too management-heavy.

When I told Duncan, he reacted immediately, loudly saying he would contact them and tell them they could not treat his colleague that way.

Embarrassed, I replied, "You can do what you like on your own behalf, but not on mine." I felt like a child.

"It's my *right* to contact them," he said, "and if you won't let me, I'll never give you information about academic events again. I'm the one who told you about this conference in the first place, and I didn't have to."

"Duncan, you're threatening me," I said, my tension rising.

"I have the right to phone them," he repeated.

He couldn't stop bullying me to get what he wanted. Manipulation, intimidation, yelling—he had no other tools in his repertoire. He didn't even recognize what he was doing.

"I don't know how I can go on living with you," he said.

I walked out of the room. He followed me into our home office, where I phoned a friend and asked if I could come over for tea. I ignored him when he got angrier and took off his wedding ring.

He went into our bedroom and, again, packed to go to a hotel. Over and over, he repeated, "Is this was what you want? I'm going to take the car. Aren't you going to talk to me?"

I said what I'd said to him before: "I don't know what to say to you anymore."

Then I closed the front door behind me and walked to my friend's house.

o o o

That night I went to bed alone, only to awakened at 2:30 a.m. by the telephone.

Duncan. Of course.

"I'm in a hotel. I'm sorry. If it seemed like I was threatening you, I didn't mean it like that."

I believed him. Not that he was sorry, but that he didn't realize what he'd done. "You've said this before," I answered. "We can talk tomorrow." I hung up.

Duncan came home but moved into the guest bedroom. He said it was his protest against my lack of caring, but it suited me. Of course, the longer he stayed in the guest room, the more he complained.

"Your son has the best room in the house," he said. "He's away at university and only using the room on weekends, so I should get his room and en-suite bathroom."

Jamie was upset at being moved from his room, but Duncan and I each having our own space helped to reduce the frequency of our louder disagreements.

That spring, separate space and the fact that Duncan had started to go to another Jungian analyst twice a week for anger management made a difference in the tension between us. His analyst advised him to just let me talk and really listen. He also gave him things to do to relieve his anger. Remarkably, when we were about to launch into yet another argument, Duncan would go for a walk or take a drive, and when he returned he would be quiet.

As Duncan began to seem less angry, the pressure in the house started to lift—and as it did, many things came out that I had never discussed before with Duncan, even old issues from before we were married. Things I had been too afraid to talk about and had just swept under the carpet—like how I felt when he wanted sexual adventures to be part of our relationship. And some of the time, he listened.

One day he commented, "You're softer now."

"That's because I'm not constantly having to defend myself," I said. "I can let down some of my guard."

Following his analyst's advice, he just listened.

o o o

Simultaneously, other changes began to occur. During our time in England, I had overindulged. Indian takeaway, fish and chips, roast beef with gravy, and sticky toffee pudding had added inches to my waistline. Duncan, too, had steadily gained weight since we'd been married. So he decided to join the local health club and I began to diet.

As I began to lose weight, I joined him at the gym, and together, we ate innovative diet food—huge prawns dipped in spicy sauce, accompanied by glasses of sauvignon blanc. When Duncan began to see results, he bought black leather trousers and a black leather jacket from a trendy boutique on the King's Road in London. I took my suits to a tailor to be altered.

Periods of calm were still interspersed with threats, however. Duncan was like a dry drunk—he could control his behavior some-times, but bullying was an addiction he couldn't shake. Just when it seemed we were making some progress in our relationship, out of the blue he said he was going to divorce me right then. This was a threat with weight behind it, since without Duncan, my residency status would no longer be valid, and both Jamie and I would be forced to leave England and go back to Canada.

A couple of days later, Duncan relented, saying he would never do that to me.

Amidst the threats, he would quiz me, asking things like, "What percentage chance do you give our relationship?"

Out of pity I would say, variously, anywhere between 1 and 5 percent, depending on how I felt that day.

"Okay, 5 percent, that's good," he would say with a smile, "I can live with that. We've got a chance."

Duncan was so unpredictable I couldn't let my guard completely down. He had been so successful in keeping me by his side with threats and criticism that if I forgot for even one moment what he was capable of, and how vulnerable I had been throughout our years together, I was doomed. I was no longer suffering from the delusion that he would change. The only reason he was working with his therapist to get his anger under control was because I was threatening to leave. In order to find out if Duncan was honestly succeeding in his effort to change, I would have to risk everything all over again and say I would stay—and I wasn't willing to do that. This time I was not going to take the chance of backing down.

Through our years together, Duncan must have thought that in between our horrible fights I recovered—that I wasn't permanently injured by any of what happened. He was wrong, of course. One day, he asked if I'd ever felt under pressure with him. I was astounded by his question. How many times had I begged him to stop yelling and cursing? How many times had I thought that if I just reworded my requests, he would be able to hear me? How many times had I thought it was my responsibility to teach him to stop threatening us? How many times had I felt afraid, frustrated, shamed, upset, fearful, as though my stomach were being ripped out through my mouth?

The only kind of person who could stay with Duncan was someone like me—a person who denied feelings, suppressed them, hid them, tried to keep them under control—or someone like his ex-wife, who had drowned her sorrows in vodka. And because I feared that, like her, I would disintegrate, I always retreated behind my hard shell. I *needed* that armor. I couldn't risk getting in touch with my real feelings, my sensitivity and vulnerability; I couldn't even acknowledge those parts of myself. Standing like stone, sometimes I looked as though I just didn't care.

◦ ◦ ◦

One night as I lay reading, I heard a thump outside what was now my bedroom. I opened the door and saw Duncan stretched out, lying on the floor of our hallway, crying, whining, begging me to give him some promise that I would not end the marriage.

"I took some painkillers," he said. "I tried to kill myself."

I kept myself calm. I couldn't risk becoming emotional, because this was clearly another of Duncan's attempts to manipulate me. I needed to go into clinical mode and be the psychologist I had been trained to be.

"Okay," I said, "how many did you take? I'll take you to the hospital but they *will* commit you. Is that what you want?"

He looked up at me. "I took seven. No, I don't need to go to the hospital."

I wondered if I was taking a risk. What if he'd taken more than that?

But Duncan got up off the floor and started to walk back to his room. "You don't care about me. And I'm not going to the Maple Leaf Ball with you." He threw this threat over his shoulder just before he closed the door to his room.

The Maple Leaf Ball is a yearly event for Canadian ex-pats, a black-tie event that even the Canadian Ambassador to England attends. In London it is held at the Savoy Hotel. That year it fell on Valentine's Day weekend. Duncan and I had bought tickets for the ball months ahead of time, and had made a reservation to stay the night in a hotel in London. We'd made plans to go to our favorite French restaurant, La Poule au Pot, for a Valentine's lunch the following day.

At breakfast the next morning after Duncan's pill incident, feeling strangely fearless, I said, "I've already bought my dress for the ball, and Frederick and Nancy are going, so I'll go with them. If you want to stay home, that's fine. I'm not going to miss this, and I intend to have a good time."

I could see he was upset with me, but his reaction also showed that his threat had been a bluff, as perhaps all his threats had been.

Later that day he approached me and said, "All right, I'll go with you."

 ❧ ❧ ❧

The ball was as magical as I had imagined it would be. I dressed in a full-length, off-the-shoulder, black taffeta gown, and Duncan wore his tuxedo. Guests entered the hotel at the mezzanine level then descended a curved staircase into the main ballroom filled with large tables surrounding the dance area. We were served a four-course meal and then the orchestra started to play. Around our table sat Duncan's boss Frederick, his wife Nancy, and several other couples. I felt detached from Duncan as he and I twirled around the dance floor until one in the morning and, thankfully, no arguments marred the evening.

The next day we walked to La Poule au Pot, a short walk from Sloane Square Tube Station. We sat facing each other over an old wooden table, fresh flowers in the center, and over glasses of cabernet sauvignon, Duncan opened the conversation.

"Your insensitivity is the problem in our marriage," he said. "You should behave differently toward me. You know, other people think you're too harsh."

I didn't just hear but viscerally felt his attempt to shame me. The coldness I felt looking at him crept up from my stomach and tingled out to the ends of each strand of my hair. "Duncan, you are now demonstrating the behavior that's causing me to leave our marriage." Every carefully articulated word I spoke was a bullet aimed at his chest.

I left him sitting at the table, walked out of the restaurant, and waited outside on a bench by the statue of Mozart. Deceptively calm on the outside, inside my heart beat madly enough for it to be seen through my blouse.

◦ ◦ ◦

And still we carried on, unwilling to break the bonds between us. Duncan was able to control his anger when we worked together and when we had weekends away. We went to the Peak District to stay in Riber Hall, an historic fourteenth century inn, where we shared a hot tub, candle-lit gourmet dinners and hikes into Matlock. In the midst of my continued stance that things could not go on as they'd been, we decided we could get along if we only made love in hotels.

The Struggle

In May 1998, Duncan and I went for a weeklong holiday to Lebanon to celebrate Duncan's 58th birthday in the land of his ancestors. We had a special lunch for his birthday at one of the riverside restaurants in Zahle, birthplace of Omar Sharif, and took a bus tour to the temples at Baalbek, the souk and mosques of Tripoli, the wine cellars of Ksara, and the ruins of Anjar. Standing amidst the ruins in Byblos, I took the picture of Duncan in his black shirt and white trousers. During a two-day side trip to Syria, I took the photo of him sitting on top of a camel at the Umayyad Fortress outside the town of Palmyra. Just over one year after this trip, those photos would sit on top of his coffin.

We stayed at a hotel in Beirut with a bar and restaurant on the main floor. One evening, Duncan said he was heading down to the bar. I told him I would follow in a couple of minutes. I dressed carefully and put on my makeup, then descended to the first floor. When I reached the bar, I saw him sitting with a drink in his hand. I slid onto the barstool beside him.

"Do you come here often?" I whispered low and slow.

After the initial surprise, delight crossed his face. We seduced each other up to our room.

On this trip, the everyday expectations of our relationship were lifted and we could enjoy each other in the way I always hoped we could—again, by making love in a hotel. If only it was always this way between us.

o o o

When we returned home to England, Duncan found a local bed and breakfast he liked, and during that spring and summer he moved back and forth between it and our house. He would call from the university and say that he felt like being alone and then he'd stay at the B&B for a couple of days. Only months later did I realize that part of the reason for him being away from home had to do with another woman.

All the while I paid close attention to horoscopes as well as my dreams.

> *You're not free to do as you wish. Even if you try, you find that, like a puppet attempting to escape the will of a puppeteer, various strings rapidly pull you back to position. The difference is that your strings are psychological strings. They are attached to a person whose moves you have deliberately chosen to let influence your own. The good news is that soon, that person will start to agree with you about where you both should be heading.*
>
> Jonathan Cainer, Daily Mail, June 23, 1998

I hoped that this prediction was correct, but even if Duncan didn't agree about where our relationship was going, me feeling that I could ignore his demands and feel stronger about my own decisions, I still felt that I had to stick to a path that was good for me.

o o o

That summer, I led a workshop on organizational change for a major insurance company. I lectured on aspects of the psychological impact of change in their organization, then the participants moved into various rooms to discuss the lecture material. I circulated among the groups of people, commenting, helping, and suggesting.

Sitting on his own was a dark-haired, solemn-looking lawyer

named Lionel who worked in London. He motioned me over to sit and chat.

"Do you ever come to London?" he asked.

"Sometimes," I said.

"Would you ever have time to go to lunch with me?" he asked.

I didn't feel attractive. I was surprised that any man would approach me or find me interesting enough to ask out. But, I was intrigued. A couple of weeks after meeting, I phoned Lionel to say I was coming to London. I didn't hide the lunch date from Duncan, but I did hide my excitement. I met Lionel at Liverpool tube station and we began what he called a "light romance."

That day, we ate in an Indian restaurant set in the middle of a park and then he showed me one of his favorite places, Leadenhall Market. He knew nooks and crannies in the city that I didn't—restaurants you entered via tiny spiral staircases, old pubs hidden down crowded pedestrian alleyways, ancient cemeteries lurking behind coffee shops, bistros overlooking major thoroughfares.

He was handsome, intelligent, and assertive, a few years younger than me. When he laughed, he threw his head back in delight, opening his mouth to reveal perfect white teeth. He had beautifully formed hands and no wedding ring. But he was married with three children and he knew I was married. Had he done this before?

I wasn't a cool Englishwoman who could take his interest in stride. I was a silly schoolgirl in my forties, a woman who had been shouted and screamed at, taken for granted, my confidence undermined too many times, and, worse, told that it was all my fault that it was happening. When Lionel hugged me, I pulled away nervously and gave him a sisterly clap on his back, afraid of my own need. I told myself I wasn't out for romance—no, I rationalized, with a degree in philosophy as well as law, he could advise me on my ideas for a book about psychology and business.

Had he come along now to help me ram down the walls in my life? Did he want a diversion in his life while providing one in mine? We spoke about poetry, philosophy, and negotiation skills. He introduced me to new authors and ideas. When I looked into the mirror of Duncan's eyes, I saw myself as difficult, bitchy, and boring. When I looked into Lionel's, I saw someone sexy, interesting, and possibly dangerous.

You could accuse me of already shopping around for a man who would fill the emptiness and loneliness I anticipated after Duncan and I separated. I was definitely trying to attract something—or someone—new into my life. Was I lying to myself about wanting to be on my own? Like the mythological Sisyphus, I had been rolling the same boulder up the hill for years and all I could see was the boulder—I needed to see what was over the hill before I *was* over the hill. But sometimes events are set in motion that are impossible to predict. It is as though they have a life of their own. Like a row of dominos, once one goes down, the rest follow.

o o o

Early one evening in July, a couple of weeks after my first lunch with Lionel, Duncan walked into the living room and said he was going out to meet a woman he worked with at the university.

"I'm getting together with Shelley for a beer at the Cross Keys pub," he said. "I won't be too late."

"Oh," I responded, "is that how we are going to do things from now on? We can accept invitations for evening dates? Well then, I guess I can do that too. When I have a male friend I want to talk with, I usually go out for lunch, but I guess the evening would be fine too."

A worried look crossed Duncan's face. "I didn't think of it that way. I'll call Shelley and tell her we can have lunch tomorrow instead."

That same night I woke up startled by a dream. *I'm driving in a car that suddenly and accidentally leaves the road. I look at Duncan because I assume he's driving, but he's fast asleep. I try to wake him up but he is too deeply asleep. I'm in the driver's seat. I'd been driving the whole time.*

Now that I was no longer quite as intimidated, was I the one driving our fate?

Later that same month, Duncan and I decided to go to the Netherlands for a bed-and-bike long weekend. After an eight-hour coach ride from Buckingham to a country hotel about fifty miles from Amsterdam, we found our room and then ate supper with the other people on the tour. The next morning we collected our rental bicycles and packed lunches—country ham and cheese, home-baked bread, apples, and a half-liter of wine for each of us. We cycled through a dark forested area, expecting to see crumbs on the path and a candy cottage around each corner. In Appeldorn we cycled around the formal gardens of Paleis Het Loo and then leaned our bicycles against a brick wall nearby in order to have tea at a lovely patio restaurant.

As I lifted an open-faced prawn sandwich to my mouth, Duncan again asked the percentage chance I gave our marriage. I knew he was trying as hard as he could to convince me to stay with him, to stay in our marriage. Perhaps he even wanted me to believe he could change. But my dreams were telling me another story.

That morning, I'd woken from a warning dream:

I'm married to an Arab-looking man who is holding me captive inside our home. My husband is restraining me, holding me down and holding a knife. I yell, "Get help!" to a woman who is there, but she doesn't have the courage to do it.

Now, finally, I was paying attention. This dream confirmed what I knew in my heart. I couldn't risk surrendering to Duncan, a half-Lebanese-Syrian man, who had emotionally imprisoned me in our marriage. Though the dream indicated that I didn't yet have the courage needed to deal with Duncan, I was more aware now. I had to stay alert, on guard, and in control, or my life would go back to the nightmare of his anger, screaming, and threats.

"Duncan, I still want to separate," I answered.

o o o

Back home in England, we were still sleeping in separate bedrooms. In the middle of the night I heard, once again, a knock and then a thump at my bedroom door. I opened it to find Duncan slumped on the floor, gasping, "I took an overdose of painkillers."

Again.

I hardened my heart and became very practical: "Okay, how many did you take? I have to know because I have to decide if you need to go to the emergency ward." I paused. "You know, when they realize you've attempted suicide, they'll put you into the psych ward for interview and observation. So, how many?"

"Eight."

"Well, then I think you're likely fine—you'll sleep it off."

Again, I didn't feel totally comfortable with this. I was gambling a bit. Maybe he'd taken more than he'd said—but, knowing Duncan, I doubted it. He was almost two hundred pounds; I thought the pills wouldn't do him too much harm. And I knew he wouldn't want the embarrassment of a psychological exam.

The next morning he looked a bit sheepish, but was fine. I had gambled correctly.

o o o

I looked at my horoscope again the next month in the Daily Mail.

> *Natural justice is being dispensed. As you watch a certain situation from a seemingly helpless point of view, it should soon become apparent that everything is working out perfectly. Resist the temptation to give this process a helping hand. Remain as neutral as you can. You can't accelerate the course of events, but you can slow it down by inadvertently getting in the way. Be a witness as far as possible and, where you have to take action, try to be wise and restrained.*
>
> Jonathan Cainer, Daily Mail, July 16, 1998

I would like to think that I always remained wise and restrained, but I know I didn't. Feelings bubbled up in me like hot lava, uncontrollable and burning everything in their path. And in addition to dreams and horoscopes, so many other messages were coming to me intuitively, my Jungian Self trying to guide me. It was difficult to discern which to pay attention to and which to ignore.

◦ ◦ ◦

Over the summer, Duncan and I traveled back and forth from England to work on a project he'd been assigned to in Milan and asked me to co-facilitate.

During one of these trips, I worked one on one with one of the German men in the group I was facilitating. Jurgen was a powerful and immensely attractive man whose energy dominated the seminar room. He was having difficulty working with some of the Italian executives and in reaction, was throwing papers, stomping around the room, and yelling insults. I sat with this man for an hour, listening to him sob with frustration. After that, throughout the week, I felt him staring at me. He sought me out to talk even outside the sessions. He joined me for breakfast when he saw me eating alone. When I walked into a room, I could feel a wall of testosterone coming from him. He was such a powerful presence that even Duncan commented on it. I felt disturbed. Off-kilter. Not in control.

Jurgen was flirting with me. Was it obvious to anyone else? How would I deal with this? Did he do it with every woman he met? After the workshop was over, the whole group went to dinner together, and everyone drank too much. Fueled by too much Limoncello and too little food, I abandoned the elegant image I'd attempted to cultivate during our time there and teased Jurgen with a flirtatious foot under the table. I barely cared if my overtures were welcomed. After so many years of unhappiness, I couldn't contain all the feelings that were coming to the surface—excitement, aggressiveness, shame, fear, frustration, and hurt.

That same month, I had another powerful dream:

There is a river, as wide as the St. Lawrence, the water rushing by quickly under the frozen surface. I'm skating on it and fall through the ice—but only up to my knees. I'm not in any danger.

My feelings, like the river rushing under the ice, had been held tightly for so long under my frozen exterior, my perfect makeup and power suits. I felt that the dream was telling me there really was no danger in acknowledging my feelings. I could fall into them. I realized with a shock how much this contrasted with the dream where I was being held captive in my home by my husband. Here I was, only one month later, having a dream of change, transformation, and "breakthrough."

o o o

During this time of turmoil, Duncan didn't share all his thoughts with me about our marriage, but he did share with others what he was going through. I wouldn't see this e-mail he'd sent to his friend Bob in September 1998 until many months after Duncan was gone.

> *To: Bob_Heffernen*
> *From: Duncan@brookton.co.uk*
> *Subject: Me and my life*
>
> *Dear Bob:*
> *It was good to talk with you after all this time, especially with the split that is occurring between Karen and I. I particularly value and need your perspective on matters, as I sometimes find it very difficult to see the forest for the trees. A good example of this is the negative feedback I got earlier this evening from Karen re how I was not a good stepfather to Jamie and how our marriage was worse than her marriage to her previous husband, Joe. This hurts and I begin to question the whole premise of us taking time to sort things out. If things are so terrible, what possible chance is there to ever have a new and different relationship?*
> *At times like this evening, I feel like a complete failure and a horrible person. How can any woman in her right mind want to have a relationship with such a terrible man? Perhaps*

I should seek out another person with whom I have no history or baggage.

And, yet, I do believe Karen is saying what she says from a lot of pain and hurt she has endured in the marriage. There have also been a lot of good things about our marriage for the both of us—we enjoy each other's company, we are intellectually compatible, we work well together, we love each other and are great lovers with each other. These are all aspects of the relationship which I don't want to give up.

As I mentioned to you on the phone, I've gone through a physical transformation—I've lost 47 pounds or as we say over here, 4 stone and 5 lbs. I've also continued with my analytical therapy, which has really been helpful. I've learned how to better manage my aggressiveness and to be a lot more patient with others and with myself. The one thing I've been working on, and it is a full-time project for me, is how to contain my strong need for affection and assurance. Sometimes this need becomes so overpowering that it scares others, especially Karen.

I have this little boy (in me) who never got the affection, love, and support he needed as a child and at times this need becomes so strong it can scare Karen and others because of its intensity. It takes up a lot of psychic space and Karen feels overwhelmed.

I've made some important changes in how I am in the last 6 months but Karen says I'm like the boy who cried wolf. Presently she has told me she doesn't trust me and is afraid of me because of my past behaviors. She is also confused because things are changing but she doesn't know if she can trust the changes. And most important she's about to turn 50 in January and she wants to go for it for herself and to stand on her own 2 feet without my support or help.

It comes down to, what kind of life do I want to lead? At times I feel beaten down by the past and I want to throw in the towel. However I do love Karen and I believe we now have

a real chance to live the kind of life we know, in our hearts, we
are both capable of. And that is why I'm going to go through
with this "separation."

  I hope these rambling notes are understandable. I do value
your friendship and whatever comments or insights you might
have. This is a very difficult time for me and I appreciate your
support.

  Affectionately
  Duncan

The e-mail, still in Duncan's "saved e-mails," revealed that he
was aware of what he was doing, yet his panicky fear kept him from
making any significant changes. He was right about my fear of him
and his overwhelming need to demand love, attention, and his own
way. But there was no mention of what form these demands took or
the effect they had on me, or our children.

◦ ◦ ◦

In September 1998 I presented a paper called "Libido in the Workplace"
at a conference in London. It was based on research I'd started at
the beginning of the summer. I was looking into whether having an
attraction to a colleague, even if it never went beyond fantasy, made
working together more productive. People jammed into the room to
hear my talk. It was standing room only. I was interviewed for an
article in a local paper. In my presentation, I referred to examples in
my own life, including my friendship with Lionel, though I didn't
refer to him by name.

  Duncan challenged me. "Why would you look to other men, not
me, to provide the stimulus to your 'libido in the workplace'? Do you
know how embarrassed I felt, standing there listening to you?"

  "He's a colleague, Duncan. That's what my research is about:
how work relationships are enhanced by attractions in the

workplace—attractions that are fun but don't go any further. Relationships that *don't* turn into affairs."

Earlier that summer when I'd begun my research, colleagues had sent me to Eric, a professor in Brookton's psychology department and an experienced writer, to discuss my ideas for turning the research into a book. I'd found Eric encouraging and easy to talk with, but in addition, an attractive man. Though clearly in his forties, the Scottish lilt to his voice and the crinkles in the corners of his eyes gave the impression of a naughty boy masquerading as a man. I'd felt an instant attraction to him and he'd invited me to return any time for a chat.

I knew I wouldn't see Jurgen from Germany again, but Lionel and Eric were here in England, and I was stimulated by their interest. My energy had changed, interested men had begun to circle, and for the first time since my marriage to Duncan, I was noticing.

The Countdown Begins

*I*n September 1998, I flew to Prague to conduct a weeklong executive training program for a medical company. Duncan wanted to come along but I really just wanted to get away from everything, including him.

John, my usual co-facilitator for such projects, wasn't free that week, so he recommended David, a consultant familiar with the programs we were running. When I arrived in Prague, I met David in the hotel lobby, and we walked to a lovely rooftop restaurant in the old town, next to the Vltava River. We needed to get to know one another and go over the project.

Partway through dinner, while we talked, my eyes were following David's hand movements as he poked at a tab of butter for his bun, picked up his knife, cut his meat, and carried it with his fork to his mouth. I felt an uneasiness creep over me—something I couldn't put my finger on.

The next morning, we met at the course location to discuss the day. David suggested an icebreaker exercise as a beginning to the workshop, and before I could stop myself, I answered in a scathing, sarcastic tone, "I'm not going to do *that* exercise. You can just think of something else."

For the next forty-five minutes, as though I was someone else, I raised my voice, repeatedly criticizing this perfectly normal, reasonable man who had done absolutely nothing wrong, and watched the growing alarm and dislike on his face. Halfway through that first morning, I finally realized what I was doing and why. A cold fear came over me, and I confessed to him, "I'm so sorry. Your hands remind me of someone, something that happened a long time ago."

David had my Teacher's hands. This ordinary man had my Teacher's hands. He had fat and white, pudgy and doughy fingers like on my Teacher's hands. My Teacher's hands were attached to the body of this otherwise normal man. Sticking out of his sleeves.

Angry, David turned away. He must have thought I was crazy.

"Please," I said, almost begging. "It isn't anything you've done."

But he didn't want to talk to me, and frankly, there was no good way to explain to a complete stranger that he had the same hands as a pedophile. What would I say?

I'd never understood why I had an obsession for looking at men's hands. But that morning, something clicked into place, like that last piece of a jigsaw you need to complete the picture. When I met a man, I looked at his hands almost before saying hello. If I couldn't readily see them, I would position myself to get a glimpse. I'd been searching for my Teacher's hands. I thought my past was locked down tight, but it wasn't. Here, thousands of miles from my childhood home, my Teacher had sprung up out of the past, with no warning.

I thought back to a day when I was eleven, the day my mother called me into the bathroom of our house. She sat on the edge of the tub. Perhaps some things are easier discussed in a bathroom, or maybe she didn't want anyone else in the family to hear. "Corrie Smith told her parents that the Teacher touched her. Has that ever happened to you?"

I knew immediately what my mother meant.

I looked down at the floor as I told her what had taken place. "One day, when I went back to school after being away with the flu, the Teacher told me I'd missed the school nurse's visit. He told me to stay in for recess. He took me to the upstairs classroom while all the other kids went outside. He took out a pen and some papers that had spaces to be filled out, and told me to stand next to him."

Hesitantly, I continued the story: "First he felt my arms. Then he wrote something on the papers. Then he slid his hand up under my skirt, slowly up the inside of my leg, almost to my panties." He'd flattened his hand—his fat, doughy hand—on my skin. I didn't tell Mother I'd held my breath and stared intently at the clock on the wall, waiting till he'd finished with me. "Then he said I could go outside for the rest of the recess period."

Mother asked, "Did you write the date down in your diary?"

Maybe. Not sure. I went up to my room to get my diary. The one my parents had given me the Christmas before. Looked to see. I showed my mother. No, I hadn't written anything down about what had happened. What had I done when I came home from school that day? Got on my bicycle and rode back into the fields as I usually did—to calm myself.

I had written in my diary the story of a loud argument that had happened in the classroom, however. The Teacher wanted Margie, a girl older than me who sat in the next row, to stay in after class. She yelled at him, "I'm not staying after class! I'm not letting you pull my pants down!"

At that outburst, silence descended, pens were held in midair, every eye on the Teacher. He had a funny look on his face. He squirmed in his chair behind his big desk. Snickered. You could see the glint of the sun on his misshapen front tooth. He looked around at every face, "I don't know what she's talking about."

But when was that? Was it in the spring, after the boy was strapped in front of the class and sent away from the school, never to come back? Billy, the orphan boy who had been recruited to work on a nearby farm. I turned to Mother. She wanted times and dates, not emotion, but I felt angry and could only say, "If he touches Bonnie, I'll kill him." Perhaps those were the words I wanted Mother to say about me.

My younger sister, Bonnie, and I didn't to school for the next while; Mother and Dad wanted to see what was going to happen to the Teacher first. There were mumbled conversations on the phone with the school inspector. Neighbors gossiped at the corner General

Store. The Teacher's father was on the school board. There were denials about any wrongdoing. Mother and Dad were disgusted with the "ignorant country people" who didn't seem to care who taught their children.

"He was let go from another school for doing the same things," Mother told me.

More girls were taken out of school. Most kept going to class. Some people just didn't see what the fuss was all about.

Mother called me into the living room for another discussion. It was out in the open now. No need to talk in the bathroom. She explained what the school inspector had told her. "In order to get rid of the Teacher, you'd have to go to a courtroom and tell a judge what happened to you. Your Dad and I have decided that would be too traumatic." My sister and I would go back to school instead. Her advice to me: "Just make sure you're never in a room alone with him again."

We went back to school—a two-room country school. I was in his class for grades four, five, six, seven, and eight. Five years. And five years is a very long time in the life of a child. Though he never touched me again in exactly the same way, I grew into adolescence under my Teacher's watchful eyes.

Now, with hindsight, I can see that this was likely when I started to endure, to shut down, and to realize that no one was going to help me. But I was too young then to comprehend all that.

I was "big for my age." That's what they called it. As though it was an affliction. Five foot nine and only eleven years old. That year my mother sewed the slim skirt I'd craved after seeing it on Betty and Veronica in the Archie comics. After I wore it once, it disappeared. She didn't know where it went. Perhaps the hope was that, in a dirndl skirt, I would look less like a woman. So my Teacher wouldn't look at me. But my mother got it wrong.

"He should have been married," she said. "That would have solved his problem."

How could I explain to her that his preferred bride would be twelve years old? I barely understood myself that he wasn't interested in women—that he liked girls.

At least he didn't follow me home in his car and park at the end of the laneway to watch for me, like he did to Marilyn, the girl who lived on the next farm. Her parents sent her three hundred miles north to her older sister's for the summer and he followed her there too.

In the winter, we couldn't go outside at recess to play baseball. Instead, every Friday afternoon, we pushed the desks to the sides of the classroom. The Teacher brought in records and taught us to dance the waltz, the tango, and the fox trot.

One January day, he motioned for me to come into the center of the classroom floor. Pressed his fingers sharply into my back as he guided me through the steps. As he pulled me to his chest, I had to place my hand on the rough woolen cloth of the shoulder of his suit. He held my slim young hand in his oversized fingers. His neck bulged, squeezed out above the stiff collar of his shirt. His round face leered at me, caught there in the middle of a twirl. I turned my face to the side so I could see out the windows. My stomach clenched. Relieved when he let me go back to dance with the farm boys in my class, I could breathe again.

Many years later, after Mom went into the nursing home, I cleaned out the drawers in my parents' living room cabinets. Amongst the baptismal certificates, wedding portraits, baby pictures, and other memorabilia, I discovered a class picture. In it, Bonnie was in grade eight. The Teacher was standing in the back row of the picture. His image had been there in our house, hiding in that drawer, for all those years. I never knew if the Teacher touched her in the same way he had me, but the photo showed me that my sister hadn't really escaped either.

o o o

I was blindsided in Prague, and so was David, my co-facilitator. I'd pushed the memory of my Teacher as far away as I could, but like many unresolved issues, it had been sitting there, waiting to attack me. David and I endured the week together. Because we were both professionals, the workshop went well and the participants were enthusiastic in their thanks to us for a job well done. But I was shaken.

I stayed a few extra days in Prague to do some sightseeing and to reflect on my future with Duncan. But all that immediately got swept aside when I came through the arrivals door at Gatwick and saw Duncan's face.

"Duncan, what's wrong?" I asked.

He just shook his head then, but as we rode the train back home, it all came pouring out. "I've been meeting Shelley. Sometimes in the evenings. Mainly we meet at a pub. She said I should leave you for her, but I don't want to."

I listened in astonishment—not at the fact that he had done this, but that I had been taken in by his deception. Or perhaps I just wasn't paying that much attention anymore.

"I'm not having an affair," he said.

That I found hard to believe. But how much did I care?

Shamefaced, he continued, "Shelley has gone too far. She said she'd tell you if I didn't."

Ah, that was why he was telling me. He'd been lying to me, and now he was afraid, desperate. He'd been visiting Shelley through the summer and early autumn when he said he was going for drives to cool off. And there was one weekend when he'd told me not to phone him because he was going on a "religious retreat." Now things were disintegrating.

I didn't believe Duncan's statement that he was not having an affair, but rather than anger, I felt sorry for him. Shelley was an alcoholic and had been an abused woman, much like Duncan's first wife. He knew he didn't want her, and now he was terrified I'd leave him.

At this point, Duncan was seeing his therapist three times a week, confiding in Shelley, and attending a therapy group once a month. He'd been keeping a lid on his anger with all this help, so I thought he'd changed, had learned to manage himself better. But it was all an illusion. He was propping himself up with all these other people. He hadn't changed anything, and now, for the first time, he'd also inten-tionally deceived me. He had no thought for me, or for anyone else for that matter. What Duncan needed, he went out and got. That's how he'd survived his childhood, and the habit had followed him into adulthood. His obsessive need for emotional support took pre-cedence over everything else—and he couldn't control it.

Duncan's old methods of controlling me—the threats, the screaming and yelling, the overdoses, the begging—weren't working anymore, but this was. Now I clearly saw his vulnerability, his des-peration, his inability to change, and I didn't think I could live with the guilt of abandoning him. It was still my job to manage him.

I felt truly caught. I couldn't leave him. But I couldn't tell him I was going to stay, either. If I did, things would just go back to how they'd always been. So now my quandary was, how was I going to create my own life—with him? We had to find a compromise.

We bought a tiny cottage in Chackmore, just north of Buckingham, so one of us would have a refuge when things got bad. Staying together while separating—that was the hard place now.

Bob visited from Canada during this time, and he gave me his honest read on the situation. "Duncan hasn't changed," he said. "He's just telling you what you want to hear. He's really angry at what's happening between you. And if you split up, he's thinking about going back to having gay relationships."

My heart sank. I knew that change would be hard for Duncan, but I'd hoped that with therapy and the modest improvement in our relationship he would see a different future for us. Bob's words made me realize to what extent I was being manipulated. I was close, but not close enough, to leaving. Every day, I watched myself slipping away, losing myself in uncertainty, sitting on a knife-edge, waiting, waiting . . .

That autumn, Eric, the psychology professor, and I did a dance of flirtation as I tried to pretend to myself that I was only interested in his professional help. We chatted briefly at staff receptions—never long enough to arouse gossip—and delight was obvious on his face every time we ran into one another in the university corridors. So dangerous, so enticing, so desired—closer and closer, we careened toward that edge.

○ ○ ○

At the end of September, I had another driving dream:

I'm behind the wheel, and Duncan is the passenger. The car lights are out. I don't have my glasses on and it's dark. I'm speeding and can't find the brake. Duncan's frightened and wants to take over, but it's impossible. I remain calm, find the brake, strain to apply it, and eventually pull into a service station, where I pay for the gas.

Again, a message from my higher Self, guiding me to believe in myself—telling me that I could handle this difficult passage.

As I wrote this dream in my journal, I thought about how passive I'd been so much of my life. I'd been told to do my best, sit quietly, not react, not do or say anything, at home and at school. And I had learned well. I knew no one was going to rescue me, but I'd still hoped. Now I was closer to dealing directly with Duncan and my feelings of desperation in our relationship. The pendulum of our marriage was poised to swing to the opposite side.

○ ○ ○

Between work projects, Duncan and I continued to exercise at the gym, ride our bikes, and take walks. He was proud of his slimmer new look, so when he continued to lose weight, it wasn't entirely surprising—but eventually I began to notice he wasn't eating very much, even less than me.

We were sitting eating dinner one evening in the kitchen, and I said, "You look great and have lost lots of weight. Aren't you carrying the dieting too far?"

"I just don't feel as though I can eat anymore."

Was he overdoing it? Being melodramatic? I wasn't sure. But when he began to throw up every time he ate apples, he went to our local surgery. His doctor thought it was likely just some sort of digestion problem, but said that at Duncan's age, it was worth investigating. He was scheduled to have an endoscopy at the end of October.

In the meantime, we continued to take two steps forward, one step back. Throwing out insults became his standard fare once again.

"I worked for ten years to support you while you studied for your degree," he snarled at me one night.

I should have walked out of the room, but I was back in the game. "Duncan, are you kidding me? Not only did I study, earn my degree, and become a clinical psychologist, I worked with you on projects, looked after the family, and went to therapy to sort myself out."

"Oh, yes, you have all the answers, don't you?" he yelled back.

Was this the same man who, only a few weeks before, had begged me not to leave him?

Later that evening, after he'd downed a bottle of wine, he told me he'd taken either five or seven paracetamol with codeine—he couldn't remember. When we looked at the bottle of painkillers, it turned out he'd only taken three. After a bit of drama, we got hold of his therapist.

In my journal, I scribbled, "I can't deal with this manipulation any longer." I still felt unable to say, "I'm leaving," but when I thought of continuing my life with Duncan I felt as though all the life force was being sucked out of me; eventually, only a thin husk would remain.

I Get Help

No longer feeling that I could really connect with the analyst I'd been going to in London, I ended therapy at the beginning of the summer of 1998, but I still needed help to deal with the issues of breaking down, breaking up, and getting on with whatever life lay ahead of me. So, in October, I decided to find a new analyst.

Lionel was the one who recommended Dr. Z. We'd met for lunch at our favorite brasserie—one that overlooked Commercial Road in London. When I mentioned that I was on the hunt for a therapist, he said, "I've heard that Dr. Z hardly ever takes new analysands—but if you interest him, he might take you on."

Sighing, I turned my foot to let the light gleam on the side of my black patent pumps as I contemplated my situation. I'd just bought them the week before at Harvey Nicks. Though I was trying to find my own way and my own life, I was still addicted to image—that of a stylish English management consultant working at prestigious international corporations. Designer clothes with matching bags and shoes still provided some diversion from my life.

I picked up my glass of white wine and held it up so the sun could shine through the golden liquid—the perfect companion to my radicchio and walnut salad. Would Dr. Z want me? He lectured abroad. He wrote extensively in respected journals. Would I interest him? The challenge was too good to pass up. Having a renowned analyst fed my need to prop up my ego in my misery. So, after Lionel and I finished our lunch, I phoned and made an appointment. I guess my story did interest him. He would meet with me in two weeks' time.

o o o

Dr. Z's office was in the west end of London, on the Bakerloo Line. The day of our first appointment, I got off the tube and followed the directions he had given me. His street was very quiet in the middle of the day. I'd arrived too early, so I stood by the waist-high brick wall surrounding a small garden next to his house, reading the paper and smoking a cigarette. Someone on the street turned her face away as she passed. I glazed my eyes over in the conspiracy; we both knew why each was there.

Exactly on the hour, I approached Dr. Z's wrought iron gate, pulled it open, entered, and then closed it with a precise exactness so he would know what a thoughtful person I was, a good person who cared that his gate was latched properly and would not swing open inadvertently.

My new analyst opened the door and greeted me solemnly, without offering his hand. He led me to his office, the front room of his house, which looked onto the street. I sat in a stuffed armchair with wooden armrests. Beside the chair, on the floor, was a box of tissues and a small woven rubbish bin. Dr. Z and I sat either side of an unlit fireplace.

"Why are you here?"

"I want my life back."

Dr. Z was my third Jungian analyst, so I knew the importance of keeping a dream journal. I wanted to share a dream with him that I had found so powerful, I'd recorded it in my journal, painted some of its images, and made notes about it:

Duncan and I are walking down a street of beautiful old stone homes. We see one with an elaborate gate that appears to be made of red, finger-like branches intertwining and reaching out from two stone gateposts. There's a ceramic Chinese woman's face on one of the gateposts. Duncan wants to go through the gate and into the house. A man comes out to the side of the gate and explains that he bought the gate and installed it in front of his house. He tells us its amazing story. It is called the Gate of a Thousand Tears, because, before the gate can open, the Chinese woman's face has to first cry one thousand tears—and that will take a long time. In the dream, it never does open.

The dream seemed important, what Jungians call "numinous." I wanted to explore whether I had an impenetrable gate in front of me. Would it stay closed until I was ready to come out and face the world? Would I have to cry one thousand tears before the gate to happiness would open to me? The only important gate I could recall in my life was the one my granny had installed in the entrance of the cemetery where my grandfather had been laid to rest.

The second dream I shared was one that had come a month after the first.

A man enters my room as I sleep. In the dream, I wake up trembling and tell him, "I haven't cried."

"Well, when you do," he responds, "you'll completely soak your bed with your tears."

As I related these dreams to Dr. Z, I could feel my chest tighten and I hesitated, struggling to hold back tears. I couldn't cry in front of him. I had an appearance to maintain. And I'd lied. I hadn't come to get my life back; I wanted him to save my life.

He agreed that it sounded as though I had spent my life trying to please men, and said he felt it was important that I not submit to anyone else, even to him, in my quest to find a new way to live my life. I needed to activate my own inner protector. But, he warned me that the way through analysis would be fraught with potholes that we might both fall into.

"And we're not going to have an affair," he added.

What? I felt chastised and patronized, but didn't raise an eyebrow. I wondered what he saw. Was I inadvertently flirting with him? I didn't think so, but perhaps this was so natural to me now that I didn't realize it. I needed help. I needed someone who liked me and would support me through my journey. I decided to wait and see.

At the end of that first session, Dr. Z and I set up appointments that would take us to Christmas, just two months away.

"Then we'll reevaluate," he said.

∘ ∘ ∘

I'd been reading *When Neitzsche Wept* and took seriously his warning to live life fully, to make it real or legitimate rather than simply going through the ceremony of life. I hadn't been doing that in my marriage to Duncan; instead, I'd been doing my duty. I'd left it to him to choose my path in life; even my becoming a psychologist was because of him. My choices in life had centered on picking one man who lived his life a certain way over another man who lived his life in a different way. But I had not been choosing *my* life. I was the canvas on which Duncan painted his life. I could have been anyone. Like my mother, who used to sing the theme song to Disney's *Cinderella* while she stood doing the dishes, I was caught in the middle of a fairy tale, still waiting for a magical prince to come, wake me up, and make my life complete.

With Eric skirting around the edges of my life, and Lionel available for lunch dates, I'd already activated the search for another man—the "magical other"—and it was beginning to feel just a teeny, tiny bit compulsive. I wasn't so sure that I would leave Duncan if I found a suitable single man, but that was the fantasy I carried.

The hard reality of my life with Duncan had reached a desperate place. On the other hand, pursuing fantasy could land me in very dangerous territory—infidelity and losing my relationship with Duncan before I was ready or able to stand on my own. At this point, it felt emotionally risky to stay with Duncan, but leaving him and getting "real" could mean facing aloneness and loneliness—the clichéd dark night of the soul. The challenge over the next few years, though I was not fully aware of it yet, would be to grow up, be real, let go of my pursuit of fantasy, and still be enthusiastic about life.

My therapy with Dr. Z wasn't just about getting my life back. It was about saving my soul.

Fate Intervenes

In early November, my friend Cathy and I were stuck on the side of the highway with a flat tire after a girls' weekend away to Aldeburgh. I'd met Cathy shortly after coming to England, at a research methodology conference at the University of Bath. Cathy was a PhD student at Bath while I was in the PhD program at Brookton, Duncan's university. She was a dynamo—when she entered the room, all eyes went to her. A big woman, highly intelligent, she was a warm and wise friend whose arms were seemingly always open.

As she and I waited for the RAC to come to rescue us, my cell phone rang. Duncan had finished the endoscopy test our family doctor had scheduled to check on his stomach troubles.

"The surgeon found something in my stomach," he said. "It could be an ulcer but it could be cancer. He's done a biopsy."

I went motionless, the blood draining away from my heart and mind. Cathy grabbed my hand when she saw the shock on my face. I knew no doctor would say the word cancer unless that's what he thought it was. But I couldn't say that to Duncan.

Four days later, we sat across the desk from Dr. Hanney, the surgeon. "You have stomach cancer."

I glanced at Duncan. I could feel the tingles of anxiety in my arms and stomach as I tried to let this information sink in. I'd never heard of stomach cancer, so there was a sense of unreality in it for me—but the word "cancer" was bad. Dr. Hanney explained that Duncan

117

would need to have tests first and then surgery. After the surgery, he said, and with a change in eating habits, Duncan could live a normal life—thinner, perhaps, but normal.

I was panicking. "Shouldn't he have the surgery now, today, tomorrow?"

"We need to see what we're dealing with first. How advanced it is. Find out if it's spread from the stomach."

Spread from the stomach?

"Did you know Duncan had cancer when you did the endoscopy? Were you trying to prepare us? Warn us?"

"Yes," he answered, "I thought it would be less of a shock."

He was wrong. Duncan was sitting so still. He looked blank. Cancer. That was what had killed his mother.

o o o

That week, Duncan and I were running a workshop at his university on change in organizations. We'd taken the lunch break to go to the surgeon's office. When we returned to the university, I took over the main part of the presentations, and Duncan sat quietly at the side of the seminar room. He didn't have much to say as we drove home that evening after the day's classes. This was so unreal, something that happened to other people.

As usual, a couple of days later, at the end of the workshop, Duncan lit into me about something and, like an automaton, I responded with a flash of anger.

The next morning he said to me, "I like you angry. You're beautiful when you're that angry with me."

I was more beautiful to him angry. Angry like his mother. Yelling like his mother. Beautiful like his mother. He could provoke my anger and then dismiss it, dismiss me, by seeing it as beautiful. Even cancer could not pierce the blindness he had about what was happening in our relationship.

o o o

We both phoned our sons to tell them the news of Duncan's diagnosis, but Duncan downplayed the seriousness of the situation. None of us, at the time, could come to grips with the possibility that he might not survive, and of course he wanted to believe that he would beat the cancer.

Within a few days of the diagnosis, both of us were doubled over with the searing pain of stress induced irritable bowel syndrome. Friends advised us to go to Dr. Leong, a Chinese herbal medicine practitioner. He gave us bags of twigs and bark, herbal medicine for the IBS, and administered acupuncture to help us deal with the stress of Duncan's diagnosis.

Every evening we each dumped the contents of our own bag of herbs into a pot of water and simmered them on the stove to make teas. We allowed them to cool and then drank half the liquid that night and half the next morning. My IBS was gone in a week; Duncan's abated somewhat, but he continued the herbal medicine and acupuncture throughout his illness to help him deal with reactions from chemotherapy, especially nausea.

Before Duncan's diagnosis, I'd been dreaming about things that were relevant to the past, things buried in my unconscious, or present issues I was facing. But afterward, I had the first of several dreams that showed me the future:

I'm in a cottage, washing dishes in the kitchen. It feels cold, like a Canadian winter. I am about to turn up the furnace when I notice that the window above the sink has a broken pane of glass. Cold air is blowing through a hole at the bottom of the window. I stuff a blue sponge into the hole. I go to Duncan and tell him my solution to the broken window.

When I related this dream to Dr. Z at my next appointment, he looked at me and said, "This is a message. He's going to die."

I left Dr. Z's office and took the tube to the City to meet Lionel for lunch at the Jamaica Wine House, a small old pub tucked away off Cornhill where we'd met many times. I arrived first, walked over to the dark wood bar, and ordered a glass of chardonnay. I took my glass to a table tucked away at the side of the room.

Lionel entered the room and walked over to me, smiling—but his smile disappeared when he saw my face. "What happened?" he asked. "You look as though someone died."

"Duncan's been diagnosed with stomach cancer."

"Oh god, Karen, I'm sorry. Let me get a drink and we can talk."

I told him the whole story and, when I finished, lifted my glass and declared, "But he's strong and can beat this."

o o o

Immediately after his diagnosis, Duncan moved back into our master bedroom. Night after night we held each other close, united against the common enemy. Despite Dr. Z's declaration about the outcome of Duncan's illness, I couldn't accept that dreams could predict the future. But as I held Duncan the first week after his diagnosis, I had a dream:

Duncan is ill and throwing up what looks like cornflakes, then painfully vomiting what looks like feces. I patiently take each filled bowl from him and pour the material down the sink.

This dream foretold exactly what would happen when Duncan was near the end.

Though I had been keeping a detailed journal for years, I now wrote as part of my own personal therapy, painfully pouring out my feelings—partly my hopes for, but mostly my fears of, the future.

Throughout the years of our relationship, sex had been the glue that held us together. As a lover, Duncan was provocative, demanding, looking always for the latest technique—but he could also be emotionally distant, uninvolved in our lovemaking. He would sometimes warn me, after getting up from the bed unsatisfied, "You owe me an orgasm." Even so, for me, our sexual relationship had always been exciting, stimulating, and freeing. Now, with Duncan traumatized from his diagnosis, that was gone.

Duncan spent the next couple of weeks undergoing blood tests, X-rays, other diagnostic imaging, and more endoscopies in preparation for his surgery. He became adept at swallowing the long tube with a tiny camera at the end.

On December 7, 1998, the night before Duncan's operation, we sat together in his hospital room, staying optimistic, reading the paper and chatting, trying to treat it as a normal evening.

Dr. Hanney, the surgeon, came into the room smiling. We had heard some of the test results earlier, but he wanted us to be clear about everything.

"Of course there's no guarantee," he said, "but I think we've caught it in time. The X-rays show that the cancer is contained in your stomach. We should be able to remove it, and, after a six-week recovery time, you'll be good as new. You'll have to retrain yourself to eat tiny meals only, many times a day, and you'll lose weight, but the outcome should be very good."

Duncan and I both smiled. His weight and love of eating had always been issues for him, but all that Dr. Hanney described seemed a small sacrifice in exchange for his life.

On my way out of the hospital—I was going home, with the plan to return the next day after Duncan's early-morning surgery—the surgeon stopped me and said, "I'll phone you as soon as I come out of the operation. If I call after about four hours, the operation was a success. We'll have removed his stomach, attached the esophagus to the duodenum, and he'll be fine. If I call after an hour, the cancer has spread too far to do anything."

That night, I only slept in fits and starts. A dream showed how closely tied I was to Duncan:

I watch a nurse plunge a large hypodermic needle into my forearm.

o o o

The next morning, while Duncan was being operated on, I sat in a room at the university scoring personality questionnaires for participants in an executive training course I was helping to run while I waited for the surgeon to call. My cell phone sat at my side.

Fifty-eight minutes after the scheduled start of the surgery, it rang.

I grabbed the phone, but the blood was pounding in my ears so loudly I could barely make out what he was saying.

"We couldn't remove his stomach," the surgeon said. "The cancer has progressed too far and has exited his stomach."

"You mean he's going to die?" I answered.

"We're all going to die," he replied. Then, after a pause, "Come to the hospital in a couple of hours. Duncan should be awake by then."

I sat motionless, trying to understand what I'd heard. After a few minutes, I went into the seminar room to tell my co-workers about Duncan. Dream-like, I walked over to the tea lady in the lounge, watched her pour tea into a cup, put in my milk, and then sat, stirring my tea, watching the spoon go round and round, clinking against the edge of the cup.

Eric approached me and sat down on the next chair. "I just heard that Duncan's cancer has spread. You can call on me for anything. I'm here for you."

I wanted to reach out and touch him, have him hold me, make it all go away, but I had to restrain myself. I just smiled weakly at the concern evident on his boyish face.

I left the university and drove the twenty minutes to the hospital. As I entered the post-op ward, Dr. Hanney caught me in the hallway and asked me to come into a side room.

"When we opened Duncan up, we could see that the cancer had already spread," he said, his voice stern. "I suggest you bring your family to England for this Christmas. It will likely be the last one you spend together." He continued, "Your husband has probably about six months to live. I'd be very surprised if he makes it to next Christmas."

Dr. Hanney warned that there was no hope of recovery, there would be no heroic measures to save Duncan's life at the end, and recommended that a DNR (do not resuscitate) note be put on his file.

I hadn't even seen Duncan yet. *Couldn't he have chosen a better moment to relay all this information?* I wondered. *Is he embarrassed that his own prediction for the operation's success was wrong?*

Duncan was in the intensive post-op ward, hooked up with tubes and wires. Even though he looked sleepy, he'd seen the clock, and had immediately realized that he still had his stomach and the cancer it contained.

"I'll fight this," he said to me with determination.

I didn't even know what that meant. To me, his chances had disappeared on the operating table.

"Of course," I said, stumbling over my words. "There are other options, I'm sure."

◦ ◦ ◦

Later that same week, I took the train to London and then rode the tube to see Dr. Z. The stations passed by unnoticed. Despite wanting to stay positive for Duncan, I wasn't hopeful about the outcome of his new situation. I flashed forward to my life as a widow and felt ashamed. If he died, I wouldn't have to make any decisions about our relationship. Two sides of me watched each other suspiciously: the kind, loving, caring, aware, anxious side, and the hurt, angry, vindictive side. But it was so much more complicated than that. I just wanted Duncan out of my life. I didn't want him to die. In fact, the thought terrified me. My grandmothers had both been widowed young. Was I to suffer the same fate?

That night in my dream, *two doctors had the drugs for Duncan's chemotherapy ready.*

◦ ◦ ◦

Had my fight to get out of our marriage caused so much stress for Duncan that cancer was the result? Just before Duncan came home from the hospital, I asked Dr. Hanney how long he'd had the stomach cancer.

"Eighteen months to two years, judging by its progress," he said. "It has exited the stomach and appears as a film over his liver and spleen."

Less than a year had passed since I'd told Duncan I wanted a divorce. I tried to be reasonable. I didn't do this. It wasn't my fault. But had he sensed even before I did that I wanted to leave him?

Our fourteenth wedding anniversary, December 21, 1998, was thirteen days after the surgery. That night, I dreamed of Duncan:

He is in full armor, complete with helmet. His visor is up. He is silver, shining, glowing with a bright aura around him, carrying a sword. A dragon is leaping out of his stomach and he is attacking it with his sword. I can see right into Duncan's stomach. The sword is hacking at the cancer, killing it. It's as though Duncan is St. Michael the Archangel.

I woke up and shared the dream with Duncan.

He listened to me with tears forming in his eyes. He believed in my premonitions.

"Karen, I can feel it," he said. "I'm going to beat this."

But when I told Dr. Z about the dream at my next appointment, his response was crushing.

"St. Michael the Archangel is the angel of death," he told me. "He is a protector of souls. He guides souls to judgment after death." He turned his face to me as tears coursed down my cheeks and said kindly, "You may have seen Duncan in the light of the hereafter."

I couldn't, and didn't, share this with Duncan.

◦ ◦ ◦

From the moment Duncan heard about his illness, he talked and thought of nothing else. He put all his energy into researching treatment, both conventional and alternative. This was natural. After all, we both knew he could die from this. But his next request caught me off guard.

"Can we sit down?" he asked me one day. "I want to talk about something. I want to have something to look forward to after my chemotherapy is over. I want us to get married in the Catholic Church."

I was shocked that this was still an issue for him. We'd been married by a Justice of the Peace, and although we'd both gone through the annulment process after our first marriages, I resisted even going to mass. I was not interested in being part of a religious community in which women were second-class citizens, and Duncan knew how

I felt. But his tendency to force, manipulate, and control now had a new angle: his cancer.

Was I wrong to fight what he wanted as a kind of last wish? Perhaps, but that is how complicated life had become for me. Doing the kind thing, perhaps the right thing, was also surrendering to Duncan, which I'd promised myself I wouldn't do anymore.

I waited a few days to give myself time to think about his request, then said to him, "Duncan, please don't use your illness to manipulate me back into our marriage."

"You're so negative," he said, disgusted. "I don't see how I'm going to be able to tolerate it. I might as well just leave now and go to the hospital."

"Can't you see? Now you're using your illness to get back at me," I said, raising my voice in frustration. "If you need to leave, then leave."

"Don't worry!" he yelled back, heading toward the front door, "in a year I won't be here anyway."

His chemo wasn't scheduled to begin until after Christmas, so there was no place for him yet at the hospital. I stood in the doorway and stopped him from leaving.

o o o

Before Duncan's diagnosis, he and I had thought we'd be alone for Christmas, so we'd made reservations at Riber Hall, the fourteenth-century inn in the Peak District where we'd stayed nine months earlier. But now, following the doctor's advice, we cancelled, phoned our sons, and asked them to come to England to celebrate what would likely be our last Christmas together.

The surgeon had only opened him up and closed him right back up again, so Duncan recovered quickly from his operation. He was able to sit at the dining table and eat some turkey with us.

Ten days later, the day before Duncan's first chemotherapy treatment, we celebrated my fiftieth birthday with a party. Adam, Jamie, and Greg helped push the dining table against the wall for a buffet lunch and laid out the wine and glasses on the sideboard. We left the

Christmas tree and all its twinkly lights up and lit the fireplace in the lounge.

The house was crowded with concerned friends and university colleagues, including Frederick and Nancy. I invited Lionel and his family and, even though it meant driving miles out of their way after a weekend visit with other friends, they came. Cathy came up from London. Though the celebration was for my birthday, that faded beside everyone's concern for Duncan.

o o o

On January 5, 1999, Duncan reported to Northampton Hospital's oncology department, a half-hour north of Milton Keynes. He was to begin two types of chemotherapy—not to cure the cancer, but to reduce the size of the stomach tumor so he'd be more comfortable and able to eat more. Every two weeks he would stay overnight at the hospital in one of the special cancer care rooms that were decorated like hotel rooms, with room service, a drinks wagon, aromatherapy, and massage.

That first time, I sat on Duncan's bed as the nurse brought in a trolley with syringes and a metal IV stand. When I looked at the huge needle and the dazzlingly bright red liquid that would be injected into him, I felt dizzy and nauseated, and had to get out of the room. I waited out in the lounge until it was over.

During this stay, he also had an operational procedure to install tubes that would directly link a small machine to his heart. Each week he was to come back so the wallet-sized pump could be refilled with chemicals that would continuously feed into his heart. The attached battery pack was kept in his jacket pocket.

Twenty-four hours after coming home from this first treatment, Duncan woke me up in the middle of the night.

"I have to go back to the hospital."

"Duncan, what's wrong?"

He was clutching his stomach. "I'm sick. I'm going to throw up."

We had been warned this might happen. I phoned the hospital

and told them we were on our way. After driving the A421 from Buckingham to Milton Keynes, I raced up the M1 and we rushed into the oncology night clinic. Pills were not strong enough to deal with his reaction, so the doctor on call injected him with an anti-nausea drug. In about an hour he felt well enough to go home.

o o o

The specter of cancer stopped both of us in our tracks. Duncan promised to help me with a consulting project but didn't. Instead, he made time for visualization and meditation. He kept Jamie's bedroom to relax and nap, used our spare room as his office, and moved back into our bedroom.

Despite Duncan's struggle with cancer, the job of getting my life back was still unfinished work that couldn't be set aside or put on hold. The challenges of my life made me realize that I really didn't know myself. I had many parts raising their ugly heads: the diversions I maintained in order to keep numb, the outer illusions I lived, my vulnerability, sensitivity, lack of self-confidence, pride, anger, sexual side, and fear—always, fear—of abandonment and aloneness. If I didn't face myself honestly, I could end up with twice the problems. I had a fight on my hands. Did I have the courage to meet the challenge?

The Last Six Months

*I*n mid-January, Duncan and I went to the Bristol Cancer Care Centre for a weekend workshop. The center encourages participants to take an alternative approach to cancer: vegetarian food, massage, reiki, group talks, individual counseling. I was one of only two non-cancer patients in the group. We were called support persons. When everyone got together for group sessions, we were a very large group in a huge room. I felt awkward, out of place. *I'm well!* I wanted to scream. But this wasn't about me.

We took turns introducing ourselves and then some people told their stories. One woman blamed her husband for her cancer. Some years before, she said, he had called her on the phone, and she'd fallen coming down the stairs in order to respond to the ring. She'd rammed her breast hard into the corner of the telephone table, resulting in a terrible bruise, and eighteen months later she'd developed breast cancer in that exact spot.

As she told this story, the woman's husband sat in the group, head down, looking at the floor, devastated. I silently scanned my body for past injuries that might turn into cancer. Later, the energy worker who did some stress relieving work on me confided, "Cancer and death don't just happen in happy marriages."

Back at home, we followed the cancer center's recommendations and started a regime of packaged nutrients and more plants in our diet. Though I welcomed this as something I'd pushed for in the past, now I felt as though my whole life was about cancer.

Duncan had a dream that month that he never told me about. Much later, after his death, I looked into Duncan's journal, then clasped my hand over my mouth and sobbed when I read his description of the dream. *He is laid out in a coffin. A beautiful woman comes into the funeral parlor and looks down at him, lying there.* By the time I read this, I had gone into the funeral parlor and looked down into his coffin.

I was so used to extrovert Duncan sharing everything he thought, I didn't realize there was much of this experience he didn't, and couldn't, share.

I didn't want to think negative thoughts because I was afraid I might cause Duncan to die. Yet death was the most probable outcome of his illness. His surgeon had said he was likely to die in less than a year. Terror and necessity dictated that I face this possibility and start preparing myself for it.

o o o

When I was with my first husband, Joe, I passed a certain point where the marriage felt done, finished, over with. Even before we separated, I began to lose weight, get in shape, make new friends, enjoy my work, and be a bit happier. I'd done so much to try to make the relationship work, but I had failed. He had made some attempts to save our marriage at the last minute, but it was too late. I'd passed the point of no return and couldn't force myself back.

With Duncan, I had also tried very hard to save the marriage. Guilt that I hadn't been able to repair my first marriage, fear that I would have to tell my parents and grandmother that I was going to divorce once again, lack of money, and a reluctance to disrupt my sons' lives again had kept me from leaving—so instead I'd tried to help him, change him, get him to marriage counseling. We'd gone to therapists, separately and together. But now, for the second time in my life, I'd reached the point of no return, and even the tragedy of Duncan's illness couldn't force me back into my previous desperate place.

o o o

After Duncan's initial stay in the hospital in early January 1999 to start his chemotherapy and set up his treatment schedule, I took him to the hospital each week to get his little pocket-sized pump loaded up with chemicals, and every two weeks for him to have his large injection of red liquids.

After the first visit, Duncan was too weak and disoriented to walk from the parking lot to the hospital, so now I dropped him off right at the door.

"Stay right there, all right?" I said urgently when I left him there. "Don't move."

I parked the car and then came back to the door. He wasn't there. I went inside and walked to the first waiting room, but no Duncan. I asked the clerk on duty at reception if she'd seen him.

"No."

Where could he have gone? I looked up and down the halls, and in various waiting rooms. Finally, I made my way to the waiting room outside his treatment room to tell them I'd lost him. There he was, sitting in the correct waiting area. I burst into tears, sat down in the chair next to him, and, in relief, circled him with my arms. He turned and looked at me with uncomprehending eyes.

We'd promised each other we would try to be as normal as we could in the face of his illness. The following day, when he said he wanted to go into the center of town, just to look around and do something ordinary, I agreed. I parked the car and we walked up the high street. As we were about to go into a store, Duncan turned to me and said in a small, gravelly voice, "I don't have the energy for this." Then, pausing, he said, "I need to go home."

o o o

Duncan had a beautiful head of thick, wavy, greying hair, but during the first few months of chemo, it slowly thinned and fell out. One of his colleagues who'd been to Africa many times brought Duncan a brightly colored Ghanaian hat to wear. The fez shape suited him and somewhat disguised his baby-pink skull with its tiny cloud of white fuzz.

Steroids, prescribed to help dissipate the nausea that came with the chemo, caused a prickliness that brought a whole new intensity to Duncan's constant faultfinding and fury. He would walk though the kitchen screaming at me, at life, at nothing.

We went to Robbie Burns Night at the university and I downed several glasses of wine.

"It would've been better if Duncan had done that," a friend commented, thinking I am sure that it was Duncan who needed the calming that alcohol could bring.

I felt I was behaving badly, but I was trying to numb the pain, the sadness, the confusion of the madhouse reality we were in.

That night, after we got home, Duncan turned to me, resentful. "You'd think you were the one with the cancer."

As Duncan was fighting for his life, I was fighting for mine, but in a much different way. At my analyst's encouragement, I resolved to maintain the boundaries I'd fought so hard to erect in the last year, regardless of the circumstances. I didn't have to panic or react angrily, or capitulate to what Duncan wanted. I didn't have to regress. This didn't have to destroy me.

As a better way to deal with my stress, I started going to the gym five times a week.

Dancing Close to the Edge of Crazy

*F*or so many years I'd nursed the illusion that the craziness between Duncan and me was *his* and that to get rid of it, I only needed to get rid of him. I wasn't admitting to my own foolishness and inconsistencies. Most of my knowledge of myself was filtered through his eyes, as it had been with Joe. Plus, I'd married him even though I was afraid of some of his sexual activities, and then I'd had to tone down my own spontaneity because I was afraid of what it might lead to with him. Now, after so many years of trying to manage Duncan, so much of my own life felt uncontrolled, unmanageable, confused, on the edge of crazy. A friend advised me to have an affair in order to distance myself from Duncan's anger. Though yoga would have been a better solution, I was considering it.

Duncan's work now was fighting his cancer. He was traveling all over the country seeking cures. He'd stopped going to his university on a regular basis leaving his office there empty, so I could use it to do my work. Or that's what I told myself. But I also knew it would put me in closer contact with Eric.

In the meantime, I visited my analyst weekly and told him stories of Duncan's search for cures and my search for sin. Dr. Z just looked at me, shrugged his shoulders, and said, "You're both crazy."

One day, when Duncan headed out by chauffeur-driven limo to the south coast for his bi-weekly immune boosting shot, I drove to his University, unlocked his office, threw my books and briefcase onto his desk, picked up the phone, and dialed the psychology department.

As I stood there waiting for Eric to pick up, a conversation we'd had months earlier ran through my mind. When Eric was first flirting with me, he'd admitted, "I want to stay married, but I find my intimacy needs elsewhere."

"So you and your wife have an arrangement?"

He looked both surprised and shocked. "No, no, nothing like that."

"So you sneak around," I concluded.

"Well"—he looked at me—"I guess you could look at it that way." Then he rationalized, "My wife isn't interested in sex. She has her job and the kids take up her time. I travel a lot."

Today, as soon as Eric picked up the phone on his end, I whispered, "I'm here." After fourteen years of fidelity, I was throwing myself at a womanizer. I felt as though I was in the middle of a bad pop tune, but I just couldn't help myself. It was dangerous, a dangerous game—and that made it exciting.

"I'll be over in a few minutes," he said.

Three or four times his secretary, Sonia, had answered the phone when I'd called. She had a cold edge to her voice every time I asked for Eric. Later he revealed, "Sonia has warned me that you're too vulnerable with Duncan being so sick."

"You discuss me with your secretary?" I asked, appalled.

"She's like family. She's been with me over ten years. She mothers me, looks after me, and she knows what I'm like."

Like Moneypenny, she could only watch.

Eric knocked. I opened the office door, grabbed his lapel, and pulled him inside. He threw his arms around me and kissed me full on the mouth. I closed my eyes as I felt the warmth and strength of his body against mine, my breath coming fast with the tingling that comes from being with someone new when you have been unhappy for so long.

He stopped and looked around. I'd pulled the blinds down on the window.

"I don't like this," he said, pulling away. "Once, a long time ago, I got involved with someone on campus and—it got complicated."

I knew his reputation, had heard the rumors. He wanted me but he had been in this position before. He paced the room with tightened lips, his brow wrinkled with stress. "I've only got a few minutes before I have to go and lecture," he finally said. "Let's talk for a bit before I go back. You know I want to be there for you, but I've never been in a situation like this before - I care for you but I respect Duncan. You *are* vulnerable. I can't trust you to hold the boundaries on us, so I'll have to do it."

In order to manage his complicated love life, he'd come up with rules and regulations to hold it all in place. He was teetering between desire and self-preservation. He knew that I was new to cheating and he didn't trust that I could keep it concealed in a separate box, away from my "real" life, like he did.

"When am I going to see you again?"

We both laughed when we realized we'd said it at the same time.

"I'll call you tonight," he promised, and left.

The office was empty again. A vacuum left in the place where Eric had stood. Though I felt abandoned, I was also tense with anticipation. My eyes filling with tears, I sat at Duncan's desk to plan my next workshop.

"Sexual excitement is the opposite of death," my analyst had told me. *Perhaps*, I thought, *it's as uncontrollable as death.*

o o o

I continued to look to astrology for guidance:

> *You are already a slightly different person to the one you were last week. The sky has not yet finished taking you through a process of revelation and discovery. More crucial changes are due. Astrologers overuse the phrase 'turning point.' It is an*

understandable tendency. Life provides us with more subtle opportunities to change direction than we realize. Sometimes it doesn't just give us a chance to do this, it compels us, too. This is such a time for you.

Jonathan Cainer, Daily Mail, February 20, 1999

o o o

Eric and I continued our flirtation. I rationalized that he was the only person who made me laugh, and that, up to that point, we had little to feel too guilty about—a kiss, a couple of hugs. But the intention of the flirting was clear. After years of Duncan veering between mechanical sex and emotional neediness and aggressiveness, I craved spontaneous lovemaking with someone else—someone who might treat me better. I had always thought of myself as an open and honest woman, but now I was clearly ducking and dodging.

While Duncan was away chasing cures, I stayed with Cathy at a Cotswold cottage that belonged to a friend of hers. She and I spent the weekend working, talking, eating, drinking wine, and putting the world to rights. She listened to me talk about my obsession with Eric. I knew she was worried about me and my frantic behavior. She shared that she would never risk her relationship with her partner for a fling. He was her rock and she knew she needed that anchor in her life.

When I went to see my analyst, I only felt worse.

"Karen," he told me, "you're repeating the pattern of feeling as though you have no choice, just like you felt with Duncan. This flirtation may feel more positive and exciting right now, but it's no different."

I didn't want to hear this. I was in control of my own life. Why was he criticizing me like this when he knew what a difficult time I was having? Anyway, it was too late to extricate myself from this obsession with Eric. I tried to deceive myself that it was not that I was afraid to get out, but that I didn't want to.

My analyst was holding up a mirror and all I could see was my bad side, the Shadow side.

"The problem, Karen, is that you feel ashamed and embarrassed rather than afraid," he warned me. "You should feel very afraid, because your tendency is to be attracted to men who aren't good for you. If you don't face this aspect of yourself head on, you'll live it all over again."

Questions about my analyst went round and round in my head. Why was I going to an analyst in the first place? He was clearly punishing and negative. I could figure things out for myself. But of course I couldn't—not then, anyway. It would still take years before I would let my Self lead me to the authentic me.

o o o

The common-sense approach regarding Eric would have been to wait—wait until nature took its course, until after Duncan's inevitable death, wait long enough so people could not find fault with me for being attracted to another man. But I didn't think in that sort of cold and calculating way. This really wasn't about loving someone else. It was about escape—now.

I was in a sea of emotion so strong, the current so turbulent, that my logical mind was muted, the sound turned down. I felt as though I was getting messages from all sides and I was open to them—too open. Again, my horoscope was eerily omniscient.

> *The moon begins to pass through your sign today. Old worries and fears are returning to haunt you. It's as if you are reviewing your progress since the last time you sat down to face a particular problem. Suddenly it seems to you that nothing has altered. That's like being released from prison and returning, of your own free will, to visit an inmate you have grown fond of. Back in those surroundings you feel trapped as you did before. But you can (and will) walk away. That's the difference.*
> Jonathan Cainer, Daily Mail, March 12, 1999

o o o

I was sitting at home while Duncan went off in search of yet another miracle cure when I heard the phone ring and picked it up.

"Hello?"

"Karen, are you alone?"

It was Eric.

"Yes, Duncan's gone to London to see John of God. Apparently he's a miracle man from Brazil who has the gift of healing."

"Well, that's understandable, isn't it? But I wanted to talk with you," he pressed. "I want you to know who I am. Really know, behind all the flirting and silly joking. This won't work if you don't see me for me."

I hesitated. I liked the flirting, the jokes, the lightness of the relationship. That's what kept me going these days. "Yes, of course, Eric, I understand what you're saying. I care for you, not just the banter."

"I don't know that you do, actually. We'll see."

Getting involved with Eric felt like a leap from Duncan to another life raft, but a leaky one—shaking off one torturer, only to acquire another. That wouldn't be progress, but the rat running the maze or the guinea pig the wheel. Was Dr. Z right that I was doomed to keep repeating my mistakes with someone else? I judged Eric for being a womanizer, but now I too was being unfaithful.

I had started the process of separation a year earlier, in February 1998, before Duncan got sick. I couldn't have known then that we might soon be facing the ultimate separation. Eric was just a distraction from the reality of my marriage, Duncan's illness and impending death, and my fear of what would come next. I knew this deep down, but refused to face it.

At the end of March, I wrote a note to Eric that said only, "I withdraw." I didn't give it to him right away, though; I was still sitting on the fence. My head said get out, but my libido said, "Stay, stay." I was in lust with him and didn't want to end things—not yet. Dr. Z said that Eric was my lover even if we hadn't actually had sex. *No, that can't be true*, I told myself, even as I recognized the truth in my analyst's statement.

I had a dream that month:

I'm talking with Eric about our relationship. He says he could tell within the first few minutes of meeting me that I am the type of person that gives, and he is the type of person who takes. He's calm, accepting that he will never change, never be a "giver." I cry and run out through the streets.

Despite this warning dream, I woke up every morning thinking about Eric. I was like the alcoholic who drinks bottle after bottle of wine, knowing full well what it's doing but not being able or ready to say, "No more."

o o o

At the beginning of April 1999, we traveled to one of Duncan's favorite places, The Lakes District. A few years earlier, while I'd gone home to Calgary for a visit, he'd driven up to the Lakes District—Wordsworth country—to spend time on his own. On this trip, he wanted to take me to Wordsworth's home, Dove Cottage, a seventeenth-century stone building that had formerly been The Dove and Olive, a public house. It was where Wordsworth lived while he wrote his most famous works, including "I Wandered Lonely as a Cloud." I wondered if we were too early for the daffodils.

We stayed in a hotel we'd been to before, the Beech Hill Hotel in Bowness on Lake Windermere. After a drink in the lounge, we sat down for supper across from each other, in front of the large dining room windows overlooking the lake. It was still early in the season and there were few others in the room. I ordered a glass of cabernet sauvignon while we scanned the menu, but Duncan drank fizzy water; his liver was no longer able to process alcohol because it was filtering all the chemo drugs from his system.

I was watchful. Like a mother hen supervising her chicks, I watched Duncan as he ate, glancing from my lake trout and mixed vegetables to his plate, to his fork lifted to his mouth, assessing his ability to swallow.

Through the weekend, I tried to manage Duncan as he railed against the hotel management. He phoned down to the front desk several times to complain that the newspaper hadn't been delivered to our room on time, and later that his bath water was not hot enough. At times Duncan was thoughtful, at times irrational. He'd always been this way, but I wondered if the steroids he was still taking to counter the chemo side effects played a part in his mood swings as well.

I drove us to Dove Cottage in Ambleside. At the end of a path there was a hillside planted in daffodils as a memorial to Wordsworth's daughter. Duncan and I sat wordless on an old weathered bench overlooking the tangled garden. Just for a moment I stopped trying to distract myself, and contemplated the battles we were both engaged in – his for his life, mine for my truth. I couldn't bridge the gap between Duncan and I but I wondered if he thought, as I did, that he was seeing this for the last time.

The End of An Illusion

At the beginning of May, as we drove home after having dinner with friends, Duncan said, "When I get well, if you still want a divorce, I won't stand in your way." Though I heard his words, I knew from past experience that he didn't really mean it.

I had tears in my eyes as I told Dr. Z about this and other things that were going on. "It feels as though nothing has changed," I said. "Duncan is in some ways the same, only with cancer it seems worse. Yelling, impatient, critical. And I am just the same—afraid, hurt, sad, angry, and so frustrated. What a mess."

o o o

Despite quiet warnings from Duncan's first surgeon, Dr. Hanney, Duncan wanted to look into new, almost experimental, surgery being done at the Royal Marsden Hospital, London. We made an appointment to see the new surgeon, Dr. Summerton. While we sat in the waiting room, we picked up and put down magazines, looked at the other patients, and smiled at each other as we noted our twin-like, matching pale lilac shirts.

In Dr. Summerton's office, I placed my hand over Duncan's as we nervously asked questions.

"What percent chance do you give me?" Duncan asked.

"About 2 percent," the surgeon said.

We both blanched.

"If this were you, would you do it? Go ahead with another

surgery?" I asked the surgeon, knowing the answer he would give us.

"Absolutely."

All in all, in a situation like this one, I think that you do whatever you can in order to cope—but sometimes you don't know the difference between coping and pretending to cope. I had a life to live while dealing with the tragedy of a dying husband and a need to keep myself well for my own and my family's sake. I had to keep remembering that I'd wanted my life back, because at this precise moment, it felt as though I had little life of my own, and what I did have was spent worrying about Duncan.

Duncan decided to go ahead with the surgery on May 16th, one day before his fifty-ninth birthday. We invited a few people over on the day before he would check into The London Clinic, a posh private clinic on Devonshire Place just off Marylebone Road, London—a luxury made possible through his university's new health insurance plan. At the party, the mood among our friends was subdued, everyone knowing what lay ahead that coming week.

We traveled down to The London Clinic so Duncan could have more tests, including another endoscopy, before the new operation. At the appointment, the technician declared that Duncan's stomach looked red and inflamed, but no more than someone who had a drinking problem. It appeared, he said, that the tumor was gone. We were ecstatic at this news, but looked at each other, puzzled. If this were true, why did Duncan even need the new operation to remove his stomach?

I asked Eric to keep me company for the afternoon while Duncan was operated on. We met in Regents Park and walked to an Italian restaurant.

"You're like a fatal attraction," said Eric as he tore his crusty bread apart to spread it with butter, a small but distinctive smirk on his mouth. "I want you to seduce me."

"Why? What are you trying to say?"

"I don't want to feel guilty. If my wife finds out about us, I can say I couldn't resist you."

The words *self-serving bastard* rang in my head, and my stomach twisted with fury. I was the bad one, the seductress. He wasn't a cheater, he was simply weak, the one who couldn't say no. His wife could keep the fantasy that her husband would never willingly betray her. In Eric's version of things, they had a perfect marriage that was being preyed upon by a bad woman.

"I don't feel guilty," I later said to Dr. Z.

"Not yet, you don't," he replied.

Dr. Z pointed out that I had two tasks now: I had to look after the practical aspects of caring for a dying man, and do so without losing myself as I had for most of my marriage.

Duncan in the MK Hospital

I woke up from another dream:

There is a small, pure white bird on the road with blood on its feathers, flapping in distress. Duncan is driving the car. He carefully lines it up to drive over the bird and I cringe while I wait for the slight bump. I look out the back window. I think I see the bird move, but it's likely just the wind.

After surgery, Duncan stayed in the London Clinic about two weeks and then came home. Hand in hand, we went out for a walk down our street. Our neighbor, her face registering surprise to see us, waved as she drove past. But after two days, Duncan was in such pain that we went to our family doctor in Buckingham. She was so concerned, she advised us to go to the emergency department at the large regional hospital in Milton Keynes, where they admitted Duncan immediately.

He was nauseous on an almost continual basis and in constant pain. I visited him every day, often twice a day. I ran hot bubble baths in the adjoining bathroom, helped him into the tub, and massaged his feet and legs. I took a large sponge and carefully washed his back, trying not to cause him any more discomfort. We could be together in these simple, intimate moments, often without speaking at all.

One day, after Duncan had been in the hospital for a week, I came into his room to find Eric there visiting. The nutritionist also came in to give instructions for eating, for when Duncan was able. She looked at Eric and me and asked us to leave, possibly thinking I was just another visitor. I looked at Duncan and shrugged, not sure what to do, and told him I'd be back later.

As Eric and I walked down the corridor, I stopped, leaned over, and kissed him. He looked around in panic at the empty hallway then laughed. "You don't care if anyone sees us, do you?"

Unsteady, I took a step back, startled into awareness, and quietly said, "Yes, I do care."

We walked out to the parking lot and I got into my car. Tears came down my cheeks as I laid my head on the steering wheel. What was happening to me? I *did* care. I drove home alone to our empty house.

Duncan didn't get any better, and his university insurance policy gave him the means to transfer to the private hospital in Milton Keynes. His spacious, comfortable room looked out onto a garden. As I walked down the hall en route to his room, Dr. Hanney, Duncan's first surgeon and a staff doctor at the hospital, took me to one side.

"If your husband's nausea doesn't stop soon, he's in a lot of trouble. We suggest he be transferred to the local hospice in order to get better pain management." He went on to explain that he had been in to visit Duncan earlier in the afternoon and tried to get him to face his impending death. Duncan had yelled at him to get out of his room.

I opened the door to Duncan's room and walked in. He was pacing back and forth, hugging his abdomen. When I came close to him, he looked up at me with eyes like those of a dog that's been whipped, and whispered, "Do you think I'm going to die?"

Pressure gripped both sides of my head, as if a vise was being tightened. I searched for the right words. "I think it's a possibility."

"Okay," he replied, "I can accept that it's a possibility, but if you gave up hope, I couldn't cope."

The message was clear. I had to keep pretending he was going to live no matter what his condition, no matter what his suffering. I could never agree to have him go to the hospice, even if it might make his physical suffering more bearable. My hope was the life raft he clung to in a sea of terror.

o o o

During my next appointment, I told Dr. Z about my latest dream:

I'm in an elevator. I have a lifetime fear that I will fall down an elevator shaft. The floor is wobbling violently. I'm terrified it will tip and I'll fall. I scream for help from my friends but they just look at me as though I don't need help. I yell frantically at them, "Of course I need help! I want one of you to come into the elevator with me and balance the platform so it won't tip!" All of a sudden, it tips, and to my shock, I'm standing on another floor—made of metal, sealed, riveted, and safe. It had always been there. I had never been in any danger.

Dr. Z confirmed that this was a message from my higher Self. "You just think you need another person to help you. When you really understand that you can rely on yourself, you won't be so compelled to turn to someone else out of a sense of desperate need."

Throughout my childhood, in my family and at school, I had looked after myself. And as the oldest child, I was often in charge of my younger brother and sister, who both seemed to need and deserve more attention and care than I did. As an adult, when my first husband walked out and left me to raise our sons on my own, he said he couldn't do what I was doing. Nor would he even try. So I'd tried to make myself believe that I was strong and didn't need any help—and all these years later, I was still trying to prove that. Even when Eric tried to tell me I was vulnerable and that he'd be there to help me, I wanted to convince him that I was cool, strong, and confident, able to handle whatever life might throw at me. But after so many years of living with Duncan, I didn't really trust my own ability to decide what was good for me and what wasn't. I was searching for the person who would look after me—who would save me from the falling elevators in my life.

I was so tired from Duncan's demands that I had no energy left to deal with Eric. I never knew where I stood with him. If I approached him and wanted to engage, he'd say I was scary and dangerous. Actually I was anxious and nervous. I tried too hard, felt unsure of myself. When he seemed reluctant to be with me, I was more and more frightened. I found myself going to Eric's office only to push him away.

"I find it difficult to talk with you honestly," I told him one day. "This relationship may not work for me."

But I was hedging my bets rather than simply being honest; this relationship *didn't* work for me.

Then he didn't want to let me go. "Why do you have so many hang ups? Just relax."

"You frighten me."

"I missed you so much today," he said, ignoring my statement.

As I listened to this, I knew clearly that this was what he said in order to keep a woman. Not me, any woman. He wanted to keep me close enough so he could pull the string any time and bring me back.

o o o

Duncan remained in the hospital. He was still vomiting and in desperate pain. I was alone. Even though he wouldn't accept that he was dying, I had to. I had to mourn the loss of the life I'd known, the person I'd loved—and at times hated—and the death of any possibility of the relationship we might have had, the relationship I'd only ever glimpsed. I watched the man I'd shared my life with die of cancer, and every day I lost another part of myself.

I felt like two people: one who kept dropping the parts and pieces of her life, and one who ran around trying to pick up those pieces as fast as she could. I tried to keep busy—get new work projects, buy groceries (only for myself now), clean the house, visit Duncan as many times as I could, weed the garden, clean up our tiny pond, buy bright flowers to put into my planters.

But even as I filled my day with activities, questions without answers swirled through my head: *Will I be able to handle the pain of his loss? Will I recover? Can I build a life of my own that is worthwhile without his support? Will I allow myself to stand alone, not controlled by my obsessive and desperate need for a man, any man, to help me?*

o o o

A few months before Duncan passed away, I read an article in *The Guardian* about a woman who called herself the Flirt Coach. She was photographed with her long blonde hair flowing past her shoulders onto an extravagantly colored kaftan. A relationship guru, she ran workshops teaching dating skills. She had a huge number of groupies who desperately wanted to learn her techniques for having a better social life. I was still working on the topic of libido in the workplace, and something in the article made me think this woman might be a good person to interview, so I called her up and made an appointment to meet with her.

Peta was unlike anyone I'd ever met. A chain smoker and nonstop talker, she was open about her infatuation with a leather-wearing biker. Shortly after I met her, she left her partner in hopes of attracting the biker and moved out of London into a garden flat in a tall red brick Victorian row house in Eastbourne. Soon I was driving regularly to Eastbourne to spend weekends with this loud, flamboyant, opinionated woman who insisted on wearing her Marigolds in the kitchen so her hands would stay soft, who ate salad for breakfast, and whose consumption of illegal smoking products was what legends are made of. So different from me.

o o o

At the end of June, I contacted Bob, Duncan's good friend in Canada, and our sons to tell them what Dr. Hanney had told me: "If the doctors can figure out what is wrong with his digestive system and repair it, he may have a window of time he can enjoy. If not, he may never get any better than he is now. His cancer has advanced to stage three and things don't look good. It's a guessing game as to what's going to happen."

I recalled what Dr. Hanney had predicted in December—that Duncan had six months to live. We were in the sixth month now.

Dr. Summerton, Duncan's second surgeon in London, advised that he be transferred back to the London Clinic, where he'd had his second operation. Duncan seemed relieved to be going back to London. He went in style, by ambulance all the way from the Milton Keynes clinic, down the M1, to London.

I visited as often as I could, usually every day, driving from our home in Buckingham to catch the train in Milton Keynes. From Euston Station in London, I walked along Euston Road to Devonshire Place and the London Clinic. If I was lucky with train times, I could manage this in just under two hours each way. Sometimes I stopped at a small corner store to choose a bouquet for Duncan from buckets of flowers sitting on the pavement. At the clinic, I'd order crab sandwiches and afternoon tea from the printed gourmet menu while Duncan fought nausea. After several days of this, he turned on me and snapped, "Do you have to eat your lunch here? Please go out of the room. The smell makes me feel even worse."

Some days I managed only a quick stop on my way to a work assignment. At times patient, other times Duncan snapped at me: "Why did you come at all if you can't stay very long?"

My voice low, trying not to provoke, "Because I wanted to see you."

He then turned his back to me and mumbled, "Oh, all right then."

From his hospital room, Duncan phoned Greg, in Canada, to tell him he shouldn't come to see him until he was better, so they could enjoy time together while he recovered. We were all used to Duncan calling the shots, but when I got home I phoned Greg to urge him to come now. He didn't. But at the advice of a colleague in Canada—"You'll regret it if your stepdad dies and you haven't had a last visit"—Adam did. He visited at the same time as Duncan's brother Davey, who had come from Toronto, and another old friend from Calgary.

"Why is everyone here?" Duncan demanded, suspicious. "What have you told them?"

I didn't need further proof that Duncan was not admitting what was happening to him.

"I told them you have a serious illness."

Calmed, he replied, "Well, that's okay, I guess."

It was the last time the brothers would be together.

But it was not all sad. One afternoon, a couple of Duncan's colleagues, Davey, Adam, and I all gathered in Duncan's hospital room and ordered up sandwiches and coffee. Duncan laughed and talked, holding court, leaning back on his pillows, surrounded by well-wishers. It was almost a party.

By this time, Duncan had been away from home for over a month. While he fought cancer in London, I carried on our consulting business alone. I wrote proposals, engaged colleagues to collaborate with, and looked for projects. Then I returned home alone every night to an empty house to feed our cats.

By this time, even Dr. Z seemed to think I needed help, not confrontation. He took ten minutes at the beginning of a therapy session to tell me what I already knew—that I was exhausted, in a state of shock, traumatized, and vulnerable. I had to find a way to have courage.

The next weekend, I attended a party at the home of Helen and Joe, Duncan's colleagues. Duncan and I had both been invited, but of course he couldn't leave the hospital. I stood on the lawn, glass of wine in hand, and asked Helen's uncle, a surgeon, what he thought about Duncan's condition. "Could he recover from this?"

I knew the truth from the way he looked at me, and the hesitation in his reply.

"It's good to be optimistic, but you have to be realistic."

I also knew that, impossibly, I believed two diametrically opposite things: yes, Duncan would die; and no, he wouldn't.

Betrayal

I rented the hotel room. Eric had decided he could overcome his reluctance to be with me if I took charge in this way.

I checked in first and took a look around at the plush bedspread, the dark framed standing mirror, the fireplace, and the mullioned windows overlooking a busy London street. As I sat on the end of the bed, contemplating the wisdom of this encounter, I heard a knock. I went to the door in an oversized white shirt and slim blue jeans. He told me later that he was confused by my clothing, as I wasn't wearing the clichéd, seductive negligee.

I put my arms around his neck and lifted my lips to his. Finally, for the first time, in this small room, we had the freedom to explore each other in the way we'd only fantasized about. He pushed me back and held my arms against the wall as he kissed me. I undressed and glanced at my body in the mirror, realizing it was the first time he had seen me nude. He looked at me, folded me into his arms, and breathed, "You're beautiful."

After a ten-month seduction, our lovemaking was hurried, self-conscious. Waiting had heightened the desire, but not the execution. Something didn't click. I'd been faithful to Duncan for over fourteen years and I still wasn't free.

◦ ◦ ◦

I moved about my house, doing my chores, going through the motions, numb in some ways to what had happened between Eric and me. I remembered Dr. Z's words: "Sex is the antidote to death." Perhaps numbness was the antidote to fear.

The day after the hotel encounter, Duncan's surgeon Dr. Summerton asked me to meet him in his office in the London Clinic.

"Your husband hasn't beaten the cancer," he said, "but he isn't in the terminal stages of the illness either. I took out his stomach and part of his bowel. He still has active cancer inside of him, especially on his bowel, but there's no way of knowing when it may grow again or how quickly."

I had done enough research by this time to know that in cutting right through the cancer in Duncan's abdomen, Dr. Summerton had released cancer cells to migrate to other parts of his body. For the time being, I supposed it was all right for Duncan to hold on to the belief that he might recover, but again it put me into a position of dishonesty. Dr. Hanney had warned me that Duncan would be in trouble if the nausea didn't end soon. It hadn't. But I couldn't tell Duncan any of this.

Despite all the negative predictions, during the first week of July Duncan seemed so much better. Instead of being irritable, he smiled when I next came into his room. As I sat on his bed, he reached over and started to unbutton my blouse. I let him take it off, and then he reached up under my skirt. The attraction I'd always felt for Duncan still hadn't wavered, despite his dry, pale skin, thin wisps of hair, and gaunt frame.

A nurse opened the door to the room. Duncan and I looked at each other and burst out laughing. With a quick apology, she closed the door. He reached over and turned on the radio. As we heard the first strains of "I Don't Want to Miss a Thing" by Aerosmith, he stood by the bed and held out his arms. I moved toward him to put my arms around him, and we danced one last time.

A couple of days later, Duncan walked over to Marylebone Road, on his own, to get a haircut. When I visited on Saturday, I was surprised to see him up and dressed. We walked down the block to Regent Park. It was a bright, hot, sunny London day. A wedding party was being photographed on the lawn and the grass was crowded with relaxed bodies sitting by the flowerbeds. We stopped at a tea kiosk, but all Duncan could eat was a Popsicle. Then we phoned my parents on my cell phone to tell them how much better Duncan was. Later, when I left him in his room at the clinic, we made plans for me to come back the next day. But when I returned, he was too ill to ever go out again.

o o o

I kept losing things. I was drinking too much sauvignon blanc, pacing the house with the glass in my hand. I shrieked to the heavens in the solitude of my bedroom. I was having an affair. I was afraid to be alone. I could no longer pretend I didn't know what was happening. I told Dr. Z only half the truth. I didn't tell him about the wine drinking, or the terror.

"You're having your own personal breakdown," he said. "There is a relentless force moving forward in you. You know, Karen, Duncan would have always stayed the same. He's giving you a gift by his leaving, his dying. He never could be part of your future journey, and neither can Eric."

I left his office in silence, the sun too bright for me to look at.

The End

On Saturday, July 17, 1999, I drove into London planning to see Duncan and then have dinner with Cathy. I sat with Duncan on the side of his bed. "I'm supposed to see Cathy, but I can stay if you want me to."

He didn't answer. Didn't ask me to stay. Didn't say a word. Just held his abdomen and turned his head to stare at me.

"I'll come back to see you after dinner."

Cathy and I ate at a little Thai place she knew in Camden. I kept looking at my watch and up at her, uneasy, and then said, "I really have to go."

"But Karen, you need time to yourself too. You need to relax and get away from worrying about Duncan."

I finished my meal and then drove back to the clinic, where I knocked on the front door, before seeing the notice: the London Clinic was closed to visitors for the night. I looked up and tried to see Duncan's room, but it was on the other side of the building. For a few minutes, I stood outside in the light of the street lamps, not sure what to do. Then I got back into my car and drove home. Only later did guilt grip me when I thought that perhaps, earlier in the evening, Duncan had been mute with pain—couldn't talk, couldn't tell me that he wanted me to stay with him.

The next morning, I went out into the garden and cut two large flowering stems from the star lilies we'd planted the previous autumn—large, fuchsia pink, and overly fragrant. I wrapped

153

the stems in plastic, took the train to London, and walked to the clinic.

Duncan looked up from his pillow at the flowers as I put them into a vase and placed them on his side table. He had a faint smile as I whispered, "They're from our garden."

He told me that an old friend, Eleanor, had been to see him on Friday. I couldn't have known then, but after the funeral she confided that Duncan knew I was trying to get him to talk about his possible death. I asked her what else he'd said, hoping to get some answers, some insight into what he was thinking and feeling.

"Nothing, really," she replied. "Our conversation just drifted to other things."

Duncan lay flat on his back, not able to hold his head away from the pillow. I leaned over close as he confided, "I'm giving up. I've told the nurses, but they won't listen to me." He looked straight into my eyes. "But I'll come back to fight another day."

Did he understand what he was saying? I wasn't sure. Nor could I ask him. He continued, "I'm afraid to be alone, but I have to face this on my own."

That night I had a dream:

I'm in a room dancing but my feet never touch the ground. I am about three feet above the floor, swirling around excitedly, as though I'm in water, treading with my arms and hands.

o o o

The next day was Monday, July 19th. My plan was to go into London to conduct interviews to further my research on libido in the workplace then go to the clinic to see Duncan. I phoned him after my first interview. A nurse answered then passed the phone to Duncan. In a small, raspy voice, he strained to speak, "Don't come. Don't come to see me."

My chest tightened. *Oh, fuck. Something must be very wrong for him to say this.* "I'll be there as soon as I can," I told him. I cancelled the rest of my interviews and headed to the clinic.

I went straight to the nurses' desk on his floor, only to hear complaints. "Mrs. Streeter, you're going to have to tell your husband we can't keep running into his room all the time. He wants us to sit with him in the middle of the night and we just don't have the time."

I went into his room, wondering why he didn't call me in the night.

He wasn't on his bed. I looked into the private bathroom and saw Duncan naked, sitting on the toilet, staring blankly ahead. Alone. I ran back to the nurses' desk, shaking and yelling in a strangled voice, "Come quickly, my husband needs help."

Two nurses stood up and hurried into his room. They moved him back into his bed. When the nurses turned their backs, Duncan whispered to me, "Pills, give me pills."

Still trying to follow the rules, afraid of asserting myself, with no real sense of how desperately in pain he was, I looked in my bag and saw some paracetamol, but said, "I didn't think I'm supposed to."

I could hear the nurses at the desk just outside Duncan's door, ringing number after number. His surgeon was away on summer holiday so they contacted an on-call physician. In about twenty minutes, the new doctor came into the room, wearing leathers and carrying a motorcycle helmet. He looked at Duncan, then at me, and barked, "Who are you?"

I registered the contrast between my royal blue suit, dark hair, and red lipstick, and Duncan—lying motionless on the bed, shrunken, bald except for his few wisps of white hair, pale as the sheets—before I answered, "I'm his wife."

Duncan was in crisis. The doctor ordered that he be taken to the intensive care unit on another floor in the clinic. I followed the gurney down the hall and into the elevator, leaving all my books and papers behind. When we arrived on the new floor, I was asked to wait behind a large white screen while he was lifted into the intensive care bed. The doctor came out around the screen, leaning his helmet against the nurses' desk.

"Is this the end?" I asked.

"No, he's definitely not near the end. We'll be installing a central line."

I didn't know what that was. I went around the screen and approached the bed. "The doctors are going to help you. I'm going home. I'll see you tomorrow."

As I walked to the door, I passed another bed in the large ward. I could hear a family whispering that there was someone else there in very bad condition. They glanced up guiltily as I passed. I turned and looked back. There was no one else in the ward. I went out the door, down the stairs, and out into the sunshine of the late afternoon. As I walked along the street, I heard a clear voice in my head, unbidden, saying, "You can go now."

❧ ❧ ❧

The phone rang at seven the next morning, July 20th. A voice said I should come as soon as I could. When I arrived, Duncan was lying on a gurney, deep in the basement of the London Clinic, attached to a machine that was keeping him alive until I could come and a priest could be called. I leaned close and said, "I love you," for the last time, and then that lie—"I will be alright"—as the nurse shut off the machines. All the knowledge, memories, joy, and despair that were in that brilliant brain of his, gone.

I can still hear Duncan quote from his favorite movie, *Zorba the Greek:* "Am I not a man? And is not a man stupid? I am a man. So I married. Wife, children, house, everything. The full catastrophe."

Duncan and I, we had the full catastrophe.

A Month without Dr. Z

I had held Duncan in my life as well as I could, and then let him go. He and I had lived with so much fear throughout our early lives and our life together that we prevented ourselves from going right to the point of intimacy before his death. To glimpse the loss while still in his presence would have been unbearable, and so unfair, as he was still there and his present self needed me. Our human frailty prevented us from achieving more, but we loved each other as well as our limitations allowed.

My horoscope on the day Duncan passed away:

> It takes a brave person to go out into the snow after an avalanche. What if another fall takes place? How can you be sure the danger is over? Tentatively, you are stepping out to see whether your world has stabilized yet. You are treading gently and carefully. You don't want to cause another upheaval or walk, unsuspectingly, into one. But try not to be too nervous. The drama is over . . .
>
> Jonathan Cainer, Daily Mail, July 20, 1999

And now I was alone. Like coming out of the house after a hurricane to see the broken trees and telephone poles on the ground, the storm was over—but the cleanup would take years. How would I manage alone?

o o o

Eric had been away on vacation but phoned immediately on learning of Duncan's death. "Should I come back for the funeral? Do you want me there? For you?"

"My family is here, Eric—my mother, my son, Duncan's son, and his best friend from Canada. No, stay with your family." I'd lowered my voice, embarrassed and confused but pleased to hear from him.

"I'll call you as soon as I get back. You know, Karen, it's our time now." He sounded upbeat. His reaction wrong. I could hear my mother and son in the kitchen, clinking dishes as they emptied the dishwasher. Eric chatted on, oblivious to my discomfort, "At the beginning of July, I asked Duncan if he wanted to come to my summer house to recover from the operation, to gain strength. My wife has to work. Will you come on your own? I'll be there with my girls. Will you come?"

Without thinking, I opened my mouth and let my reply slip out, "Yes."

o o o

After the funeral was over, my friends and family went back to Canada, and the aloneness crept in around me in every room. I wandered from the kitchen to the dining room to the living room to the garden, often with a glass of wine in my hands. I stood in my kitchen and leaned my forehead against the wall, screaming, "Oh, no, no, no, Duncan. You can't be gone. Come back." Then, louder, "Come back to me."

Again and again, sobbing, my eyes squeezing stream after stream of tears down my face and onto my clothes, I tried to command him back into this life, his mortal life. I buried my face in his sweaters, breathing in the scent of Aramis, his favorite cologne. I howled like a dog caught in a leghold trap, helplessly pulling and tearing at myself. My head ached every time I did this, but I couldn't stop, couldn't help myself. The bouts of tears and pain washed over me relentlessly, so that I was tossed again and again back onto my despair.

Duncan had been gone almost two weeks, but in my dream life, he was alive and well:

He is sitting in a café with his hat sunk down over his face. I take it off his head and see his face, young and handsome again, his hair black. He beams up at me. His jacket and shirt slip off and I caress his warm chest and shoulders.

I jolted upright in bed. The dream was so vivid that, with tears in my eyes, I yelled, "You came back!"

o o o

To escape, I drove east, through southern England, to Cornwall. As I passed mile after mile on the motorway, I thought about what I was embarking on. If I were horribly depressed, barricaded myself in my house, and baked cookies nonstop, I could understand, other people could understand. But this? What was I doing? I tried to find a little bit of grit within myself as I contemplated seeing Eric again. I would have rules. If he stayed with his wife, eventually I would see other men.

I followed the directions Eric had given me to his summer home. It was on the outside of an historic village, a large stone country cottage set off by an acre of lawn and towering trees where he and his wife could entertain up to forty people for dinner. I had barely stopped the car in the driveway and stepped out when Eric grabbed me by the hand and took me around the corner of the house for a tour of the grounds. He turned to me, his hands encircling my waist, pulling me close to him, whispering a cliché in my ear—"You look beautiful, good enough to eat."

All I wanted was his attention, to know that he desired me. He kissed me eagerly and I could feel his growing enthusiasm through my gauzy summer dress. I wanted the escape, the diversion, the excitement.

Later that afternoon, Eric told me he'd invited a woman—Jeanette, a neighbor—for dinner. She had a casual, easy way with him. They had a history, a friendship. He offered sauvignon blanc, which I downed like lemonade. After dinner, I went outside to his children's swing set and sat down on one of the swings. Pumping harder and harder, I went higher and higher, up and down, the roof of the house swirling, the grass too green, the sky too close, my stomach heaving, sobbing and angry, my desperation exposed, my embarrassment obvious. I went up to the guest room to sleep, but stayed awake—crying, mourning, alone.

◦ ◦ ◦

The next morning, Eric tried to reassure me, "I've known Jeanette for years. I've no interest in her. I kissed her once, years ago. There's nothing there. I just need women to like me, to flirt with me." He told me he had invited about twenty of the neighbors for supper that evening. I couldn't attend a party like that—a gathering with normal people, strangers who just wanted to have a good time. I was desperate. I needed his attention. Alone.

This time Eric's charm wasn't working. I shoved my clothes into my suitcase and threw it into the backseat of my car.

"You're overreacting. You're not the only woman who's ever lost her husband. You don't have to go."

"Yes, Eric, I do."

As I drove back across southern England, the urgency I'd felt about Eric before was mixed with so many other feelings. Was what he offered only a sham? He said we weren't right for each other, or at least we wouldn't end up together, so why tell me it was "our time"? Did he want me to be his bit on the side? No matter how much I romanticized the relationship, I wasn't going to be one of those women who sat alone, hidden away every holiday, while her lover spent time with his family—or other women.

I'd never learned how to dodge Duncan's barbs, but perhaps I could take myself out of Eric's way.

◦ ◦ ◦

I couldn't take time off. Couldn't relax. Had to work to pay the bills. John, my friend and work partner, felt it best to keep me working, if only for a few days at a time. I stood at the front of a room full of executives looking for guidance in changing the culture of their organizations. I imagined their gasps if I were to share that I'd just lost my husband to cancer. I knew I wasn't ready to be leading workshops. What was I doing?

A week later, in London after a business meeting, I just couldn't get on the train and return to my empty house, so I walked to the Maple Leaf Pub, a Canadian-themed pub with Molson's on tap, lacrosse sticks, and hockey posters on the walls. A little bit of home.

As I sat nursing my glass of chardonnay, a gentle-looking man started to chat with me.

"Are you Canadian?" he asked. "Is that why you're here?"

"Yes, but also, I didn't want to go home. I just lost my husband."

"Oh, what happened?"

"Cancer. He died of cancer."

He looked at me in utter amazement. "I'd be walking on a lonely beach by myself for the next six months if that happened to me."

I could hear judgment tinge the edge of his voice. I felt as though he was saying I didn't know how to behave, to mourn, to mark Duncan's passing. He didn't understand that I was trying to run from the horror as I had done in the last few months. Escape was what I craved.

o o o

Guilt is not one of those emotions that creeps in around the edges of your life—it swoops in and clobbers you, beats you down until you don't want to raise your head. I was racked with guilt about how I handled the whole of the time Duncan was ill, but particularly his last four days. I hadn't seen the signs that he was leaving so soon, or I saw them in that way I have of not comprehending or responding immediately. I didn't see the full extent of his pain, or his fear of being alone. I couldn't have taken away even one tiny piece of the pain, but, even though I was there nearly every day, I felt I could have been there more.

He did his death like he did his life, trying to bully it into sub-mission. We did no crying in each other's arms about our fear and grief at his impending death. I tried to tell him how much I was going to miss him and his only answer was, "Well, I'm going to miss you too." He'd had faith that his human emotions would per-sist beyond death.

How can he be gone? How could I have gone to supper with Cathy on that last Saturday? How could I have left him in the intensive care ward on his last night? How could I have taken energy away from him and put it elsewhere—on another man?

o o o

August was the month my analyst took his holidays—bad timing for me. With no one to talk to and the house empty, I searched for meaningful things to do. I knew that Duncan's energy, his spirit, was no longer in our house, so on Sundays I went to the Abbey, where we'd held the funeral. Perhaps his spirit would be there, floating in the chapel. I tried to reconnect with my Catholicism, and searched the Sunday gospels for messages that would keep me going through the following week.

I weeded the garden, bought fish for the tiny pond, and played Van Morrison to fill the empty spaces of my rooms.

The days stretched before me, hot and humid. I lost weight. I'd open the fridge door, stare at the food, and then close it again.

I over-exercised. I went to my tiny local gym and rode the station-ary bike for twenty heart-pounding minutes, followed by an ever-increasing weight regime. In the locker room I ran into someone I used to see regularly.

"Where's your gym partner?"

"That was my husband. He died in July."

"Oh god, I'm so sorry."

I'd leave the gym exhausted and dripping with sweat. To let my muscles rest, every other day, I forced myself to stay home from the fierce workouts that the gym coach said were anaerobic—my body's demand for oxygen exceeding the oxygen supply available. I wasn't coming up for air.

How can he be gone? I phoned my mother and choked on the words, "Where is he?"

"Oh, Karen."

"No, Mother, it's all right," I said, coming to my senses. "I'll be all right."

She didn't know what to say. No one did. I hung up, walked into the kitchen to make tea, and stood crying, sobbing, aching.

o o o

The eight months of Duncan's illness went by so quickly I didn't have time to catch up with the fact that I was not in control of when our marriage ended. Duncan was the one who left. Even in the face of the obvious, I could not face that it *was* the end. We moved so quickly from broken marriage to dying and death, I couldn't switch tracks fast enough. Instead, I derailed.

I acted as though we had all the time in the world, that nothing had changed, that he was still as capable as ever, even while on chemo. If someone tells you your husband is going to die in six months and you believe it, you make certain choices, maybe spend more time together. You don't waste time on insignificant things. But in order to make those decisions, you both have to accept that he's going to die. Instead Duncan had said to me, "If you gave up hope I don't think I could cope."

The adult part of me had rationally prepared for his death. I'd notified relatives, taken over business projects, planned our last trip to the Lakes District. But like a child, I had been furious and impatient with Duncan for dying. So I'd been thoughtless. And I hadn't really believed that he would die, because I couldn't.

Only bottle after bottle of clear golden liquid slipping down my throat would take away the swirling of my thoughts. One evening, I filled my glass with sauvignon blanc, opened the French doors from the breakfast nook, and stepped out into the dark. The humid August air closed around me as I walked across the patio stones and then stubbed my toe against an Italian stoneware pot. The wine glass tumbled end over end and then dropped onto the grass, wet and empty. I lay on my back, my head soothed by the damp coolness of the grass, staring at the stars, smelling the night-blooming jasmine, my arms stretched out on either side of my body, reaching nothing.

I ran away from death as fast as I could and in as many ways as possible. I loaded the fridge with Tesco sauvignon blanc and slipped, night after night, into an alcohol-induced stupor. I lay on the couch in the lounge, the television on, letting its noise lull me to sleep, unwilling to go up to my empty bedroom.

But the soothing coolness of yet another glass of wine couldn't protect my mind from the thoughts that bombarded it. Duncan's life and my life had intersected for seventeen years. I'd loved him, been afraid of him, obeyed him, disappointed him, pleased him, tolerated him, betrayed him, infuriated him, and "contained" him. I'd been his emotional punching bag.

My intense emotions gave me only a false sense of reality. I couldn't make these feelings go away, but I could start to accept that I was something other than just this set of feelings. There had to be something more to me than this pain, and over the next few years I would fight to find out what that was.

o o o

I relived Duncan's illness in my dreams:

I walk into a house where two women are looking after Duncan. He has diarrhea. I go in and start to take him home. It's raining and we're out in the back garden. I support him and take him to our house. I get him inside and he's upset and looks down. The back of his jeans is brown, soaking, stinking, and weighed down. I take off his jeans and he lies back, facing me with his eyes closed.

I visited our family doctor, who had asked me to make an appointment every two weeks so she could keep an eye on me.

"How are you doing?" she asked.

"I can't sleep. I'm afraid to go to bed and I'm awake most of the night."

"Are you eating?"

"I'm not hungry most of the time."

"I'll give you some sleeping tablets. You're not depressed, just in normal mourning, so this should help."

No one tells you what "normal mourning" feels like, so how can you know?

o o o

While Duncan was sick, like Siamese conjoined twins, I had shared symptom after symptom of his illness. But instead of the two of us being properly surgically separated, we'd been ripped apart. Now my guts were hanging out to bleed. During the first month after his death, I felt a pain as though someone were punching me, hard, in the stomach. I read something years ago that said that sometimes when one Siamese twin dies, the other dies too.

In September my doctor sent me for my annual mammogram. It came back showing an ambiguous spot. I had to go back to the clinic and have an ultrasound done. Then my PAP smear had to be redone. There were suspicious-looking cells, the letter said—quite common, but I had to return to the clinic so my doctor could arrange an appointment with a specialist.

"It's not unusual for a new widow to have health scares," the gynecologist said. "It's the stress. It's usually nothing, but they need to be checked out." After a full anesthesia and a cone biopsy, I was declared "good to go."

My final health problem turned out to be a very upset stomach—upset to the point where I was in almost constant pain. I was sent to Dr. Hanney, Duncan's original surgeon. He booked me into the same clinic that Duncan had been in for a short time, where I was administered a light sedative before an endoscopy.

When I woke, Dr. Hanney said that I had some small lesions on the inside of my stomach. These were the result of taking very strong pain pills for a number of years to deal with my almost constant neck pain. Years later, X-rays confirmed that the neck pain was the result of my ex-husband Joe's parting gesture to me—his using me as a punching bag.

If I stopped taking the pills, Dr. Hanney said, the lesions would likely clear up.

o o o

I spent much of my time wandering around the rooms in my house. Duncan and I had chosen the things in them together, but they were mine now—not ours, but mine. I looked at the art on my walls. The Margaret Keane print with hand-applied gold leaf, signed by the artist, bought in Lahaina, Maui, on our first vacation together was mine. The Dalí prints we bought in St. Petersburg, Florida, at the Dalí museum were mine. The hand-loomed silk carpet bought in a tiny carpet shop on the main street of Palmyra, Syria, was mine. The antique French tulipwood sideboard with the marble counter-top, bought by Duncan and his first wife in Cleveland was mine. The glass dining table and chairs, the dishes, the cutlery, the books, the sofas, all were mine. Our lovely house, a model home in a new English housing estate, was mine. The back garden, with the stone patio and the small pond, mine. The bleakness of the kitchen, the loneliness of the lounge, the futility of the fireplace, the starkness of the lamps shining on the walls, the emptiness of the bed were mine. The physical pain, the emptiness pounding at my stomach, my heart, my gut—all were mine.

o o o

I'd been trying to get away from the pain of mourning by using the fantasy of easing Eric into my life to take the place of Duncan. Was I mad to think that I could avoid the pain? No, I was in the middle of a breakdown. Now I realized this was something I had to face.

In September, I went to my first therapy session with Dr. Z since Duncan's death. It had been almost a year since we started therapy together—since I'd arrived at his door with a desire to get my life back. But my own personal, transformative work had been interrupted by Duncan's illness and death. Now that Duncan was gone, my own personal work was beginning.

Though it was a huge temptation, I actually didn't want to just quickly relieve the pain I was suffering by taking a pill or distracting myself. In addition to the misery of grief, there was so much else to explore with Dr. Z. Did I have a dark side that compelled me to search out men who would ultimately hurt me? Did I want to get even with those who betrayed me? If Duncan had never told me about Shelley, his pub-going colleague, would I have pursued Eric as I had? Was my anger as irrational, as childish, as Duncan's? Getting well, getting clear, finding out what my true Self was—all these were my goals now.

The New Struggle

*I*n the first week of October, I phoned Jim, the man who'd been Duncan's analyst, to tell him, "I have a book of yours, one that Duncan borrowed. I just want you to know that I'll get it back to you as soon as I can."

He seemed only mildly interested in the book but obviously wanted to talk to me.

"Karen, I'm so glad you phoned," he said. "I want to share some things about Duncan that may help you now. He was a man with incredibly deep pain. His anger toward his mother for having caused that pain led him to have anger toward all women." I listened quietly to what I knew was true. "He was very vulnerable and sensitive but couldn't really face that part of himself. He had to appear as though he was always in control and could handle anything. That was how he survived. But as much as he couldn't really face his inner torment and pain, he also couldn't come to terms with how much pain he inflicted on you, his family."

"Jim, thank you for sharing that. I know Duncan didn't really want to hurt us. It was as though he couldn't help himself."

"Yes, you're right—he did as much as he could in terms of facing the truth about the effect of his anger. I don't think he had the strength to accept the full impact."

I put the phone down silently, sat in a nearby chair, and rested my head in my hands, shaking and crying. Jim's call helped put Duncan's rage and pain into perspective. He did understand, in theory, what

I'd gone through with Duncan. As tears ran down my face, my heart filled with sadness and compassion for Duncan. He had loved and hated his mother. I remembered the pain on Duncan's face as he described the torture inflicted by Aunt Cubie at his mother's bidding. He wanted me to be the mother he dreamed of having—and then the angry child in him inflicted rage on me when I didn't fulfill his expectations. But should this information make a difference in how I felt?

Duncan's demons had dominated our lives for so long. If I empathized too much with him, I might shove my own pain aside yet again and not come to terms with how the boys and I had been affected. I might understand him and his motivations, but was that going to help me now in my struggle to find out why I had been attracted to such a damaged man? I recalled how Duncan would often quote Werner Erhard: "Understanding is the booby prize of life."

o o o

I entered a surreal time in which the horror of my situation mixed with my attempts to relieve my misery. I was desperately lonely. I continued to check in with my family doctor every two weeks. She monitored my various physical problems and test recalls. She renewed my sleeping pill prescription. My routine of going regularly to the gym was much better than going to a pub.

In addition to going to the gym five times a week for workouts, and losing weight, I was smoking. One day, an old friend turned to me in disgust and said, "Given that Duncan died of cancer, how can you smoke? Are you crazy?"

I think we know the answer to that one.

Most nights, I was still sleeping on the living room couch with the television on, even after taking sleeping pills.

After going with her and Cathy to the Nottinghill Carnival, my friend Aileen said, "You seem all right until the sun goes down, and then you wilt."

I joined a local support group for widows and widowers so I could get some peer counseling. I was paired with a woman who had lost her husband at age thirty-three. She just listened. That was all she had to do. I needed to talk about Duncan—talk about his illness, and my reactions to it. Tell the story over and over and over again.

I'd heard admonitions that it was not good enough to just be coping, that you had to be thriving. But at this point, just getting up every day and putting one foot in front of the other was my version of coping. And sometimes that was as good as it got.

o o o

I went to Duncan's university one day in October to pick up materials for a course I was teaching and dropped in to see Marnie, a colleague. Marnie's father had recently died and her mother had been admitted to the inpatient psychiatric ward of the nearby hospital. I was terrified of falling apart like that.

She gave me a book she'd bought for her mother, a report of academic research on English and Canadian widows. Apparently those who fared the worse were widows whose husbands had suffered a great deal of pain and had not gone into hospice. Like me, these women had witnessed, but could do nothing to relieve, their husbands' agony. The front cover showed the bleak outline in black of a woman sitting up in bed, awake in the middle of the night. I was that woman, up at midnight screaming at the blackness.

I prowled the local bookstores looking for other books that would help me and picked up *A Widow for One Year*, by John Irving. Perhaps if I read this book, I'd be a widow for only one year. It didn't seem that much of a stretch. I didn't have to try to locate would-be suitors. Men I'd thought were friends now labeled me a "right bit of crumpet." One of Duncan's colleagues predicted I'd be married within a year's time.

Dr. Z raised his eyebrows in a flippant manner when I told him of the men in my life, but to me it seemed obvious that I really had no life of my own without a man—without Duncan—to fill it. He had won our work contracts, dictated my style of clothing, and taken up most of my energy. His job at the university had been our main source of revenue and social life. What did I have without him?

I leaned on my friends and their hospitality. I spent time in my friend Cathy's tiny apartment. After sharing a bottle of wine, eating takeaway Chinese, and setting the world to rights, I slept on cushions in her living room to have companionship and a sense of safety and security. Sometimes I would just call her when things got bad and ask if I could come and sleep on her floor.

An old friend, Bev, flew out from Canada and helped me with a course I was teaching. Then she and I flew to Ireland. After landing in Cork, we rented a car and set off to find attractive B&Bs and good pubs. We explored the Dingle Peninsula and sat in a tiny pub chatting with the locals. We sought out ancient stone cairns and interesting pie shops, and visited Blarney Castle. Neither of us would risk leaning backwards over the abyss to kiss the Blarney stone as my Granny had done in the 1930s on her widow's tour. We explored Tralee and Killarney, drove along the south coast, and slowly made our way to Dublin. After we checked into our B&B, we took the tram to Temple Bar.

Bev had known me for so long, from the time I'd been married to Joe.

"You don't just need to get over Duncan's death," she told me over a pint of Guinness, "you need to get over your marriage."

She was right, and if she'd said it a couple of years down the road, I could have heard her advice—but at this point, I could barely put one foot in front of the other. Logic found no foothold in my brain. The thing I could do best was respond to the lively Irish music with its melancholy longing and tap my foot madly to the beat. As the link to my Irish heritage was reignited, I had a tiny glimpse of me, the real me, the woman underneath the heavy shell of my power suits.

After two weeks together, Bev returned to Canada and I to my life in England.

o o o

I was on the university campus again, walking to the library with a stack of books, when I saw two women who'd worked with Duncan from the time he first arrived at Brookton. One of them reached out and touched my arm to stop me and said, "Hello Karen, how are you doing? How are you coping? How are you keeping busy?"

I tried to open my mouth to respond but she seemed so far away I was afraid my words wouldn't reach her. Her face was in a haze. She looked at me—waiting, at first, expectant—but then an impatient scowl crossed her face. She turned to her companion and said, "Let's go get a coffee," leaving me just standing there.

"Wait," I wanted to say, "I'd like a coffee." But that day I couldn't react in a normal fashion. Instead, I stood frozen to the spot and watched them walk away. Confused, I felt the pressure of tears welling up inside me, but I wouldn't let them fall down my face where someone could see.

o o o

Jungian analysts are people you can speak to about the big questions of life. That is their territory. During one of my sessions, Dr. Z advised, "Don't try to sort out the last year. You'll just have to be at peace with the unknowable and the unfathomable. You've been dealing with the mysteries of the universe."

Sitting there in his office, I could feel that I wasn't to blame, that I shouldn't judge my actions and reactions. No one was criticizing me anymore, at least not to my face. Duncan had left, leaving me to get on with my life.

My efforts to get my life back and become calm and centered were hampered by the fact that, despite my doctor's assertion that I was in normal mourning, I was actually experiencing many of the symptoms of post-traumatic stress disorder (PTSD). My repeated dreams about Duncan ill and dying, severe guilt, excessive drinking, feelings of being abandoned and alone, constant agitation, and physical pain were all typical of PTSD—something I didn't realize until years later, when a psychologist friend made the connection. During this time, I often felt as though I was sinking in quicksand as I blamed myself for not being able to cope, and for not being able to avoid what I judged as the dark and murky parts of myself. My ability to judge what was good for me and what was harmful was so skewed that I often did things that made no sense.

 ◦ ◦ ◦

At the end of October, Cathy, Aileen, and I decided to go to a country hotel north of Hove for a weekend away. Cathy had seen an advertisement for a murder mystery weekend, but there were not enough people signed up for murder—so I settled for seduction. We were sitting in the lounge on Saturday night, doing a musical quiz, pondering who had sung "I Will Survive," when a male voice yelled out from across the room, "Gloria Gaynor!" The three of us turned to see a handsome, middle-aged man sitting in the corner of the lounge reading a paper. Cathy asked him to join us. Later, Peter confessed that he felt it was fate.

He was supposed to be staying at a hotel right on the seafront in Hove with his sons from a former marriage, but all the hotels were full, so he'd ended up here at the South Farm Hotel. Tall and slim with thick, slightly graying hair, Peter bore a slight resemblance to Hugh Grant—and, according to Aileen, he only had eyes for me. That night in the lounge, after Cathy and Aileen said good night, Peter and I sat, had a couple more drinks, and talked.

He was English—from Brighton—but had lived and worked in Nigeria for many years. He was returning to Lagos the next day on an early-morning flight from Gatwick. This had been his routine for several years since his divorce. He offered to "walk me home" to my hotel room. When we reached my door, he leaned over to kiss me and I wrapped my arms around him and passionately returned his kiss. He smiled broadly then laughed and said, "Maybe we should go to my room."

I should have said no.

In Peter's room, we undressed and sat on his bed. I looked at him and slowly moved my fingertips down his arms. We were gentle with each other, slow and deliberate. I ran my hands across his shoulders and upper back, noticing the contrast between his deep tan and my pale white skin. As I did so, I thought about how present and close I felt to this stranger—this unique, irreplaceable human being.

After, he spoke about his work and daily routine back in Lagos.

"Monday to Thursday I work on my project sites," he said, "but Friday is for me." His voice caught just slightly as he said this and I looked up at him, but he had turned his face away. I knew something then, though I didn't know what I knew.

Peter gave me his business card and we exchanged e-mail addresses. Then he left before first light for the airport. When he'd gone, I went back to my room for a couple hours of sleep.

Despite a heavy head, I managed to get up at a decent hour to meet Cathy in the dining room for a full English breakfast. We chatted about our plans for the day. She and I would go to Folkington Manor gardens to have a wander without Aileen, who had to go back to London. Then the conversation turned to Peter.

"So, are you going to keep in touch with him?" Cathy asked.

A look on my face must have given me away, because she immediately followed with, "Oh, Karen, you didn't."

I smiled at my naughtiness.

"Aileen said you might. My goodness, I didn't see that one coming."

"Yes, we've agreed to keep in touch. Don't know where it can possibly go, as he is so far away."

But her face showed concern, not delight. "Just don't let yourself become like those expats in African countries. You know, I went to Ghana one time because, since I'm from the Caribbean, I thought I might feel more at home there, might like to live there. But I couldn't relate at all—I found out I really am English."

o o o

I was still bombarded with dreams that were helping me to come to terms with what had happened, like this one, on November 17, 1999:

I see Duncan in a building all made up for Christmas and I approach him. I hold his face in my hands. It is ashen. I hold him to me and tell him he is going to die. As I do this, I phone my mother. In a mirror, as we talk, I can see my mother's sister as a young woman in her twenties. She is only in the mirror, not in the room. I speak with my Mom about this and we are both frightened. It's a sign that death is impending.

Two steps forward, one step back. Four months after his death, I knew consciously that Duncan was gone, passed away. But the knowledge had to seep down, down into my unconscious, because there he was still alive. Possibly my dream was trying to tell me of another death as well. But whose?

In public, I could still put on a professional front. The undercurrent of agitation and stress that was always present only came out in full force when I passed safely through my front door after a day of being out in the world. I was still self-medicating with sauvignon blanc. I often looked in the fridge to refill my glass only to realize I'd finished the whole bottle. I ached for Duncan to be there—the wise side of him, the Duncan who had been my friend. He'd been good at advice if the issue didn't involve him. My first analyst in Calgary had said it would've been better if we'd just been friends. Much too late for that now.

Distraction didn't always work to keep the desperation at bay. It would creep up on me when I didn't expect it. A feeling of hysteria would prompt me to yell out in my empty lounge, "Duncan, I didn't want you to die, just to stop screaming and insulting me! Please don't leave me, don't go away! Come back!" Louder and louder, I'd sob the words. I didn't take into consideration that these reactions might affect all I would do in the next part of my life.

Before I'd met Peter, I'd already bought my ticket to go back to Canada for Christmas. He was coming to England to see his sons for the holidays, and we wouldn't even pass in the airport. But I watched every day for his e-mails. He'd warned me that the infrastructure in

Lagos was virtually nonexistent: he could only e-mail when he was in his office, there was no postal service, the electricity went out at least once a day, phones were unreliable, and he had no cell reception in his home. He had to go to a certain restaurant and stand outside to get reception. But we agreed that he would call me every Sunday evening.

During those Sunday talks, we had long conversations about how we'd met, how strange it was that he happened to be at that hotel on that weekend, that perhaps it was meant to be, and how he'd not had a relationship since his marriage broke up two years before. Thinking of our meeting as destiny fed my illusion that this was more than just a casual encounter. I put my hopes and dreams onto Peter, once again hoping for a fantasy prince who would save me from pain and loneliness.

The possibility of having Peter in my life made it easier to maintain my distance from Eric. He and I had met to discuss our relationship about a month after I'd left his summer house in mid-August. He was still critical of my sudden departure and my mistrust of him.

"Yes, Eric, I do feel uneasy about seeing you. And I really can't understand how June stays married to you. I admit that."

His face veered from anger to shock. "I didn't expect you to be so honest with me. I admire that in you, but now I don't know if I can trust you." I remembered him saying that he needed to be admired and flirted with in order to feel good about himself. "I was so supportive of you during Duncan's illness, and now you're being unreasonable . . . Remember, I'm not going to leave June and break up my family."

Eric said we should see how we felt in the next few months. I still felt attracted to him, which I knew made no logical sense at all. I was excited about Peter, but with him so far away, I would have to be patient and give it time, whereas the temptation of Eric was right on my doorstep.

Another Year of Loss and Pain

Before Christmas, I flew back to Ontario to see my parents. This was the first time I'd been home, or seen Dad and his sister, my Aunt Barb, since Duncan had died.

My aunt asked me to join her in the den so we could talk about how I was doing. I told her stories. Stories about coping, and friends, and work projects. Not stories about despair. Not stories about empty wine bottles. Not stories about waking in the middle of the night screaming. Not stories about the men in my life or my belief that if I married again quickly my problems would be solved. Later, I leaned back on the living room couch and closed my eyes while the TV blared and my family sat and chatted. It was so comforting to have people, noise, and activities around me.

After a while, my dad approached the couch. "If you're going to sleep, why don't you go up to your room?"

My room was still set up with twin beds, twin dressers, and my old school desk, just as it had been when my sister and I had lived at home as young girls.

"No thanks, Dad, I want to be down here."

A few minutes later he returned. "Karen, wouldn't you feel more comfortable and be better able to sleep if you went to bed?"

Impatient, I raised my voice. "Are you trying to say you don't want me here?"

"No, no, I just thought you'd be better off there."

"Dad, I'm alone all the time. I want to be with people."

My aunt motioned to him to just leave me alone.

◦ ◦ ◦

After a week, I flew on to Calgary to spend Christmas and New Year's with my sons and old friends. Peter called every day from England and said he'd posted a Christmas card to reach me at my son's house. He wrote emails about feeling tingly in a way he hadn't for a long time. He said he'd given up the possibility that this could happen again, though he wanted to think he had kept the door open to a new relationship, just in case. He told me he liked being the caveman and being in a traditional relationship with a feminine woman. I flashed to a vision of me standing in a kitchen with a frilly apron on, mixing drinks for my hubby. I knew that wasn't me, but I wasn't ready to give up the fantasy.

I brought in 2000, the new millennium, with old friends Natalie and Norman. When I returned to Adam's house at about two in the morning, his roommate asked if I wanted to go with him to pick up Adam, Jamie, and their friends from the party they'd gone to and go out for an early-morning meal. At about three in the morning, we all sat around a huge table in Chinatown, eating, chatting. I was thrilled to be part of my sons' lives.

"Why do you keep calling her Mom?" said one of the young women to Jamie.

"Because she's my mom," he answered.

She looked a bit surprised.

Adam laughed and said, "My boss doesn't think you look old enough to be my mom either."

I smiled. At nearly fifty-one, I still felt young.

Perhaps not surprisingly, drinking too much was not an issue on this trip. Surrounded by friends and family, my sons especially, I had no urge to drown myself.

I arrived back home in England in time for Peter's bouquet of red roses to reach me on my birthday. Maybe he was the one who would save me after all.

❀ ❀ ❀

At the end of January, I met Peter at Gatwick. I kissed him as he came through the exit gate at the airport, but it felt awkward and forced. As we lifted his bags into the boot of my car, I tried to picture myself as his partner, but despite all our phone calls and e-mails, he was a stranger. Every time I imagined myself at his side, I had the feeling of being "the little woman."

First we drove to the South Farm Hotel, scene of our first meeting, where we spent a couple of days with his children. Then we returned to Gatwick, flew to Calgary, picked up a rental car, and drove the ninety minutes to Banff for a ski trip. We'd booked a chalet on Tunnel Mountain and agreed to split the cost, but as we headed into the lobby to check in, Peter turned to me.

"Give me your half of the money," he said. "The man has to be the one who pays." He flashed his huge smile at me as I reached into my wallet for cash.

On the mountain, when Peter asked someone to take our picture, the man didn't hesitate to refer to me as Peter's "wife." We were a handsome couple: slim, fit, and attractive. Standing at the base of the Strawberry chair lift at Sunshine Ski Resort in my new white ski suit, I felt ladylike and feminine beside Peter, the rugged adventurer. I struggled to squeeze myself into the image of being a fragile ornament, Sleeping Beauty beside the handsome prince.

Sitting in the ski chalet, Peter excitedly explained how long-distance relationships had worked for him in the past. I listened quietly as he outlined a possible future for us. "You could come down to Lagos every three or four months and I would come to England the same. I have a friend who's had a relationship with a woman in England for about ten years and it works well. Maybe at some point you could stay longer and find some work projects in Lagos."

Everything went well until we went out for a posh dinner at a nearby lodge. I only had two glasses of wine, but on an empty stomach, they hit me hard. At first Peter didn't notice, as he was too busy explaining, "My sons are coming to Lagos for Easter, so you can come in June or later."

June? That was five months away. I couldn't last until June without him. Why was I being shoved aside for his children? Why couldn't we all be there together? If I was going to be part of his life, shouldn't I be there too?

I knew I shouldn't do it, but with my emotions bubbling to the surface, I started to complain—whine, even—that I was being left out. I watched myself sulk, desperation driving me to push too far. The couple of glasses of alcohol I'd had fueled my arguments. I hardly touched my steak. Peter said he had routines with his kids that he didn't want to interrupt. He wanted to spend time with them on their own. Of course. Neither of us knew if our romance would last, but his relationship with his children would.

Just in time, I caught myself in my anxiety and apologized to Peter. We walked back to the chalet and ended the evening talking in the hot tub. He agreed to have me come at Easter and overlap my visit with his kids'.

At the end of this trip, we drove back to Calgary and had dinner with Adam and my friends Natalie and Norman. Then we spent a day shopping. Peter wanted to buy his sons some souvenirs and to buy a dress and hat for Teni, his children's nanny in Lagos. We spent hours searching for just the right dress. After we flew back to England, Peter went back to Lagos, and I went home.

o o o

In my dreams, both the future and the past plagued me:

My father is terminally ill. I am angry and challenge my mother, "How do you think it feels for me to live so far away and always miss everyone's birthdays and weddings? Doesn't anyone realize how much I care?"

And later that week:

Duncan is sick, and in treatment. I bring him to a room where he is to get an injection for pain. I don't want to look at his bum because it's so thin and bruised. I hold him, caressing his hair and forehead.

I woke up from this dream with tears running like a flood down my face, my head aching from visions of both the past and a possible future.

Even as I struggled, however, I continued making contacts for work projects, and spoke with Peter in Lagos every Sunday evening. In addition, I'd decided I had to start getting out of the house and establishing a social life for myself. I decided to volunteer at The Stables, the theater just outside Milton Keynes started by John Dankworth and Cleo Laine. I'd attended some concerts there, and someone suggested that if I were to volunteer I could see all the performances for free and meet some interesting people, too.

Almost immediately I met Tracey, who was also a new volunteer. Like me, she was an independent trainer in organizations, owned her own house, and lived alone. We decided to have dinner at a local pub. I told her about losing Duncan, my on-again, off-again romance with Eric, and Peter, my English love interest in Nigeria. She'd been having an affair with a married man for over fifteen years. A few years before, he'd been stationed in Lagos for two years by his employer, a British oil company. His wife had accompanied him, but Tracey flew out to meet him at a place distant from Lagos while he was there. I couldn't believe the coincidence.

Tracey was a very angry woman—called her lover's wife "Wifey" in a disparaging tone. I pointed out that his wife had been there first, and likely would be there until the end if he hadn't left her by now. Silently, I congratulated myself on the wisdom of my decision to avoid being Eric's bit on the side.

○ ○ ○

One of Peter's great passions was sailing. I wanted to be able to do more than just sit on a lawn chair at the Lagos Yacht Club while he sailed, so in preparation for my trip, I took a beginner's sailing course. Our class headed off in dinghies across a small lake to learn the basics. Though not mechanically adept, I loved being in and on water, so I thought surely I could at least manage to tie knots.

I also went to my doctor for advice about malaria medication. Peter had warned me that, while the chance of contracting malaria in the city of Lagos was small, the risk of serious illness if I should contract it was high. He himself had almost died from a bout of malaria. My doctor gave me a prescription for Larium. When I went to my local Boots pharmacy to fill it, I also bought the strongest form of bug repellant I could find.

In preparation for my early-morning flight from England to Lagos, I asked Cathy if I could sleep at her apartment the night before, as her place was much closer to the airport than mine. She and I went out to an Italian restaurant in Richmond that evening, and once again she reminded me of her advice when I first met Peter: "Karen, tell me you aren't going to become like those expats in Africa."

I had no idea what she meant, but assured her that nothing was going to change me. How do you know what to say when you have no idea what you're walking into?

◦ ◦ ◦

The next morning, I sat in the airport waiting room next to women in colorful long dresses and headdresses tied in large bows. Men were in suits and traditional African hats. I wasn't just setting out to see Peter, my handsome lover, I was off on an adventure. Into deepest Africa. I'd bought a lovely new silk dress and matching jacket so we could dine at the yacht club, packed coordinated shorts and T-shirts to wear on the sailboat, workout clothes in case I had time to go to a gym, lovely shirts to wear to parties at other ex-pats' homes.

When I landed in Lagos, I saw Peter and his two young children on a high bridge, waving and watching the plane taxi to the terminal. As I disembarked, baggage handlers ignored the luggage carousels, which didn't seem to be turning anyway, and threw the bags out onto the floor. I grabbed mine, went through customs, and headed out the door into a world of chaos and heat.

My first introduction to Lagos was through the window of Peter's car, sitting beside his sons in the backseat. Peter sat in the front next to his driver. From the airport, we drove onto the most crowded motorway I'd ever seen: six lanes of cars moving so slowly that young men and younger boys, loaded with goods to sell, made their way between the cars. They smiled as they tapped on the windows, showing their wares—toothbrushes, combs, sunglasses, underwear, fruit, and vegetables. You could do much of your shopping while you drove home. I looked beyond the roadway and saw large puddles of brown water tinged with gasoline highlights and edged with garbage, shacks of wood and metal, young children sitting by the sides of the road. As the freeway rose to cross over a river, I could see for miles. The shacks went on and on, right to the horizon.

When we finally turned off the motorway onto smaller roads, there were whole families who seemed to be living on the grass and mud at the side of the streets—sleeping, cooking, squatting to relieve themselves, all within view. Chickens wandered down the roads, dodging dogs and cows. Some people were selling vegetables and fruits. The driver stopped the car. Peter got out and approached a woman he seemed to know. He told her he wanted tomatoes and some apples but argued with her aggressively about the price. He pretended to walk away several times, but in the end made the purchase. He laughed as he got back into the car and bragged about how little he'd paid. The driver looked straight ahead as Peter waved at him to drive on.

As we drove home, Peter's kids fought and yelled at each other. As an elbow caught me in the shoulder, I asked them to tone it down. Peter turned in his seat to glare at me.

We entered Peter's walled compound through a gate guarded by three men sitting on chairs and boxes set outside a small gatehouse. The top of the cement wall was inlaid with razor wire and broken glass. The courtyard was empty, but more than that, it felt deserted.

Peter explained that all the other apartments' residents had gone back to England for a few months. Expats received very generous holiday packages to compensate for having to live in Lagos.

In addition to his driver, Peter had a staff of two women, Teni and Efe. They stood side by side at the door to greet us as we entered the main floor apartment, then took our suitcases.

Peter explained that Teni had been his boys' nanny when he and his wife lived together in Lagos. When they returned to England, Teni had gone back to her own family, but when Peter came back to Lagos after his divorce, he went to the slums and searched until he found her. He had, in his words, "rescued" her. And he still referred to her as "the nanny," even though his children were only there twice a year.

Teni was a tall, solid young woman, who offered a defiant, unsmiling, even surly look when introduced to me. Oh boy, this was going to be fun. Thankfully, Efe, barely beyond girlhood, was helpful, kind, and polite.

Peter had done some painting and redecorating in preparation for my visit, but it was up to Teni and Efe to clean, and very little of that had been done. During the time I was there they barely seemed to do more than put out cereal boxes and milk on the dining table for breakfast and ignore requests to cook meals.

The apartment was cavernous. To counter the sub-Saharan heat, all rooms had terrazzo floors with no carpets. At one end of the huge main room there was a dining table that could have sat twelve. The large window was barred and looked out onto what had been servants' quarters. At the other end, two large couches, two stuffed chairs, and a table made a U-shape facing the five-foot widescreen television that blocked the light from the patio doors. These glass sliding doors, with a view of the garden, were permanently locked and chained. The windows in every room were covered with bars. The phone didn't work, and the electricity went off every day for at least five hours.

Peter showed me to his bedroom. He had emptied drawers so I could use them for my clothes. I hung my lovely silk suit in his closet.

That same evening, Peter, his kids, and I piled back into the car to go to the yacht club for supper. Peter introduced me to members as we made our way into the clubhouse, and then out onto the large stone patio that jutted into Lagos Bay. It was a lovely scene—tables with umbrellas, tiny lightbulbs strung on the trees, pinpoints of light flickering across the bay from buildings too far away to be seen. Peter was at ease, ordering drinks at the bar, smiling, laughing, nudging the shoulders of old friends as he moved past them, then leaning back and relaxing in a patio chair. The club had a well-stocked bar, and you could order meals any time of the day.

Peter had booked no time off work. He said he'd planned to, but an emergency had come up at one of the building sites he managed. It clearly irritated him when one of his chums at the club chided him, "I can't believe you haven't taken any holiday time to spend with Karen after she's come all this way." Peter glanced at me and then turned to the man, mumbling that he needed his holiday time later in the summer to be with his boys. Obviously he'd never meant to take time off to be with me.

When we arrived back at Peter's apartment, we watched a bit of television and then his kids went to bed. Teni and Efe rolled out mats in Peter's office to sleep on. He explained that when his children weren't visiting, the house girls used their bedroom.

Peter was an enthusiastic and seemingly inexhaustible lover. He woke me several times during that first night to have sex. But he never said a word. Never chatted with me. Again, I felt as though I was with a complete stranger. But I had decided to be patient. We'd get to know one another.

o o o

There was a race day every week and regatta days periodically at the yacht club. I was there for a race day. As we raced his sailboat up Lagos River, I tried my best to remember how to tack and jib, and to respond promptly to Peter's sharply barked orders. But his impatience at my failures showed that I fell far short of adequate.

During my visits to the club I met several of the expat wives. Louise from Scotland, married to a senior oil executive, invited me to join other wives for lunch and an afternoon party later that week at the compound where she lived. Danielle from Austria invited me to join her for a workout. Peter seemed pleased that, within a few days I had been adopted by the other expat women.

A couple of days later, Peter called his driver to the house to tell him to take his children and me to the afternoon party. His kids would come with me, but Teni, their nanny, was staying home. When Peter undid his shirt, took it off, and handed it to Teni for the laundry, it was clear they would both be staying home. I looked at Teni as a smirk crossed her face. I looked away and then back again, sensing I was missing something. There, across Peter's face, the word "evil" was printed as though in black ink. I blinked to make it go away and, shaking my head, went into his bedroom to change. *What did I just see? Was it real? My stress? The heat?* I remembered that the Larium I was taking to reduce the risk of malaria sometimes caused hallucinations. *That must be it.*

The compound where the women's party was held had a large lawn, huge swimming pool, and a patio with a wooden gazebo shading tables holding plates of tiny snacks. In the center of one table was a huge punch bowl. The menu was clear: very little food and lots of drink. A deadly combination for me, especially in this heat. The other women had already eaten lunch before they came, but no one had told me to do so.

The punch was very fruity. You couldn't even taste the alcohol.

It appeared there were many young, attractive women stranded in Lagos with nothing to do. They sized me up. As each guest arrived at the table, more and more questions were aimed at me about my relationship with Peter. Where did we meet? Were we engaged? What did I do? Would I move to Lagos? I explained that it was much too early in our relationship to speculate on any of that.

"Should we tell her about the dead bodies?" asked an athletic-looking blonde with perfect makeup.

As I took another cup of punch, one of them told me that a man's body had been thrown just outside the gate of her compound during the night. Another day a body washed up on the rocks that edged the yacht club patio. No one seemed to care or think it was unusual. The Lagos police didn't investigate all the deaths that occurred within the city because there were too many to count.

Nannies lounged on the side of the pool, sometimes laughing among themselves, sometimes attending to the children. Children walked back and forth from the pool to talk with their mothers. All the women had brought their children's nannies so they could visit, eat, drink, and gossip without worry.

Late in the afternoon, Peter appeared at my side as I was sucking fruity vodka from a large piece of pineapple. He'd taken a look at his children as they played in the pool. They were old enough to manage for themselves, so they were fine, having fun.

"Where have you been?" I giggled. As I turned to him, I announced to the women, "Peter's five months younger than me; he's my toy boy!"

I was taken with my own joke, but Peter's face was rigid.

When it was time for Peter and me to leave, Louise and I chatted for a few minutes about the lunch date she and I had made for the following week.

We arrived back at Peter's apartment, and I went to his bedroom to change into pajamas and a robe. I came back to the living room to see Teni lounging on one of the couches, dressed in a shiny pink night-gown stretched tight against her full figure. Peter sat in one chair, his kids taking up the other spots on the couch and one other chair. No room for me. I stared at them. Peter just stared back. I went back into the bedroom, sat on the side of the bed, and started to cry. I was alone. I'd had too many drinks. I was confused about the messages I was receiving, especially the frightening vision earlier on Peter's face.

Peter came into the room and sat down next to me.

"What is Teni doing out there stretched out on the couch in her underwear? Why is there no room for me?"

"Keep your voice down. You've had too much to drink and I don't want my kids to hear you. Teni is their nanny. She always watches television with us, which is more than you're going to do in your condition."

Insulted, I threw back, "You wanted me to go today. Why did you give me your children to look after? All the other children had their nannies there to look after them." The problem wasn't that I was wrong about what I was saying, but that I'd had too much to drink and Peter had been keeping track.

"This isn't the first time, either," he said. "You had too much to drink the first night I met you."

No, this wasn't a new situation for me since Duncan's death, but here it mattered. Just the previous week I'd spoken with Dr. Z about my hurt, demanding, selfish side. Usually I could keep it pretty well under wraps but not when I'd been drinking. That's when that side of me spilled out in plain sight. For Peter, drinking too much trumped any real concerns I had.

"Just keep quiet and sleep it off," he said. He got up, turned, and walked out of the room.

Had I had such a crazy relationship with Duncan that I hardly knew how to behave? Or was there something else at work here? And why, though the days here were hot and sunny, did it always feel dark to me? The barred windows, the chains on the doors, the walls around the grounds—they blocked out any sense of lightness, happiness, or freedom. Much later, a colleague of mine back in England described Lagos as "hell on earth."

o o o

The first Sunday I was there, Peter took his children and me to a restaurant called The Cookery—the place he went to every Sunday evening to get phone reception to call me in England. Long picnic tables with benches that could seat ten people were set up outdoors under strings of lights on the edge of a dirt parking lot. People sat in whatever seats were available. I sat next to Peter's kids, down the bench from him. Very young, attractive Nigerian women were serving behind the counter and sitting out at the tables with older white men, mostly English. There were no older Nigerian people, male or female, and no young white men. I was the only white woman.

One of the young women slid onto the bench beside Peter and stared at me while she said, "Hi, Peter, how are you?"

"Fine, I'm fine, why don't you get us some of the 'plates of the day'?"

"Sure, Peter, four plates?"

He nodded.

She touched his arm in a familiar way and slid away. Everyone knew Peter.

"Have you taken Karen to any of the dance clubs?" asked Jim, also English and the owner of The Cookery. Jim, in his mid-fifties, had been in Lagos for over thirty years. He turned to me. "You should see how those women dress! They leave nothing to the imagination."

As I sat there in the gathering evening darkness, I caught pieces of conversation from the various tables. One man I remembered from the yacht club complained about the "ladies of the night" sitting at the tables alongside regular customers. Ladies of the night? These young girls? Some looked no more than fourteen or fifteen. I noticed one older, grey-haired man speaking urgently with one of the young women. When she walked over to the counter to order food, the man turned to his friend and said, "Suzie says I have to get a place big enough for us to live together or she might hook up with someone else."

Poverty and desperation in Lagos prompted women to snare white men to support them and set them up in apartments in exchange for sex. Here, these men, many in their fifties at least, could have young girls they could only drool after back home. Kept women are everywhere, of course, but here it was blatant. Did Peter assume I wouldn't know what was going on? Had he been here so long he was immune? Didn't he see that this was not a place to bring a new girlfriend or his young children? And did he participate in any of this?

o o o

Halfway through my visit, Peter's sons flew back to England. Peter was only home in the evenings, so I had hours and hours to fill. Some days I read and prepared work documents, but I needed company. I got in touch with Louise and made plans for our lunch.

To meet Louise, I had to go out of the apartment, cross the deserted compound, and ask the guards on Peter's gate to call a taxi. Like Peter, all the expats had their own drivers that they trusted, but Peter had left me with no means of transportation. I got into the taxi his guards called and hoped that the driver would actually take me where I wanted to go. I'd been told that most cabs in Lagos were unlicensed, and that a stop under a bridge for buddies to rob passengers was not unheard of.

In Lagos, traffic lights were few and far between, and people crossed the roads whenever and wherever they pleased. Sidewalks appeared periodically and scattered shops mingled with vacant lots filled with garbage, so it was a relief to see that the café Louise had chosen for our lunch was modern and clean. As we ate sandwiches and drank coffee, Louise asked me about my life and sons and then shared stories about her husband and family. She'd been in Lagos five years and hated it.

"Nigerian women just throw themselves at white men," she said. "We were at a party one night and a woman tried to pick my husband up while he was standing right beside me. We're due to go to Pakistan next and it will be a relief. The women will be covered up."

I confided my concerns about Teni, the nanny. "I don't really know what's going on, but she seems to resent me."

"Well, I wouldn't worry too much about that. If you were to come here to live, you'd choose your own house staff and they would have to do what you want."

I had been thinking Peter was such a catch, and that I was the one with the problems, but Louise was blunt: "Peter is always in the bar drinking, and the men he hangs out with are rude and crude. You can do better."

o o o

I sat alone in the apartment much of the remaining time I was in Lagos. I could see the deserted garden through the patio doors. It was clear it hadn't been looked after for years. The pool had been filled in, there were no flowering plants, and no grass grew between the few palms that still stood. I took a kitchen chair outside to sit in the shade and read one day, but it was too hot. Another day I tried to sit out to get a tan but the sun was too bright, too intense. Once I stood out in the compound and phoned my son, Jamie, back in London, and began to cry over the phone. He had met Peter and thought he was a nice man, so was completely surprised to hear that the visit was not going well. He was concerned but could do nothing to help me.

Even when Peter came home, I still had no one to talk with. When he came in the house, he'd walk right by me without saying a word, go to the television, turn it on, flop down on the couch, and start watching.

I needed to go somewhere that felt like "me," so I went to a large, well-equipped gym with Danielle, whose husband was stationed in Lagos for two years. She echoed Louise. "I'll be so glad to leave here," she said. "It's the worst posting we've ever had. I have a cook, a maid, and a driver. Every afternoon I shut myself in my bedroom and read just to have alone time, to be by myself. When expat men come to the gym to exercise, Nigerian women deliberately take the machines next to them to start conversations and offer their services. Sometimes when men stop their cars at intersections, women try to get right into the cars."

Yikes.

o o o

On the Thursday after Peter's kids had returned to England, he came in early from work. "I just came by to pick something up. Then I'm going to get some lunch for us from The Cookery."

"Wait," I said, "I'm coming too."

"Why? What do you want to do that for?"

"Peter, I've been shut in every day. I just want to get out."

I could tell he was reluctant. "Oh, okay, you just want to come along."

What was so odd about that?

When we arrived, Jim, the restaurant owner, looked at me, then at Peter, then back at me. "Peter, I need you over here." The two of them walked to the side of the building.

"The shipment's arriving," Jim said, making an effort to lower his voice.

"When?" asked Peter.

"Tonight, come back tonight."

Perhaps they didn't think I'd hear them, or possibly they thought I wouldn't attach any significance to what they were saying. And they weren't entirely wrong—I knew something was going to happen, but didn't know what.

After Peter's conversation with Jim, we bought sandwiches and returned to the apartment, but we went back to The Cookery for supper that night, and this time we sat inside. The outside tables were even more crowded than the time I'd been there before, and with even younger Nigerian girls. Partway through our meal, Peter left me sitting at the table and went outdoors. I could see a very young girl standing among the tables—she looked no more than fourteen. She looked as though she'd had her hair professionally done, with curls and braids on top and a long fall of dark hair to her shoulders. I watched Peter through the window. Standing there. Just staring at her. A chill went through me as I realized that the "shipment" was a new group of young girls, about to be sold to the highest bidder.

The next morning, I was still in bed when Peter came back into the bedroom. He'd been up early to shower and get ready, he said, for work. As he leaned over to kiss me good-bye, I smelled cologne he'd never worn before. And he was wearing a new shirt.

Friday. His day for him. Not work.

The words came back from last October, when we'd first met. I knew. I wasn't sure what I knew. But I knew.

Late in the afternoon, Peter came home, the collar of his shirt undone and his sleeves casually pushed up. I'd spent part of the day sitting out in the garden reading and writing in my journal, and part of the afternoon packing. I knew I could pay a fee of fifty pounds and take an earlier flight home. I'd been in Lagos just over two weeks, and didn't want to spend another day there. I wanted to go back home, to England.

"I'm going home tomorrow, Peter," I said when he walked in. "I've realized it's too early for me to have a relationship."

"Yes, it likely is for me too," he replied.

On that, our final evening together, Peter and I dressed to go out to one of the few elegant restaurants in Lagos. We stood in his lounge while Efe took our picture. When I look at that picture today, I see a handsome, smiling couple. I see an attractive professional woman in an expensive teal silk suit, slim, dark-haired, with red lips and flawless makeup, a smile frozen on her face. She looks as though she doesn't have a care in the world. As though everything in her life is an amazing adventure.

That night, after we returned to Peter's apartment, I dreamed of Duncan, and woke up missing him horribly. I wanted him there so I could talk to him about what to do about Peter, to tell him that I didn't know this man at all—that I'd fallen for a handsome face and the fantasy adventure of flying off to Africa.

I had romanticized my first encounter with Peter, thinking of it as fate that we both happened to be at the same hotel on that particular weekend—but it was an illusion, not real. I had diverted myself from the obvious with Peter, just as I had with Duncan and Eric.

o o o

When I landed at Gatwick, I drove directly to Cathy's and sobbed in her arms about Peter's betrayal, the young girls who would soon go to the highest bidder, and my lost illusions.

"Are you angry because he was having relationships with Nigerian women?" quizzed Cathy, ever sensitive to racial prejudice.

"Cathy, the girl was only a young teenager, a child little older than his son."

"Are you jealous of them?"

I was. I was eaten up inside with jealousy, drowning in pain, and fearful of my inability to judge anything clearly when I was still so devastated by Duncan's death.

o o o

After almost a year since Eric and I had called off our relationship, I threw caution to the wind and resumed seeing him. Spending time with him was comforting. I could talk to him. He knew me, knew what I'd gone through. I convinced myself that he was just an old friend I was still very attracted to. I told him about Peter and going to Lagos, and he confirmed my fears.

"He was stupid to have taken you to that place," he said of The Cookery. Eric knew Africa. He knew about the "flesh trade."

But he was still married, so we saw each other every few weeks at most, and sometimes months went by without us seeing each other. In many ways this was the best of both worlds for me. I could still feel I had Eric's support, but I was on my own most of the time, which allowed me to get on with building my own life.

And Duncan was still with me too, in my dreams:

Duncan is lying in bed next to me, wearing jeans and a shirt. I look down at the bulge in the front of his jeans and laugh. He has clearly stuffed something into his jeans. He asks me to feel it and I see a bit of my pantyhose at the top of his jeans. We both laugh hysterically at the joke.

o o o

My glamorous friend, Peta, was spending her days in Eastbourne writing the definitive book on flirting, and still plotting to trap the biker she was attracted to. To further both projects, she decided to throw a party at the end of July and invite every interesting person she knew. I booked into the Cherry Tree Guesthouse down the block so I could stay the weekend, and arrived early to help her organize her space for the guests.

I told her that after the disaster with Peter, I wanted to meet someone I could just have fun with. She pointed to a man's picture stuck to the wall behind her desk, among tens of other photos. "What about him?" she asked.

I unpinned the photo to take a closer look. The image was a bit blurry, but even fuzzy the man looked like he would be on the low side of interesting. My eyes scanned the rest of the pictures and lit on one of a handsome man in an arrogant pose, his hand in one pocket and the other in mid-air as if he had been twirling it above his head.

"Oh, that's Lawrence," she laughed in delight. "A couple of weekends ago, I invited him down from London to see if I fancied him, but there was no way!"

I, on the other hand, was intrigued.

As the sun went down, the guests arrived. There were nutrition specialists, tarot readers, New Age healers who were cheating on their wives, a celebrity journalist named Pam, a society page writer named Mary, and a middle-aged astrologer who wore red velvet even in the summer. Someone named Rex brought a very large snake in a basket and a performing dog. A colorful marquee stood in the large garden. Small sausages and meatballs from Tesco were roasting on the braziers on the patio, overseen by one of Peta's young admirers.

I sat on a low garden bench with a glass of chardonnay in my hand, and a man approached me that I recognized as Lawrence. His voice was so smooth I could see myself in its reflection. Low and slow. Knowing. He and I chatted, had another glass of wine, and then walked to the beach, only a couple of blocks away, carrying a bottle of chardonnay and two wine glasses. Our feet crunched across the shingle. We sat on large rocks out off the shore talking, trying to impress each other as the tide came in up past our knees. Then we traipsed clumsily back through the water to the shore. I made my way to my B&B and he bunked with someone in Peta's building.

The next morning Peta made brunch for the small group of

partiers who'd stayed overnight and served it under the garden marquee. Afterward, Lawrence and I drove to the top of Beachy Head and sat with our feet dangling over the edge of the cliff. Later, Peta told me he came back to her house from our outing grinning from ear to ear, and told the dwindling group we were going to see each other again.

He drove to my house the following week, and, during long walks and pub outings, tried to impress me with his knowledge of human behavior, from a Neuro-linguistic Programming point of view. I thought I'd met someone who could share my interests, but he wasn't interested in sharing. He was competing. Later, he said that he was disappointed he couldn't teach me anything.

In August, I flew to Ontario to see my parents. My father wasn't well. The previous summer he'd had an operation to relieve pain in his legs caused by clogged arteries—a complication of smoking. At first, he seemed to be doing well but then became sicker and sicker and had test after test to see what the problem was. An infection in his blood, blood poisoning. He had a superbug picked up during his operation.

We went for a drive and I asked him to take me to see the ferns in the forest up one of the country roads. Usually so eager to share everything with me, this time he was agitated, irritated with me for asking. He said he really needed to get home.

Later, as I sat reading under the trees in the front garden of my childhood home, Dad came out and sat down beside me. He asked if I believed in the afterlife. I suspected that he was fearful about his health and so told him the truth—that I honestly didn't know. He nodded, a sad look on his face. He then shared something he had learned from a buddy in AA. "You know, Karen, when someone says 'I love you' and the other person answers, 'I love you, too,' it really doesn't mean anything. It only means something if you're the first one to say it." My father took his dedication to abstinence very seriously and valued the things he'd learned about human behavior in AA.

I thought back to the dream I'd had in the spring. In it, my father was terminally ill and I'd called out in anguish, "Doesn't anyone realize how much I care?"

After I returned home from this trip, my father's fears about his health again came out in my dream life and also seemed to foretell his death.

Dad falls and I cradle his head. I yell for someone to call an ambulance. He is saying his last words to me—"Tell your Mother . . . " but I can't hear what he's trying to say.

I'd already bought tickets to go with Lawrence to Edinburgh and Dublin in September for NLP events. But when he found out that he couldn't impress me with his knowledge, there'd been a cooling of the relationship. However, I ended up with a definite bonus – a woman who would become very important in my life. While sitting with Lawrence and Peta at the Last Drop Pub in Edinburgh, I saw Pam again, the journalist I'd met at Peta's party during the summer. As we only lived about ten miles away from each other, we planned to find a pub half way between our homes and meet up for a meal.

o o o

The men were beginning to pile up. I still met Lionel regularly for lunch, and I was seeing Eric intermittently—but they were both married, and therefore unavailable. Peter and Lawrence, meanwhile, had been attracted to me because initially I seemed to fit their fantasies. When they found out I really wasn't their dream woman, like Duncan, they were uninterested or angry.

I could hear my mother's question to me—"Are you promiscuous?" And my answer—"No, but I could be."

I barely understood what I was doing myself, so how could I explain to her that each time I met someone I thought he was the answer to my prayer for a man to cherish and take care of me? I naively jumped into each relationship, idealizing that man, not holding back my emotions, not discriminating, and not demanding anything real for myself. I was in denial, possibly willfully avoiding the clues to the real person.

Did I really need a man, a prince, to help me, to save me? Dr. Z said that when I realized that I could help myself, my quest for a savior would dissolve.

Friends and Lovers

When Duncan and I worked together, he'd get the gigs and we'd do the projects together. Now I had to continue what I started when Duncan was ill—make new contacts and get work for myself while I worked on other contracts. I had to get out into the business community, meet potential clients, and form new work alliances. I joined a consultants' network and continued to work on projects with John at the insurance company he worked for. He and I also co-wrote some articles on teamwork and change in organizations.

I'd broken off the relationships with Lawrence and Peter relatively easily, but Eric worried me. I felt more bonded to him. With him, there was that reassuring feeling of love and familiarity in my life. After all the months together, going through Duncan's death, and still feeling an incredible attraction to him, I couldn't say no, but it meant I was still hooked into an unhealthy relationship with a married man.

I continued to meet Tracey, my theater volunteer friend, for regular bike rides. We either rode the local town bike paths or joined others for group rides out to country pubs. Other times we would get together at her home for drinks or meet for pub dinners. She tried her best to rationalize her fifteen-year relationship with a married man but I couldn't buy it. He'd never even hinted at leaving his wife for her. Dr. Z warned me I could end up like her if I didn't break things off completely with Eric while I still could. If I truly wanted my life back, I couldn't stay tied to someone I would have to share.

o o o

I began meeting Pam, the woman I'd met at Peta's party, for drinks and meals. The Flying Fox Pub—or FF, as we called it—was about halfway between Buckingham and Dunstable, where she lived. It soon became our regular meeting place.

Pam was a successful journalist. After starting out as a junior reporter on Fleet Street, she'd quickly made her reputation as a television and movie critic. There was no one in British television she hadn't interviewed. Very blonde, with flawless, English rose skin, she was the poster girl for Britishness. And Pam lived the glam life: she could get tickets to the BAFTAs and belonged to the Groucho Club in Soho, a private club for celebs and media types.

We soon discovered we'd both been married twice, both had two children who'd been deserted by their fathers, both had received no child support, and both were single and looking for a meaningful relationship. Her hairdresser in Dunstable became my hairdresser so we could get beautiful while we chatted. Topics ranged from raising our children to books we'd read to nasty exes to hopeless dates to men we had to be careful of to the latest fashions. It was a relief to meet a woman who had gone through so many of the same things I had. She was bright, fun, empathetic, and thoroughly comfortable to be with. A new friend to help me through the dark days.

o o o

In November, I held a supper at my home for independent consultants I'd met at networking meetings. One consultant, Darla, an American, stayed overnight. After the rest of the group left, she and I talked until late into the evening. She'd married an Englishman she'd met in Australia and moved to England a few years earlier.

"Are you seeing anyone right now?" she asked.

"Well," I replied, "there's someone I see every once in a while, but nothing serious." I wondered if she was thinking of setting me up with someone, and realized with a bit of a shock that I was willing to completely let go of Eric in order to meet someone suitable.

She described her friend Jim, who was newly separated. "He's just been to visit. He's an Aussie, back in Australia now, but he's coming back in February to live in the UK. When he comes, I'll have a party and you can meet him."

The following month I flew to Canada to spend time with my parents before going on to Calgary for Christmas with my sons. I knew my dad had been continuously ill since the summer when I'd last visited, but I didn't realize how serious it was until I arrived at my family home. Mom surprised me by saying, "Your dad's in the hospital. He's chosen to have another operation. They'll operate first thing in the morning. You can call his room and speak to him."

Dad picked up on the first ring as though he knew when I'd call. "Hi, honey," he said, "I'm going to go for it. I can't go on like this. The doctor said there's only a small chance it will fix things, but I have to do it."

Dad explained that his quality of life at this point was so bad he would try anything—echoes of Duncan's decision before he'd gone in for his last operation.

My father came out of the operation the following afternoon and was in the ICU. My Aunt Barb was there, as well as my brother, sister, niece, and mother. We spent the time pacing the hospital corridors, drinking coffee, and eating from vending machines. When Dad woke up, I saw him through the plastic surrounding him, hooked by tubes to large black machines with digital screens mapping his vitals. I looked at him and, remembering his admonition of the previous summer, said, "I love you, Dad, and I said it first."

He responded with the tiniest of smiles.

I flew to Calgary on schedule, thinking that perhaps I should stay, but that somehow Dad would recover. I couldn't allow myself to see the signs that he would surely die, just as I had done with Duncan only eighteen months before. As with so many things in my life, I allowed my judgment to be swayed by wishes and fantasy rather than facing facts and reality.

o o o

On December 23rd, 2000, while staying at my son's house in Calgary, I had a dream:

I'm out on a boat with a medicine man on Glenmore Reservoir. The boat suddenly spins and I close my eyes. It stops. I open my eyes and now seem to be at my son's house. Suddenly it spins again. I close my eyes and have a powerful sensation of spinning in the boat again.

My mother phoned on the afternoon of December 24th. "Karen, your dad is gone."

Tears filled my eyes and poured down my face onto the phone receiver I held in my hand. I spoke with my mother for a few minutes, assuring her I would get the next flight back to Ontario.

Gone at seventy-five. My father, always with a cigarette in his hand, whether he was reading in his armchair, talking, fishing, or just contemplating. I'd been told my dad resembled Lee Marvin— tall, slim, elegant, and handsome, with prematurely grey hair. He looked like his mother and I looked like him. Always a nervous man who didn't like any kind of confrontation or upset, he'd sought the comfort of the bottle to relieve his anxiety. At age fifty-six, he went into a twenty-eight-day program after threatening to blow his head off with a shotgun. He finally found his own strength through AA. Then he dedicated his time to others who needed to find their way to sobriety.

He was a romantic. The greeting cards he gave my mother for her birthday or their anniversary were always large and flowery, filled with poems of devotion. I'd pick them up off the top of the television and read the lovely verses inside, puzzled by the contrast between this and how my parents interacted. When he would get home from the night shift at the motors, my report card would be waiting for him on the kitchen table. In the morning, there would be a letter telling me all the things he could never tell me in person. Though I needed much more from him than this arm's length love, I knew he loved me in his own way.

I flew back to Ontario on Christmas Day so I could be home in time for the funeral. By the time I returned, he had already been placed in a closed coffin resting at the front of the funeral home chapel. My Aunt Barb suggested I ask the funeral home staff to open the coffin for me, but I didn't want to cause any trouble, any upset, for anyone, so I never saw him that last time. I realize now that that is likely why I couldn't cry, either at the funeral or in the months following. Though I was aching on the inside, outside I just felt numb.

At the visitation the night before the funeral, the chapel overflowed with family, neighbors, and many older men my father had helped through AA. I stood, shook hands repeatedly and heard, "So sorry for your loss" as I replied, "Thank you for coming."

An elderly First Nations man approached me, introduced himself, and said, "You don't have to tell me who you are." I thanked him for coming and he confided, "Your father was a great man."

One month after my father's death, on January 22nd, after returning to my home in England, I had a dream:

Dad is coming into the kitchen of our family home with papers in his hands. He says to me, "Now we can deal with this issue of the Teacher."

It was only after my dad was dead and gone that I realized I'd needed him to be my hero, the one who would save me from the Teacher, all those years ago. I'd been blaming my mother for sending me back to my elementary school to be taught by the Teacher while ignoring the truth—that my father also could have stepped in and been there for me. It was wonderful that he was there for all those men in AA who needed him, but he'd left me to face a pedophile alone.

o o o

I returned to the UK shaken and rudderless after my father's unexpected death, spinning as in my dream.

Eric asked me to spend the night with him in his London flat. He bought treats from Tesco for supper and we sat eating salads and shrimp in his tiny studio apartment. He held a cold glass of sauvignon blanc, turned to me, and asked, "Should we be monogamous?"

I naively replied, "You mean you wouldn't have sex with your wife?"

"No, I have to continue to have sex with her or she'd be suspicious of what I might be up to, who else I might have in my life."

If he didn't mean his wife, he meant other women. He was asking me if I would be monogamous and he would eliminate other lovers from his life—which confirmed he had other women in his life. I had suspected that all along. I'm certain he could sense my uneasiness with our discussion and what it revealed about him.

"Karen, if I leave my wife, will you marry me?" he asked.

I looked up at him, my breath caught in my throat. I had held him at an emotional distance so that I wouldn't want him so much, wouldn't dream of a life with him but was he now offering what I had wanted? I was cautious. I stayed calm. "You have to leave her first, Eric. You have to get a place to live and then we can start to see each other, to date like normal people. We would see where it went from there."

"No, I can't do that. I have a position, a reputation to maintain. You have to agree to marry me before I leave her."

"No, Eric. We've been sneaking around. We haven't had a regular relationship. And, given your past, I'm not sure you could ever be faithful."

"Why would you think that? You see how I am with you," he started to plead.

I was skeptical. I'd heard the rumors about all his affairs. He had admitted as much to me, and now I knew for certain there were other women.

After we made love, I lay awake wondering again about the wisdom of planning a future with a man unwilling to leave his wife until he secured promises from me.

The next morning, we walked to his car and then drove north out of London. Along the way, he planned our next visit together, telling me how we'd go shopping to buy lots of sexy lingerie. I sat listening and knew he had done and said all this to other women—to many other women.

When I got home I had time to think. I was afraid to be alone, and I recognized that in the past I had traded my integrity to be with someone, anyone. I didn't want to keep doing this. I wanted to be happy on my own. I wanted my life back.

I remembered what Dr. Z had said—that I could be caught with Eric as I had been with Duncan. Even though I'd managed to distance myself from Eric, in recent months I'd opened the door to him again. I had to break it off immediately, go cold turkey, while I still had my wits about me. Not dither as I had with Duncan, only to still be with him eighteen years later. Dr. Z was right; that could happen to me, just as it had with my friend Tracey and her married man. Two years ago I'd said I wanted my life back. Now I had to actually do it.

I phoned Eric. "Hi."

"Hi, what is it? I'm driving down the M1 right now and can't talk."

"Eric, I need to see you. We have to discuss something important."

"Karen, I'm off to Bristol for a weeklong workshop. Can't you just tell me now?"

I didn't want to do it this way. Our relationship was too important to me to end it like this, but I had no choice. I was overcome with a sense of urgency. "I don't think we should continue."

"Yes, I agree." Relief permeated his every word. "It's too risky. You're too much for me. Too dangerous."

I didn't believe that I was too much or too dangerous. I was sensitive and vulnerable. Too sensitive and vulnerable to be in a relationship that wasn't honest. The shell was beginning to crack.

° ° °

I was still spinning from all the death and loss: first Duncan then my dad. My shell was cracking, and underneath it, I was a walking open wound—too raw, too open.

In February, my consultant friend, Darla, phoned to say that her friend Jim had arrived back from Australia and was staying in her home north of Oxford. She and her husband were planning to host a big dinner party in his honor and, as she'd promised, she was inviting me to attend.

Jim phoned a few days before the party and we spoke for over an hour. He was newly separated and eager for a complete new life. Since he'd been born in Scotland, he had British citizenship, so he'd decided to start his new life here in England. He wanted to find a flat in London and was looking for an executive job to replace the CEO position he'd had in Australia. He never wanted to get married again, but was looking for a woman to share his life. He invited me to meet him in London that Friday evening, the night before the dinner party. I gave him the name of my favorite coffee place on Leicester Square, the Rendezvous.

Standing at the counter ordering a cappuccino, I heard, "Karen?"

I turned to see a tall, slim, grey-haired man tilting his head and smiling at me.

"Yes, it's me," I replied as I held out my hand to him, a bit tentative. "Why don't I get a table for us while you get your coffee?"

I waited at a nearby table as he ordered and then paid for his coffee. It gave me a chance to study the man I had spent time with on the phone. He was not handsome, kind of a John Wayne type, but he gave the impression of a solid, mature individual. I could feel an impatient, powerful energy in his presence.

He came over, set his coffee on the table, and sat down. We picked up our conversation where we'd left off a couple of days before. He explained that he'd left his wife about ten months ago. Five months after that he was let go from the top executive position at a large insurance company in Australia. "I wasn't happy in my marriage, but if I'd known I was going to get fired, I'm not sure I would have left Trudy just then," he said.

He wanted me to know all about his rise in the insurance company, the fact that he knew the Prime Minister of Australia, and how much the woman he'd married looked like a movie star. He described her as opportunistic, harsh, and critical, so he had finally said good-bye.

Jim asked if we could continue the evening over dinner, so I suggested an intimate restaurant I knew in Soho, just a short walk away. He explained that he wanted someone to travel with, to spend time with, while he found the perfect executive position commensurate with his past status. He was interesting, well traveled, charming, and, with every glass of wine he drank, more and more flirtatious. After he accompanied me to Euston station, I boarded my train to go home.

o o o

The next day I packed a small bag and drove to Darla's home, north of Oxford, for the dinner party. She and her husband lived in a sprawling thatched-roof house set in three acres. They were hosting a large group of people who were aware of Darla's matchmaking efforts. I could hear whispers to Jim of, "Oh, she's lovely," and, "You two look so natural together."

Later in the evening, when everyone had either left or gone to bed, we sat in front of the stone fireplace. Jim put his arm around me while he balanced his glass of chardonnay in the other. Then I noticed him carefully place the glass on the side table. A jolt of desire ran sharply up from my thighs into my chest as his large hand parted my knees when he kissed me. Just that movement, nothing more, opened something in me that felt absolutely new.

"I've put a vase of flowers in the room you are to have tonight," he whispered.

"Do I have to sleep alone?" I replied, too quickly diving again into a romance in the hope that it might take away the pain of the last few years.

Jim took me up to the room that was to have been mine to get my things and bring them into his room. From the first time we slept together, I nestled close to him, my arm around him. A limpet, he called me. Sheltered safely in the lee of his back, I slept deeply for the first time since Duncan had died.

Like my father, who'd only been gone two months, Jim was a drinker, a smoker, and a fisherman. Over the next months he would set the hook and I would be caught—hook, line, and sinker.

After the horror of Duncan's illness and death, and now in the aftermath of the death of my father, I felt helpless, like a tiny child learning to walk—take a step, fall over, grab a chair to pull myself up, fall all over again. A couple of days after the dinner party, I had this dream:

My new lover, Jim, sees me walking, naked and vulnerable. Jim approaches, is mildly chagrined at my nude state, and gives me his overcoat. He wraps me in his coat and puts his arm gently around me as we walk.

I could feel my false front, my barrier, my protective shell, dismantling, but that meant my wounds were even more exposed. I wanted someone—a man—to protect those wounds. Some might have said I needed my father. But I was also afraid. I knew I needed that man more than he needed me.

o o o

At the beginning of March, Cathy and I went to Morocco for a week's vacation. Jim phoned me the night before I left and asked me to come to see him before I flew out.

"I can't, Jim," I said. "Our flight to Marrakech is first thing in the morning. I'm headed to Cathy's tonight."

He seemed sad that I was leaving. "I really think that, at this stage of a relationship, it isn't good to be apart," he told me. "Promise me you'll phone as soon as you get to your hotel."

I phoned him every day for the first four days of my stay in Marrakech, until he said he was going away for the weekend to see his nieces.

"Okay," I said, "you can phone me, then."

"No," he said. "I won't be doing that."

Startled, taken aback—there are many words to describe how I felt at that moment. I had diligently followed through on Jim's request to phone him, but he had no intention of reciprocating.

I didn't hear from Jim till my return to England. My uneasiness, my better judgment, told me there was a control game being played here and that I didn't know the rules. Again, as so often had happened in my life, the signals were there for me to see, but I chose to look the other way.

◦ ◦ ◦

Jim wanted to travel, so over the next couple of months we took weekend breaks to the Peak District, Paris, and Barcelona, and went for a week to Malaga on the south coast of Spain so he could golf. Then he took a month-long trip back to Australia on his own, to arrange for his belongings to be shipped to England.

Right after his return, at the end of June, we were sitting having a glass of wine in an Amsterdam bar and Jim asked, "What if I said it was all right with me if you had sex with anyone else that you wanted to?"

I replied without hesitating: "I guess I would figure our relationship was over."

He took another mouthful of wine, turned to me, and said, "I'd feel the same."

"Then why did you say that?"

He drew another cigarette from his package and paused before putting it in his mouth. "I thought you'd been with someone else while I was away."

For all his surface confidence, he clearly didn't understand how attached I felt to him.

"Well," I replied, "I thought you might have slept with your ex one more time while you were in Australia, just to see if you'd made the right decision."

"Good god, no. I had dinner with her one night and that was enough."

For that brief time, we were one. Swallowing the last of our drinks, we went to our hotel room, almost too impatient to wait until we got through the door.

I spent the next couple of months inadvertently discovering Jim's "rules" for the game of relationships. I discussed my consulting career; he said he wanted a "traditional" woman. I mentioned my love of traveling in the Middle East; he disparaged "rag heads." He asked if I knew what "Rosetta" was, and when I explained to him what the Rosetta Stone was and that it was in the British Museum, I could see I'd made a mistake. He didn't want me to know. I hadn't realized until I saw the look on his face that this was another test. He took me into stores to see if I would ask him to pay for my purchases. I paid my own way. He criticized my car ("a shit box") and the town I lived in ("horrible").

"I didn't think your house would be so large. Even your music collection is better than mine," he complained.

I loved the theater. He preferred to play golf. He felt frightened about being jobless. I pointed out that it was an incredible opportunity to find out who he really was without the executive persona. But he needed to be the expert, the teacher, the one admired for his accomplishments. Almost accusingly, he said, "You don't care that I was the president of a company."

No, I didn't. I wanted to find out who he really was, what he truly valued and thought. I wanted a spiritual seeker, someone who wanted to understand more about himself. Not a golfer.

Jim explained his strategy for his life, a plan that would guarantee he wouldn't make the "marriage mistake" again. He wouldn't divorce Trudy, so he wouldn't be free to marry again. The last time he did that, he said, he'd ended up unhappy, with a wife who spent all his money and made a fool of him.

Although he was separated, he was like Eric—a married man who didn't want a divorce. Through his own choice, he wasn't free to simply fall in love. He said he was a man who had "given" all his life. But had he? Or had he walled himself off, as he was doing with me? Jim kept his distance from women. He liked to charm and entertain them—to be the center of attention, but not get emotionally close.

Jim would sit back in his chair after ordering an expensive bottle of New Zealand Sauvignon Blanc, strike a match and, with a sweeping gesture, light his cigarette and take a long drag. "Ah," he'd say, "now I feel almost human." Our romance was fueled by alcohol and cigarettes and plagued by my lack of confidence and his attempts to show off in front of me and other women.

After meeting a friend of mine, Jim confided to me that he would like to bend her over a table and give it to her from behind.

He's just kidding, I told myself, just as I had done with Joe's taunts so many years earlier.

Another day, we met in the City for a drink and he said, "I just met a secretary with a low-cut blouse. I know if I asked her out she would say yes."

I was upset at his crudeness and teasing, but instead of dealing with him, I tried to figure him out. I pondered whether he was trying to impress me, or trying to prove something to himself. I felt desperate about this relationship in a way I hadn't since my days with Duncan. Every time I was upset, I would phone my friends and go on at length about how I felt. I was miserable. He was playing with me, just like a fish he'd caught, running the line out and then, just as I thought the romance would dissolve, pulling me back in.

After we'd been seeing each other for about six months, however, Jim reached a point where he seemed more relaxed, said he might be able to give me the companionship I wanted. Said he was opening up. I was staying overnight with him more and more in his London flat. He offered me my own drawer space so I could leave some of my things in his bedroom. Introduced me to his nieces. Said, "We should think about going to Edinburgh to meet some old friends of mine."

When I told my friends all this, Mary said, "Well, Karen, now you have the power." Mary played relationship games too and felt that now that Jim had become a bit more emotionally open and vulnerable, I could call the shots.

◦ ◦ ◦

Near the end of August, Jim and I went to Brighton for the weekend. While having dinner, I talked with him about moving to London. I'd already been looking at some flats in N16, the same area of London where Cathy lived.

"I hope you're not moving to London because of me," Jim said harshly.

Whoa, that was unexpected. I wanted to defend myself, but why should I have to? I loved London and often traveled in and out on the train for work, meeting friends and going to the theater. There were some attractive loft conversions close to Cathy's house, which was miles from Jim's flat. What made him so angry? Later, he carelessly commented, "I look on us only as fuck buddies."

A fuck buddy. Not someone who meant anything important to him. Not a relationship that would mature into permanency. Someone to flirt with and impress, have sex with, and then put aside when he grew tired of me. I was angry with myself for again having ignored obvious messages.

Still we continued to meet, and I continued to push for some sign that we were more than fuck buddies. Over a drink in All Bar One in Leicester Square, I muttered, "I love you" and he jumped to his feet. He shouted to the other patrons, "She loves me. She loves me!" But there was no reassurance that he felt the same.

Later that week, after several glasses of wine during another dinner, I flirted with a colleague, right in front of Jim, and feared that it marked the beginning of the end. While it might have been unconscious retaliation for his numerous unkind comments, by then I knew full well what would scare him away.

On a weekend trip to Cornwall, he was very distant. Then he didn't want to see me every weekend. I was distraught and told my analyst I was losing him.

Dr. Z said, "But surely you know what to say to win him back."

I didn't. And should I try? Deep down, even though I was still caught up in the fantasy of a caring man who would look after me, I knew that this relationship was not right for me.

However, despite the obvious writing on the wall, I was unprepared for the emotional shock of the end of our romance. I came back from three weeks in Singapore and Hong Kong, where I'd been consulting for a major bank, and Jim refused to come to the airport to meet me. He had to play golf. Though exhausted from jetlag, I agreed to come to London to see him and go to a party he'd been invited to. A man who'd asked me to dance asked, "Is Jim your friend or your boyfriend?"

I didn't know anymore.

Later that week, Jim phoned. I could tell from the sound of his voice that something was wrong. "Karen, can we get together tomorrow?"

"What is it?" I asked. "What's the matter? Please just tell me." Desperate, I pleaded, "Don't make me wait until tomorrow."

"Well," he started, "I want to see you just as much, I just don't want to . . ."

"Have sex?" I replied, wanting my heartbreak straight—no ice, no water.

"I was going to say, 'Be intimate.'"

He didn't just want to close the door on our relationship; he wanted to slam it in my face. He was adamant that I was never to come to his apartment again. But he said he wanted to return the things I'd left there, in person. I should have told him to put them in the post, but I had to see him. I met him at the Coal Hole Pub on the Strand and he put a brown paper bag on the table with my blouse and make up inside. We sat opposite each other, and with each glass of wine and each additional cigarette, I kidded myself into thinking I could bear this. Bear that this would be the last time I would sit with him in that familiar way we had.

I naively thought that if we didn't see each other for a while he would miss me and want to rekindle the relationship. So, when he called the following week to see if I wanted to get together for a drink, I turned him down. But I wasn't playing games; I honestly couldn't switch tracks that easily, couldn't be near him.

"You're a hard woman," he muttered as he hung up.

He called again several months later, so drunk he was slurring his words. "I miss you," he told me. "I think we should go to dinner, see each other." After a few minutes of catching me up with his life, he said, "I'll call you again soon." But it was six months before he phoned again to ask me to dinner.

We met at Covent Garden. "Are you over the romance yet?" was his first question. I just stared at him. Over drinks, he explained that he was lonely and had no one to travel with. His plan was for us to travel together but stay in separate rooms.

"So you want to travel as friends?"

"Well, Karen, if we had sex, it would just be sex."

I stared at him in disbelief. "Jim, sex between us could never just be sex."

Perhaps he was right, and we were only "fuck buddies," two people who needed to feel needed in a time of hurt and loss. When I'd said "I love you" to him, I was saying, "I need you. I want you." He had been right to end the relationship. We didn't have much in common. But I would have hung on to him as a life raft and not let go.

Several months later, I woke up crying, gasping from a dream:

A man sets up a sound system in a park and a Scottish song is playing. I'm riding my bicycle and singing at the top of my voice, "Oh, ye'll take the high road and I'll take the low road, and I'll be in Scotland afore ye. But me and my true love will never meet again on the bonnie, bonnie, banks of Loch Lomond."

I never made it to Edinburgh with Jim, but I had said good-bye.

Following the
Slender Threads

Slowly, but surely, my dreams told me that I was coming to grips with the fact that Duncan was gone. In one, *Duncan is lying on a bed facedown, his hair as black as it was when he was young. I say to him, "But you're dead," and he looks at me in disbelief. I point out to him that his body is gone; only his head and feet remain.*

Duncan's time on earth had come to a close and I'd been left alone—but not with my life back. He'd been abusive, but had he been the whole problem? For so long I thought he was. Because he demanded so much attention, there was little time for anything else. But was my husband's last gift to me the space and freedom to find myself, unencumbered by the illusion that it was he who stood in my way?

So far since his death, I'd been too afraid of being alone and too passive to assert what I wanted in my life—to really give myself the opportunity to find myself. My methods of trying to get my life back were not working. Finding a new man, keeping myself obsessively busy, shopping til I dropped, over-exercising, drinking and smoking too much—none of these activities were helping me.

In November 2001, I was asked to write a book about management consulting that would be one of a series of six books, each on a different business concern. It was an interesting and exciting project, and something I could immerse myself in. I would be the editor: I'd set the theme, plan the topics to be covered, and choose the contributing authors. It was a challenging project that would take just over a year to complete. And I was able to fit all this in and around my freelance work.

In the following months, I needed this type of distraction. I was still mourning the end of my relationship with Jim, and not fully acknowledging the emotional impact of the death of my father. With feedback from lovers that I was dangerous, always said the wrong thing, couldn't be taught anything, was too intelligent and too competent, I was realizing that it was not going to be easy to find another partner. I knew, of course, that the comments I'd received reflected more about the men who'd said them than they did about me, but they also made me search within myself for the grains of truth that had prompted them. And then there was the question of whether finding another man would solve my problem anyway. I didn't just want a lover. I wanted a life I could feel good about, contentment, friends. Perhaps a man who could be both a friend and a lover.

Sometimes in my search for distractions I was misunderstood. This was the case when Will, another of Duncan's old friends, was in London about eight months after Duncan's death and we had dinner together. Afterward, he dropped me at Euston station so I could catch the train home. When I turned to say goodnight, he kissed me. On the lips.

A bit disconcerted, I walked toward the station, but then turned back and watched as he got back into his cab. *What just happened? Did I miss something there?* I liked and admired Will, but I didn't fancy him. Was this why he phoned every time he came to London? I just thought he didn't want to eat alone. I hoped this wouldn't cause a rift in our friendship.

o o o

To quell my loneliness, I would often call Pam: "Want to meet for a meal at the Flying Fox tonight?"

We'd meet at the pub and trade stories of our life struggles, families, and careers. Over cigarettes and chardonnay, we'd commiserate about our single status. Sometimes we would meet Peta in London at Groucho's, and sometimes our other friend, Mary, would join us as well. We dubbed ourselves the *Sex and the City* girls; four single, older, talented women who proved the cliché—we were looking for love in all the wrong places.

Since neither of us was dating, Pam and I would often have dinner at her house or mine and finish the evening by watching a film. One such night, I asked her, "What are two intelligent, accomplished, and attractive women doing watching a movie at home on a Saturday night? Again?"

"Well, I've been dying to tell you about Sue, a friend of mine who's met someone really interesting through Internet dating," she said. "A helicopter pilot. Come on, it wouldn't hurt to look."

The appeal of this suggestion was definitely enhanced by the couple of glasses of wine we'd had over dinner. We went upstairs to my home office, turned on the computer, looked up "Internet dating sites," filled out the online forms, and posted our pictures. Within days, each of us was receiving e-mails. And invitations.

At first I agreed to meet every man who sounded interesting for dinner, but after a couple of excruciatingly long evenings, I started suggesting drinks. If the man turned out to be interesting, we could always go for dinner. It only took a couple more dates for me to realize even drinks weren't necessary—I could assess the suitability of most men over a quick coffee.

Perhaps women in their fifties shouldn't tell their mothers everything. When I told my mom what I was doing, she actually gasped.

"That could be so dangerous," she said. "I've heard that some men doing Internet dating are murderers."

Actually, I reassured her, if any of them had been axe murderers, it would have been far more interesting.

Mary invited Pam and I to try a singles' dating club with her. We went on very expensive outings to posh restaurants in London with other unattached men and women in the hope that something might click. I had only one follow-up date from this endeavor, and the man spent the entire meal discussing his upcoming singles trip to the Cotswolds: Easter with complete strangers. Some people were lonelier than I was.

A couple of weeks later, I stood with my friends at yet another singles' event, this time in London at a fashionable King's Road club. As we chatted, a small, stooped, white-haired man came by and leered at me. "Aren't you a nice one," he said, reaching out his hand to grab at me. I slapped him away, thinking, *This is not working as we'd imagined.*

After a couple of months of this organized pursuit of single men, Pam asked the question that was to change my life: "If you could meet someone anywhere in the world, where would it be?"

I immediately blurted out, "Maui."

Oh, wow, where did that come from? Intuition? Some memory from the dim and distant past? I wanted to find out.

I immediately went onto the computer and found the international singles' listings. Only one man was listed as living on Maui. I typed an e-mail to him: "You are likely wondering why a woman in England would write to a man on Maui, but if that woman can move from Canada to England, anything can happen."

Amazingly, David wrote back. And I wrote back to him. We exchanged pictures. We phoned each other. He had a lovely, deep voice with an American accent. He had moved from South Dakota to Maui several years before to pursue a relationship that hadn't survived. Now he lived in Wailuku with his Afghan dog and worked in his own dental lab in his house.

One day, as I was turning the key in my front door, my neighbor came rushing over with a huge plant. David had sent a bromeliad to introduce me to the exotic flora of Hawaii.

He would phone my cell as I was driving and I'd describe the poppy fields in the English countryside as I passed them on my way to work. I walked around my house and garden chatting with him, describing all the details. He said he was looking for a sincere, committed, monogamous relationship.

Sometimes when he phoned, I'd be at a pub with Pam or Tracey and all three of us would chat.

David said he couldn't get away from his dental business, so in June, after four months of e-mails and phone calls, I made arrangements to go to Maui to meet him.

o o o

If you dig a hole straight down through the earth starting in England, and come out the other side, you'll be in Hawaii. It's an eleven-hour flight from Heathrow to Maui, with a layover in Los Angeles. I knew I would look pretty rumpled by the time I landed, so I packed a change of clothes—white trousers with a pink-and-white-striped T-shirt, white sandals, and a pink suede and leather bag I'd bought in Hong Kong. I struggled into the tropical outfit in the tight confines of the plane toilet, then applied a new coat of makeup and redid my hair, just before we landed.

When I came out of the gate at the Kahului Airport, David was standing there, waiting for me by a huge planter filled with the Hawaii state flower, yellow hibiscus. Tall and slim, with prematurely white hair, he had a face that was not handsome, but was striking and interesting. He smiled warmly as I approached, but there was a tiny look around his eyes—perhaps concern, or disappointment?

He drove me up the hill from the airport in Kahului to Wailuku. His home was a small, three-bedroom clapboard house, almost invisible behind a twelve-foot hedge of green and orange crotons intermingled with fuchsia bougainvillea. Pitcher plants, succulents, and stephanotis crowded his front porch. Two huge plumeria trees and a mango tree shaded the back garden. His patio faced the West Maui Mountains, and had a spectacular view of what David called "my mountain." Rows and rows of orchids competed with each other for space on the patio, from tiny chocolate oncidiums to showy white and purple cattleyas. His babies. Every evening, after he finished in his lab for the day, he loved to sit out with a glass of good wine and watch the sun set over his mountain.

At fifty-three, I was seven years older than he was. I read voraciously and was in the process of writing a book. He read magazines. But we shared a love of wine, eating out, art, and Maui. He introduced me to the music of Hapa, a group that played modern Hawaiian music. We drove up to Haleakala, the volcano, on his motorcycle, visited one of the large orchid greenhouses near Makawao, and ate shrimp and mango salad at Kula Lodge, his favorite upcountry restaurant. Later, we swam at Baldwin Beach and ate seafood at Buzz's Wharf. But as we spent time together over ten days, it was clear that we were not romantically suited to each other.

"I'm very particular," David hinted as we sat on the patio of Kimo's restaurant in Lahaina. It was obvious that, for him, I was not young or cute enough. I was in love with Maui, but being with him was not romantic, rather more comfortable, almost like being with my brother.

After I went home to England, David continued to phone me. It made no sense to me to remain friends with someone half a planet away, but he didn't want to let me go.

"Don't push me away," he implored. And I agreed.

I was back in England, lonely once more. My sweet memories of Maui would come rushing back when I played my Hapa CD. Tears filled my eyes as I remembered the smell of plumeria, the lushness of the ferns, the palm trees, the sound of the waves on the beach, and swimming in crystal clear, turquoise water. Though my trip to see David was the first time I'd been to Maui since my vacations there more than twenty years earlier, my love for the island hadn't diminished.

o o o

At the end of July, I attended a week of Jungian lectures and workshops sponsored by the Champernowne Trust held in Windsor Great Park, just west of London. The first evening of the event, I sat in the lounge in Cumberland Lodge in front of the fireplace with my glass of chardonnay. A tall, dark-haired, attractive Englishman approached, sat down in the chair opposite me, and began to chat. Clearly flirting, he said he was shocked to learn I was over fifty. He was living in New Zealand and was back in the UK for his father's funeral. He was married with two young children. We said goodnight but the next morning he joined me at breakfast and began a conversation with a clear purpose.

"I think if someone had an affair very far from home that would be fine. What do you think?"

I pointed out that his wife was equally far from him. "Would it be all right if she had an affair while you're here?"

"No," he replied. He looked at me as though he might say more, but then rose, took his tray, and left the dining room. I saw him later that evening, dancing with a blonde in a skin-tight dress.

Something had changed for me. In the past I might have accepted an offer to have sex with a handsome, intelligent man, caring little if he were married or not, but now I was disappointed that that was all he wanted. I spent time at the huge lily pond a distance from the lodge, writing in my journal and thinking about David, a man who wanted to be a friend, not a lover.

Despite this small shift, however, I was still spinning—teetering two steps forward, one step back—still finding it hard to just sit quietly and be alone, still attempting at times to fill that inner empty place with alcohol and men. I wept bitterly on Pam's shoulder as I tried to raise my head above the despair and frustration that swirled around me.

In early September 2002, Will and I met again for dinner, this time at a lovely Thai restaurant in Soho. We ordered spicy seafood soup and discussed the chapter that Will was writing for my book project. Then he said, "So, tell me what's been happening. Are you dating anyone?"

"Actually I met someone, a man named Paul, in Ontario when I went back to visit my mother last month," I shared. "He runs a small pub at the end of my aunt's street in Port Hope. He's bought a ticket to fly over and see me in October. He's a musician and we hit it off right away, but he's a bit pushy, so I'm not sure how that's going to go."

Will put his wine glass down so quickly, the chardonnay spilled onto the tablecloth. "Karen, you don't have to go to bed with him."

Where did that come from? I felt unnerved and self-conscious, as though everything around me had increased in intensity. "Well, no," I said, "but that's not actually the issue." Then I changed the subject so he wouldn't bombard me further with his judgment. Inappropriate, controlling men—*that* was the issue.

o o o

After having read my horoscope in the newspapers and cutting out the relevant ones to paste into my journal for more than three years, in the fall of 2002 I decided to actually consult an astrologer. Pam had been to see Suzanne a few times and gave me her phone number. I made an appointment for the following week, giving Suzanne only the date and time of my birth so she could prepare my astrological chart.

Pam and I walked into her studio for the appointment and Suzanne looked straight at me. Even before I could sit down, she began, "You've had a difficult three and a half years, haven't you? In fact, you've had an extremely difficult time."

Even though I believed in the power of the planets, I was not prepared for its preciseness. Nearly three and a half years had passed since Duncan's death, and Suzanne had no way of knowing this. Yet the stars had predicted—foretold—this time in my life.

Had I been destined to meet and marry Duncan, watch him suffer and die, and then have this time to mourn and be in despair? Or was this time of trial larger than my relationship with Duncan? Perhaps my path in life had led me to this time—a time when I would have to examine my behavior, beliefs, and choices. Dr. Z had warned me that I would have to get out of my "victim stance" and come to terms with my early experiences with the Teacher, my parents, my first husband's cruelty and abandonment, and the abuse I'd suffered with Duncan. Was this the time in my life when I would finally sort things out and heal from all I had known? For the first time since Duncan's death, I was struck by a profound sense that everything that happened was meant to be.

◦ ◦ ◦

During that winter of 2002 - 2003, I was again waking up in the middle of the night to wander around the house—examining things on the shelves, rearranging things, visiting all the rooms, drinking too much wine, playing Van Morrison too loudly, sometimes phoning friends in Canada to break the loneliness. Two steps forward, one step back. Even though I was beginning to see glimmers of progress, I knew now, more than three years after Duncan's death, that my healing would not be quick. This was confirmed for me by a colleague who had lost his wife many years before; he told me it took him five years to really heal from the loss. And my task was bigger than just getting over my spouse's death.

One night I called my mom and burst into tears. Sputtered into the phone. She hesitated and then, as before, said, "Oh, Karen." It was all she could manage.

I didn't want to hang up and lose that thread to her, but no advice she could offer was going to help. Under the surface, I suspected that my mother was also lonely now that my father was gone. Was she driven by grief and loneliness to wander in the night as well?

One night my wanderings took me into our guest bedroom. I examined all the books on the shelves, and discovered again that book I'd meant to return to Duncan's analyst nearly three years before, Robert A. Johnson's *Balancing Heaven and Earth*. It was a book Duncan had been reading just before he became ill. It was still crammed with his yellow sticky notes and handwritten scribbles in the margins. I took the book off the shelf, took it to my bedroom, and began to read.

Johnson, a Jungian analyst, explained that when he had ordinary decisions to make, he drew up lists of pros and cons, positives and negatives, but when he had important decisions to make, he waited for what he called the "slender threads." He said that the slender threads were messages the Universe sends to all of us. These messages or threads come in various ways—meeting unexpected people, gifts, dreams, intuition, an inner knowing, being in the right place at the right time, inspirations, and synchronicity. Jung had said much the same thing, but the messages he talked about came from the Self, that inner guide meant to help you toward individuation, whereas Johnson's slender threads could also come from the outside. The slender threads can appear in life like this book had, this gift Duncan had left for me.

I knew that I received intuitive messages, and I paid close attention to my dreams. But this book said that I had to listen more consciously for, and trust, the slender threads in my life. I wasn't to control the process, only pay attention, listen, and receive. I didn't know what form these threads would take, but in order to hear what messages the Universe had for me, I would have to quiet my life and heighten my awareness. And, most important, I would have to learn to trust.

Johnson felt that the Universe has a plan for each of us that will lead to greater wholeness in our lives. I thought I'd been looking for an answer—find a new man, get more work, drown my sorrows in chardonnay, keep busy with girlfriends, travel around the world. But these were *my* answers, *my* ideas that *I* controlled, answers that came from a desperate place in *me*, not ones that came from universal wisdom. Possibly the plan for my life was one I had never considered—a new career, a new country. I had to stay open to something I might never imagine for myself.

In the meantime, when I was alone at night, I would still uncork a bottle of wine, lie on the couch, and watch *Bridget Jones's Diary*—again. I'd seen it eight times and yet still it made me laugh out loud.

o o o

Early in 2003, Will and I met again, this time at a fish restaurant just off Covent Garden. He was staying overnight in London on his way to India. Waiting for the arrival of two orders of the grilled "catch of the day," we exchanged news over a couple of glasses of sauvignon blanc.

Then, ever the process psychologist, I said, "We've never talked about our relationship."

Will's words jumped out without hesitation, launching themselves off the tip of his tongue: "Well, don't think I'm going to fulfill your sexual needs."

I set my glass down on the table and stared at him. Tears sat on my eyelashes, skillfully caught before they could drop down onto my cheeks and be revealed. Had he been waiting for an opportunity to say this? An excuse to shatter me with his harshness and misunderstanding?

With that statement, Will hooked into all my fears and shame about my life. I was a widow. I'd had affairs. I felt guilt over the difference between this life I was leading and whatever I wanted my true life to be. Was his response to me a slap on the face I deserved? Or envious projection and jealousy?

Whatever his personal motivation, his words threw me right back into my old way of dealing with Duncan—self-recrimination and wordless disappearing. Appetite gone, I heard my inner voice say, *Just be quiet. Keep it all to yourself.* I did as I had learned to do all those years ago in my family home and in school with my Teacher.

I realized that, though almost four years had passed since Duncan's death, my life was still much like it had been when I was with him. I was living in our house, sleeping in our bed, wearing designer suits, working at our business, in a career that was really his. I was still overspending at expensive boutiques, wearing Versace, Prada, and Ralph Lauren, and dabbing Jean Paul Gautier behind my ears. And, perhaps most importantly and disturbingly, I was still reacting in ways that I had when I was with him.

I went home and Will left England, but my doubts and fears remained.

◦ ◦ ◦

In February 2003, I hit a low I couldn't shake. I went into Dr. Z's office and told him I couldn't cry. I had no tears. I didn't care anymore—about anything. I felt empty. I was exhausted, worn down. Up to that point in time, through my ceaseless activity, I'd avoided that type of low, even though I would have sworn I'd spent the previous four years in hell. But feeling lonely, hurt, and desperate is so different from feeling nothing. I had sunk so deep I was below the waves, in a place where there was no light and no life. All I could remember, all I could cling to, was the idea that for the big questions in life, I should not do anything. I should wait and listen, listen for the slender threads.

Of course, my inclination was still to do something. Get rid of this non-feeling. Bring energy back into myself through any means. So, on a weekend in early March, I drove south past London, around the M25, west on the M4, and south through Marlborough to a place Duncan and I had visited a few years back: Poole, on the south coast of England. As I descended the last hill into the north part of town, I was startled by a feeling so strong it was like a clear inner voice, telling me that I would soon meet a man who would be important to me.

I took a room at the Antelope, advertised as the oldest pub in Poole, and spent the day wandering, having the odd cigarette, and sitting with my feet hanging over the stone edge of the harbor. I decided to forego DaVinci's, the Italian restaurant Duncan and I had eaten in so many years ago. Instead I ate at another, more upscale seafood restaurant, and, by catching snatches of conversation, discerned that it catered to young couples with good incomes, older people trying to revive their relationships, and widows with books to read and a desire for a good fish meal. I ordered the crab starter accompanied by a cold glass of sauvignon blanc, then enjoyed a baked salmon fillet covered with hollandaise sauce, served with tiny potatoes and fresh salad.

The night before I'd come to Poole, I'd had what felt like an important dream:

I can see David from Maui on top of a huge building that looks like a monument. I climb up many steps to join him there. He's pointing far into the distance.

When I woke up I wondered did he hold the key for what lay

ahead for me? A slender thread? That night, back at my room in the Antelope, I dialed him on my cell phone. By this time, we had such a relaxed relationship this seemed natural to me.

"You sound down, like something's the matter," he said.

"Yes, really down," I admitted. "I was wondering . . . do you want a visitor?"

"Sounds like you need another holiday in paradise," he replied.

It had been a year since my first trip to see him. But this time I had no illusion that he was the answer to my loneliness. He was a safe friend, a harbor in the storm. I told him I'd make reservations to fly out in four days' time.

The next day, Sunday, I took the tiny ferry from Poole to Studland, in Swanage, where I parked at the north end of the miles-long beach and began to walk. In the middle section of the beach there was a sign that politely tells you that the area is "naturist"—British for "nude." Some elderly women were looking deliberately seaward to avoid catching sight of male bits, but it was overcast and cold, so there was no one lying naked on the beach.

Partway down the beach I was sometimes following, and sometimes ahead of, one particular man. I watched his back as he walked ahead of me. When we both stopped as part of a group gathered to look at a cuttlefish washed up on the shore, he used the opportunity to say, "Hello."

"Hello," I responded.

"Oh, you're American," he said.

We set out at a comfortable pace to walk the remaining part of the beach as I explained that I was Canadian and he introduced himself as Nick. I could hear the Irish lilt in his voice as we chatted. He asked if I wanted to join him for a cup of tea, so we queued up in a small tea shop on the beach. As I looked in my pocket for money, he paid, and answered my look with, "I'm only paying for tea. It's not a commitment."

I could feel heat rise up my neck and into my face, accompanied by a trace of excitement mingled with puzzlement.

We carried trays of tea and biscuits outdoors to the tables on the sand. Then he asked how I came to be walking on Studland beach.

"My husband died nearly four years ago and I'm at a low point in my life. I remembered this beach from the last time we came down to Poole."

He replied, "I came here meaning to do some sunbathing on the naturist end of the beach. But it's too cold today so I gave up. What do you do for a living?"

"I'm a clinical psychologist who took a segue in my career. I've been working in large organizations since I came to England and it's tiring work. No matter how much time and effort I put into my projects, the companies make little or no change, leaving the employees frustrated. I'd like to do something different, but don't know what. Besides, I have a lovely house and need to pay the bills. I guess I'm waiting for some sort of sign to guide me."

He told me about the drastic change he'd made about two years earlier when he started to study craniosacral therapy. "I'm still working part-time as an architect but hope to move into therapy full-time when I finish the training. My wife has just graduated as a psychologist and is in the process of setting up a private practice."

He retrieved a white plastic cigarette substitute from his pocket, put it in his mouth, and sucked on it as though it were a cigarette. He took it out of his mouth and motioned toward me with it. "One of the other changes I'm making. This is to help me quit smoking."

As we continued to look at each other, he said, "I want to give you one piece of advice. You're so attractive, you shouldn't settle for anything except exactly what you want."

I sat quietly and tried to make sense out of what Nick had said. I'd become so used to insults and judgment from men that I couldn't quite process such a positive reaction from this man. Could he see what others couldn't, or had something changed in me to attract compliments rather than criticism? I felt disappointed he was married, but realized that this encounter was not about starting a relationship—it was about compelling me to pay attention. He got up to leave and I stayed behind, watching as he walked toward the parking lot. Wondering . . .

My intuition, that inner voice, had been right that I would meet someone significant. Nick from the New Forest was the wrong man for me on the wrong nude beach, but even so, I felt a chill of excitement. I had the distinct impression that an angel had visited me—and the message he'd delivered was to continue listening to slender threads.

I drove home and prepared for another eleven-hour journey to Maui.

o o o

This time, I told myself, I was in Maui just to relax. David was too busy to go anywhere with me most days, so I explored on my own or read, lounging in his garden under the plumeria tree. I don't remember who recommended it, but I was reading *Why Men Love Bitches*. Another slender thread. The author recommended that women just live their own lives, for themselves, and not change in any way for a man—and said that men preferred this anyway. "Make them earn you," was the book's advice.

I realized, with a shock, that I had never done this. I sat on the lounge and, after every sentence, put the book down and looked around, taking in the flowers, the beauty, the peace of the garden. I felt a sadness well up in my chest as I thought back on my life so far. I realized that for so much of it, I hadn't even known how I felt, hadn't reached underneath the shell I'd carried to staunch the flow of blood as each wound had been inflicted. But that had been slowly changing. Perhaps I hadn't quite put the shell down, but it was light and transparent enough now, cracked in places and broken around the edges, so that I wasn't so much of a mystery to myself anymore.

One morning over coffee, David asked me, "Where are you going this morning?"

"Oh, not sure, I'll likely just go over to Kihei to the beach."

"Have you gone to Little Beach yet this trip?"

Little Beach, the tiny jewel of a beach to the north of Makena where Duncan and I had gone on our first vacation—a nudist beach and hippie haven accessible only by climbing over a high spit of hardened lava.

"I haven't," I said. "That's a great idea."

"Sit at the back of the beach under the trees, where the locals sit," David advised. "Then you can see all the action."

Without realizing it, he'd given me another slender thread.

I drove across the island, climbed up and over to Little Beach, took off all my clothes, and organized my towel on the sand where David had suggested, under the trees. There was an assortment of men sitting nearby—the locals. Sam, a Vietnam vet with long stringy hair and a deep tan, asked me my name and told me about the drumming and fire dancing that took place there on the beach every Sunday. Alex—a tall, tanned, athletic-looking man with his long hair pulled back in a tight ponytail—offered to pass me a spliff, but I motioned, with an apologetic smile, that it was not my thing. I noticed a man with long hair flowing in the wind as he ran on the beach, clearly showing off his manly bits. There was also an interesting-looking man on a towel close to mine—a good-looking guy with short, shiny, wavy hair, and a golden tan.

With only mild embarrassment, I walked into the ocean to swim, and when I returned to my towel, my cell phone rang—a colleague from London. We chatted about an upcoming project and then I put the phone down. By this time, the shorthaired man had moved his beach towel to within a conversational distance. His handsome face was smooth-shaven, his hair plastered to his head with ocean water. He introduced himself as Bill. He had a friendly smile, was slim with toned muscles. When you're sitting on a nude beach there are no secrets, of course, but there was an innocence about him. He later told me he didn't think that much would come of talking to a woman with long, red-painted nails who was speaking on her phone while sitting on one of the world's most breathtaking beaches.

"Are you on vacation?" he asked, looking intently at me, as though my answer mattered to him. His eyes crinkled shut as he shared a funny story about how he also came to be on the beach that day, and then, "I'm usually up early each morning and walking the beach by now. Also, lately, I've spent time up on the cinder cones looking for deer antlers. I like to collect things."

He was relaxing to be with. He told me he had first moved to the Big Island of Hawaii and then to Maui after having been badly bruised by a painful divorce back in New Mexico. He'd spent some time living in his van, but at this point was renting a studio apartment, upcountry in Pukalani. "I tell people I'm homeless and unemployed on Maui," he said, laughing. He laughed a lot.

He was a craftsman who, for thirty years, had built up a reputation for designing and creating historically inspired jewelry. He had traveled the country, setting up his booth at festivals set up by the Society for Creative Anachronism – a society of people who dressed up in medieval clothing and reenacted the Middle Ages. He'd sold his business in order to stay home and try to save his marriage. After that dissolved, he'd sold most of what he owned and set out in his van. When winter set in on the mainland, he'd flown to the Big Island.

Bill's story touched on several things that had been lurking around the corners of my thinking for some time. He'd given up his work. He'd rid himself of most of his personal possessions at the end of his marriage and was now living in a tiny apartment. I was intrigued. Would I have to let go of my things, my house, my ways of doing things, my ways of creating my identity, my excuses for not doing so? I wondered, *If I were to change my life entirely, what would I keep?*

I'd reserved a place with a tour business, Hike Maui, for their hike in the Haleakala volcano crater the following day. At the end of the afternoon, Bill and I walked to the parking lot together, and I invited him to join me.

"I'd love to hike with you," he said, "but the organized hike isn't something I can afford." He gave me his phone number. "Will you give me a call if you have time to hike on a different day?"

When I got back to David's, Hike Maui had just called and left a message. There weren't enough people to do the hike into the crater. I could go to Hana with them and hike to Waimoko Falls, but I'd already done that hike. I phoned Hike Maui.

"We can't hold you to your reservation," the girl on the phone said. "You wanted the crater and we can't deliver. We'll refund your money." A slender thread.

I called Bill and asked if he was still interested in hiking with me. When he said he was, I gave him David's address. He'd pick me up early the next morning.

David was skeptical. He'd lived on Maui for seven years, and knew the transient population attracted to the beaches and hot weather. "Is he one of those guys who lives in a van?" he asked. "I want to meet him. If he's a loser you can't go anywhere with him."

I laughed at his protectiveness, but he was right. I was over fifty, and still didn't have very good radar about what my friend Cathy called "poorly men."

° ° °

At seven thirty the next morning, Bill pulled up in his green van. I introduced him to David but before I went out the door, he pulled me aside and whispered, "I'll keep in touch by phone in case he's a lunatic."

Then I headed out to hike Maui.

We spent the next couple of days together, hiking, talking, and swimming in Maui's crystal clear water. He took me to secret beaches and showed me how to balance rocks. He'd been inspired by a book of nature art by Goldsworthy, an artist from Scotland. He took photos of me draped in ferns, sitting by the water's edge.

"How old are you?" he asked.

"Fifty-four."

"Really? So am I. I thought you were about forty-four. That's great. It's good to know that women my age are attractive. But," he stressed, "I'm never going to be in another committed relationship. I've learned my lesson. I've had three marriages that didn't work out.

I went for intensive counseling to save my last marriage and learned so much about myself, but it didn't help save the marriage. My first two were open marriages, and if I ever enter another relationship, it will be an open one."

He explained that his last marriage had been monogamous, but he'd never had a relationship with a full commitment that had lasted. He just didn't want to take another chance, and had come to the conclusion that he simply was not good at relationships. I was to find out later that he was a man who was in love with love, and that had gotten him into trouble more than once.

Bill had completely broken with convention. He'd changed his way of life and moved to Maui. There was a sense of fun and a relaxed understanding between us, but I was uneasy about his desire for an open relationship. By this time I knew I was not willing to bend myself and my life into whatever a man wanted. Plus, I lived on the other side of the world. With promises to keep in touch by e-mail and text messaging, Bill and I said good-bye and I flew back to England.

A Leap of Faith

"The perfect holiday romance," Cathy said, gasping at the photos I'd taken on the nude beach in Maui when I returned to England—"His bits are showing!"

But her advice was, "Now, back to work!"

But I wanted to see if my intuition, my slender thread, was right—that Bill was someone I needed to get to know further. Was he the right man, on the right nudist beach? With Bill I saw myself as someone another person could find fun and exciting. With him, I wasn't standing on the sideline hoping to have fun like other people. It was a strange feeling, one I'd never fully had before—happiness.

We kept in touch, and when a work project that was supposed to have started on July 1st was cancelled, I phoned him and said I could come back to Maui for another visit.

But then things ran into a snag. One night Bill called and, after a couple of minutes of chitchat, he told me that I should feel free to explore any relationship that might come along.

"Why?" I asked. "Is that what you're doing?"

He told me he'd recently met and spent time with a woman he'd met there on Maui. I was disappointed.

I went over the situation in my mind. If he'd met someone just after I'd left Maui, of course I wouldn't have minded. We barely knew each other. But he'd started something with someone else knowing I was making the return trip to see him. Then again, he'd been honest with me. He'd said he didn't want a committed relationship. Ever.

And I hadn't listened to him. Perhaps this was his way of emphasizing that to me.

Possibly I'd put too much emphasis on the fact that we seemed so compatible. If he wasn't excited enough about seeing me again to hold off on another possible relationship, he might not want to explore what we might have together anyway.

A few days passed and I still I didn't know what to do. I talked it over with Pam. Her advice? "Don't go. Can you cancel your flight and get your money back?"

My earnings from the freelance management consulting projects I'd been doing were so good that I had money and time on my hands. I could support my home, my travel, my car, my lifestyle, as long as I continued to do about ten days of consulting per month—and the last year had been busy. From a financial standpoint, there was no reason for me not to go.

In the end, I decided to return to Maui at the end of June. I couldn't change my flights or get my money back, and I still wanted to see Bill. But I was wary—and perhaps, I thought, that was a good attitude to take. Like a mantra, I repeated to myself that I would just live my life, take time and see what happened, not cater to any man—go in with my eyes wide open.

o o o

Bill met me at the Kahului airport, and he honestly seemed excited to see me. I told him I'd stay with him in his apartment but would also visit David while I was there.

The next day, David and I went out for lunch to a restaurant that overlooked Maalaea Harbour to discuss my situation. I told him that Bill had dated someone while I was back in England and I had no idea where that relationship stood at the moment. I was too nervous to ask.

"He was in long-term open relationships, Karen," David said. "He's not going to change. You couldn't consider that kind of arrangement, could you?"

"No," I had to admit, "I couldn't."

"Well, then, get out now," David said. "He might be with someone else right now, while we're having lunch."

I hadn't even considered that possibility.

For a day I looked around Bill's apartment and van for clues, indications of his other relationship. Finally, I just asked him openly about the woman he'd gone out with. He said it was one time only and hadn't turned out very well. He'd been very close to being intimate with her, but it hadn't felt right to him. They had nothing in common. He'd decided not to see her again.

I was relieved, but puzzled about why he'd even told me about the whole thing.

"I was completely transparent with my partners in my marriages, so that's what I felt I should do with you," Bill explained. "But I haven't changed my mind about not wanting a committed relationship."

Despite my reservations, when I was with Bill I felt more alive. It might have had everything to do with being on Maui, or a new understanding of who I was and what I wanted out of life, but I knew Bill played a role.

He and I discussed our childhood experiences while we hiked across lava fields and along the Maui shoreline. We discovered we'd both collected rocks and minerals and that each of us had a rock hammer at the age of twelve. We were almost exactly the same age. He was an artist, a kind and gentle soul, a seeker. Not a golfer. One day, he took me to Iao Valley for a spirit walk—something he'd learned to do in a men's group he'd attended back in New Mexico. As I walked through the jungle, I had to close my eyes, hold Bill's hand while he led me, and just trust. For the second part of the walk, I had to just look straight ahead, not at my feet, and, again, just trust. I had never felt I could trust a man before.

Back at Bill's apartment, I lay face up on a blanket in the middle of the living room floor so he could lay stones up the center of my body, in a line. Smooth, rounded stones of different kinds. Over my heart he placed a huge piece of Baltic amber he'd polished himself. As he gently put the amber down onto my chest, I felt a huge shudder, and a jolt of energy ran from the base of my spine up through my chest, and out of my head. My arms felt loose and free. My body jerked spasmodically until the surge played itself out. It was unexpected, startling, beyond my control—but not unpleasant. I'd never felt such a thing before. Not pleasurable in the same way as an orgasm, but energizing. I lay there, not logically understanding what had happened to me, but sensing that this was not something to fear. Bill had never had an experience like that, nor had he helped anyone to achieve it.

Only much later, after I did some research, did I understand what I'd experienced. This energy jolt is called kundalini, and people spend much time and effort trying to achieve a kundalini awakening. Some think this energy, or chi, is dangerous and mentally disorienting but I somehow intuitively knew that it was an awakening of something in me, and that Bill had facilitated this. In some traditions, he would be called my guru. It is thought that when kundalini energy is released or freed, it can potentially destroy our filters, allowing us to feel all of the feelings around us, but I knew I'd already started that process. I was already consciously allowing myself to become aware of the slender threads all around me, as well as the feelings—my own—that I had ignored for so many years. My journey toward wholeness had already begun.

o o o

Things continued to shift for me. After I returned to England, I decided I wanted adventures on my own. In the past, I'd sat home weekend after weekend unless I had someone to accompany me some-where. Now I wanted to simply enjoy my own company. One weekend in mid-July, I booked myself into a small tourist hotel in Aldeburgh, on the east coast of England. I walked the beaches where amber occasionally washes up, borne on the currents from the North Sea.

I bought a small dome tent, a blow-up mattress, and a small lawn chair so I could do some camping and hiking. Then I pulled my old hiking boots out of the back of the closet, looked over the ordnance map of England, and decided to drive to a campground in Langton Matravers, near the south coast of England.

After I'd set up my tent in the campground near the coast, I checked the map for easy walking routes. I walked over to Worth Matravers, where I stopped for lunch at the Square and Compass, right in the middle of the village. After a pint of ale and a plough-man's lunch, I continued on the trail down to the coast and sat on the rocks by the sea for several hours before I made my way back to my tent. In the evening, I had the curry special of the day with a single glass of chardonnay at the Ship Inn in the village of Langton Matravers. Later, I snuggled down into my sleeping bag in my tiny tent back at the campground—finally, after four years on my own, feeling content with my single life.

In the meantime, a Scotsman had contacted me through the dating site I still belonged to. He called my cell to chat while I was camping. A photographer and music lover, he sounded interesting. A wealth of male riches again, but this time it all felt very different. As though life was slowing down—not rushing by like a new mountain stream but meandering and exploring, like a river that had finally reached flatter ground.

Though things had been changing all along my personal journey, even before Duncan's death, emotional changes often don't register as quickly as physical ones. Dr. Z said that my higher Self had been protecting me all along. He marveled that, when I could have gone off my path, away from my goal to have my own life, something had always happened to prevent me from doing that. I could have com-mitted to another unsuitable man. But I didn't. I could be sitting and waiting for Eric, my married lover, to take time away from his legitimate family and spend it with me. But I wasn't. I could have turned a blind eye to Peter's exploits in Nigeria or joined him in his search for sexual adventure. But I hadn't. I could have agreed to a one-night stand with the handsome man from New Zealand who wanted a guilt-free long-distance affair. I hadn't. In addition, with Bill, I'd started to explore my spiritual side.

After I returned home from this camping trip, Bill contacted me to say he wanted to do something he had always longed to do—visit Britain. He planned to spend most of the time traveling and touring museums on his own, but his visit would let us see each other again. He'd only ever been out of the States once—to Banff, Alberta. He didn't have a passport, so his trip would have to wait until he applied for and received one, a process that would take months.

In the meantime, Alec, the Scot who'd called while I was camping, decided on the spur of the moment to drive his sporty red car south all the way from Falkirk, halfway between Glasgow and Edinburgh, to visit me. He and I had been e-mailing sporadically over a period of about six months, but all of a sudden, there he was on my doorstep. He had long, dark hair, was several years younger than me, and had a love of classical music. He stayed in my guest room. My son, Jamie, and his fiancé were visiting that weekend. Jamie declared Alec "pushy and overbearing."

Alec asked if we could visit Cambridge, as he'd never been there. It was his birthday, so I treated him to lunch at The Galleria, a favorite restaurant of mine that overlooked the Cam. Afterwards, we walked up and down the riverbank, taking photos. Before he left for his drive home, he invited me to come to Scotland to see his part of the world.

I felt awkward about this visit, as I knew that Bill was planning to come to see me as soon as he got his passport, but in September, I flew to Glasgow.

Alec didn't want to pick me up at the airport, so he instructed me to take the shuttle bus to the center of town, find the large Starbucks on the high street, and wait there for him.

When he arrived, he put his arms around me and pecked me on the cheek. "The car is this way," he said, walking quickly away. I followed, trundling my bag along the cobbled street. "We won't be going to my house," he explained.

Why? I wondered. Did he live with someone? Was it a mess? Was he ashamed of it?

"I want to take you north into the highlands to see the real

Scotland. Oh, here, this is the car," he said, pointing to a small blue compact. "I borrowed it for the weekend."

Our first stop was Colquhoun's restaurant, only a short drive north of the city, overlooking Loch Lomond. The waitress showed us to a table near a roaring fire. *Okay, well, maybe he's trying to make up for me having to find my own way into town by treating me to a meal in this lovely, historic restaurant.* I ordered roast pheasant with small white potatoes and a side salad. The whole-grain buns were made onsite. But Alec had no credit card. He asked if I could please pay for the very expensive meal.

We stopped at an ancient pub in a small village. I was thrilled at the opportunity to have a wee dram beside a field stone fireplace, sitting on a chair that'd been there from the time of Mary Queen of Scots. Wary when I wanted to sample the scotch, Alec muttered, "All right, just one." But no sooner than I had my drink in hand, he was already saying, "Okay, drink up quick then. Let's go now."

He wanted me to see the places that were important to him, but balked when I wanted to see nearby stone circles. Most of our day in Oban was spent shopping for a good white shirt for him. He had a wedding to photograph the following day and needed to look smart. We drove south to Inverkip. From the shore I could only glance long-ingly at the castles on the opposite coast. We had to go to the wedding.

When Alec left me at the Glasgow airport, he said that he might call me in January. It was September. *Okay,* I thought. *He's not interested.*

But I was wrong. A couple of weeks later, Alec called. He wanted to come to my son's wedding in December, and suggested that he take the pictures. I told him that only family members were invited to the wedding.

I didn't need another unsuitable man. I let Alec go without know-ing what would happen between Bill and me. It didn't matter. If things didn't work out with Bill, I was all right alone.

o o o

Bill came to England in October 2003. He told me that, when he went through British passport control, they'd asked him what the purpose of his visit was, and he'd replied, "Love."

He spent a few days with me at my house and then, while I worked on a consulting project with the Royal Mail, he took the train up to York on his own. He phoned while there and described the wall around York, the Roman museums with carved jet jewelry, and the Viking site in the middle of Old Jorvik. Then he confessed that he really wanted to explore with me rather than just have a quick visit to England.

He came back to my house by train, and on the weekend, I drove us to Tintagel, on the west coast of England, the legendary home of Arthur and the Round Table. We stayed in the huge Tintagel Hotel, visited the Witchcraft Museum in Boscastle, and saw magical wells and stone circles. Though we were having a wonderful time together, Bill stressed over and over again that he was only offering an affair, a fun sexual encounter, not a relationship. I'd had enough affairs to know I didn't want another. I told him I didn't want him if he wasn't at least open to the idea of a relationship.

When we returned to my home, Bill spent day after day at the British Museum in London while I worked. My mother and oldest son flew in at the end of November in preparation for Jamie's wedding in early December, so Bill met my mother, both sons, and my future daughter in law. They all liked him, and he was invited to join us at the wedding. My mom asked what we intended to do with Bill living in Hawaii and me here in England. I had no idea.

After the wedding, a week before Christmas, Bill and I drove to Ireland together. Bill knew about the sacred sites of Ireland and wanted to visit New Grange, a stone-age passage tomb, north of Dublin. We arrived there on a grey and dripping Winter Solstice afternoon, and found that it is precisely on that day that the light of the sunrise reaches right into the back of the chamber. A slender thread. Later we traveled to the Hill of Tara, where ancient Celtic kings and queens had been crowned. Bill took me to places that had been important to my Irish ancestors long before they sailed to make their new home in Canada. I'd been to Ireland many times, but I'd gone to oyster festivals and NLP workshops, sat in pubs and sung along with fiddlers. Not until Bill came along had I ever explored the ancient spiritual sites of my ancestors.

We were driving through a small village toward the end of our trip when Bill decided to tell me once again that, while he enjoyed spending time with me, he didn't want a relationship. "I'll never commit to anyone again," he said.

I stopped the car on the side of the road, lowered my head onto the steering wheel, and felt the weight of heavy tears come to my eyes. I needed some space. "Get out of the car!" I yelled.

Eyes wide, Bill complied and walked a little ways down the road.

All I could think was that he had deceived me. I'd asked him, again and again, before his visit, to only come to see me in England if he could remain open to whatever might happen. I had repeated the same while he was visiting. But once again, he was saying that he was closed—closed to the possibility of anything between us. I wanted reality in my life, not fantasy. Not an affair. Not another broken heart.

After a few minutes, Bill got back into the car and we drove back to England. The last week of his visit was awkward, but I was adamant that I would not settle for a life of short-term romance and long-term pain.

At the beginning of January, I said good-bye to Bill at Heathrow. As he turned and walked away from me, I had the feeling that I would never see him again. I accepted this more calmly than I ever thought I would. I walked back to my car and drove home.

◦ ◦ ◦

About two weeks after Bill left, I walked into my house and saw my post on the carpet. On the top was a thick envelope. With Bill's return address on the front.

I took the envelope into the kitchen and sat at the table. Slowly I opened the envelope, took out the pages-long letter, and read. The gist of it was this: *I want to take a chance on our relationship. I can't promise anything. I've been a failure at marriage and don't know if I have it in me to be a success. But with you perhaps there is a chance.*

I laid the letter on the table and spread my hands to smooth out the pages, almost as though I could feel the hard-won words, like Braille, under my fingertips. I sat quietly for some minutes trying to take it all in. I contemplated his message as I pictured the many hours this letter must have taken him to compose. Like the Fool in the tarot cards, he was stepping off the cliff in a leap of faith, trusting that I would catch him.

I remembered what Nick, that other man on the other nude beach in England, had said—that I shouldn't accept anything except exactly what I wanted. Now I had come to the crossroads where I could explore what I wanted with someone who was willing to explore with me. I wanted to see if my quest to get my life back included a real relationship, such as I had never known.

In the meantime, other things in my life had begun to unravel. After having withdrawn from the Ph.D. programme at Duncan's university, I'd applied again to do a PhD, but then realized that the woman who would supervise my research was someone I could not spend the next four years with. Also, I had no clear idea what research topic I wanted to pursue. There was no slender thread pointing me in that direction. Also, the management project I'd been involved with for nearly four months turned out to be a small disaster. We were working twelve-hour days but only getting paid for eight. Clark, the man in charge, didn't show up on time for meetings then expected us to stay up with him until all hours. The team finally met together for a clearing session, but the issues brought forward turned out to be more personal than about the project. Clark laughed and said that all his projects turned into therapy sessions, with people crying and running from the room. I was exhausted. When I realized I wouldn't get paid for some of the days I was contracted for, I quit. Was this another slender thread designed to confirm that this was not the life for me?

I phoned Bill to discuss his letter and to let him know that my project was finished, and he invited me to fly to the States so he could show me the Southwest. I agreed. I, too, it seemed, was ready to step off the cliff into uncertainty.

o o o

After we spent a month holidaying—traveling and camping together in Arizona—Bill stored his camper van and returned with me to England.

I decided to sell many of my things, put some in storage, and rent out my home in England to provide an income. Bill and I organized garage sales—quite a surprise for my English neighbors, who only sold things at car boot sales. I sold most of my designer pumps, suits, and floor-length gowns. Those that didn't sell, I donated to the local charity shop.

Bill built a small storage room in the corner of my finished garage so I could store the things I wanted to save—some antiques inherited from my grandparents, dishes and silver cutlery, carpets and art. With this arrangement, I could rent the house and store my valuables. A property company would handle the rental while I was gone. I wouldn't sell my house. While I was willing to try a new life, I wasn't willing to burn bridges.

o o o

Now that we had made the decision to see where our relationship might go, Bill and I needed to spend time together and really get to know each other. I flew to Phoenix and then on to Albuquerque. Bill had already returned to the States before me to get his van so he could meet me at the airport. In the green camper van that had served as his temporary home before he ever moved to Maui, we headed out to visit sites in New Mexico that were important to him.

We drove north to Jemez Hot Springs, where he'd bought property in his early twenties with his first wife, Sherry. He showed me the house he'd built in the same village with his second wife,

Lorraine, and subsequently sold. Adobe and stone, with a skylight in the kitchen and a full porch across the back, facing a full acre of garden, it was a beautiful home, now a B&B. But as soon as I went into the house, I felt as though I'd been punched in the stomach. I had to get out. The feeling of discomfort stayed with me for several hours as we visited Soda Dam and Spence Hot Springs, special places Bill had lived near for twenty-five years of his life. My feelings were a sign that something needed to be addressed, but at that point I didn't know what. However, I knew I was past the point in my life where I would ignore such messages.

Bill had had open marriages with both Sherry and Lorraine. Consensual agreements, in which each was free to pursue other relationships in any way they wanted. He confessed to me that he'd been increasingly depressed during that time and sought extra-marital relationships with more and more desperation. He explained that when he was in his twenties and thirties, he rationalized that he honored the women he had affairs with. They were lonely like him. Some of those relationships lasted years and even evolved into friendships. But the older he got, the more he grabbed at whatever sexual encounters he could to avoid feelings of emptiness and despair.

At the end of Bill's marriage to Lorraine, he felt that they were better off as friends than partners. But when he married his third wife, Sue, and moved to Ruidoso, New Mexico, she strongly objected to his ongoing friendship with Lorraine and asked him not to see her again. He did as she asked but resumed the friendship as soon as this marriage dissolved. Even when Bill first visited me in England, he would phone Lorraine to talk about England and about me.

On our drive south from Jemez to Ruidoso, we stopped in Truth or Consequences for me to meet her. She was a tiny woman with short dark hair and a trim figure, living in a small dog-eared house on the edge of a small dog-eared town, dry, dusty, and blistering hot in the summer. When we arrived, Lorraine immediately pulled out old photo albums with pictures of when she and Bill had been together. She engaged him in conversations about times and people from their past, leaving me completely out. The message was clear, "You may be here now, but I was here first."

To help pay the bills she'd been renting her living room to a couple who'd been driving around the country trying to find a place to call home. Shakti was a self-declared mystic and vegetarian who went one step too far with her landlady. She came out of the house, saw Lorraine on the front porch and made a joke at her expense. Lorraine didn't hesitate. She punched Shakti right in the face and the two women battled it out, trading punch for punch. Lorraine screamed at her tenants to, "Pack up and get out. Now."

Luckily, I had missed this incident, but Bill told me the story with a smile on his face.

"What's so funny about two middle-aged women in a fist fight?" I questioned.

Despite the fact that he'd ended the marriage because of her constant anger, Bill was so used to Lorraine's eccentricity, he had no sense of her inappropriateness. But I had lived with bullying and assault so I didn't find it funny at all. I went out to his van and sat inside. Bill opened the back door with a puzzled expression on his face. I looked him straight in the face and said, "I don't think this is going to work."

"Wait, yes, it will. You don't have to be friends with Lorraine. I want you to, but you don't have to. Come on, let's just leave."

We spent the last part of our trip in Ruidoso, in the southern part of the state, where Bill still owned a house he had shared with his third wife. He and I spent a month painting and cleaning to make it more saleable. I wasn't happy that I was helping clean up after her, but if it would speed up the process of us being together, I was willing to do it.

Finally, in September 2004, after his house sold, Bill and I boarded a plane and flew to Maui. We were filling out the landing cards while in descent over the Kahului airport, and in response to the question, "Number in party," I wrote "1." Bill looked at my card just as he wrote "2" on his.

"I thought we were a party of two," he said, a sad look on his face.

"Bill, this is an official government document we're filling out," I said. "We aren't married. I'm a party of one."

o o o

David had agreed to let us stay with him until we found an affordable rental house. We pitched a tent in his back garden and began to search the papers for properties to view.

One evening, we stopped and parked our car to sit on a beach in Kihei and watch the sunset. Bill looked at the ocean and then back at me. I had the feeling he was building up to ask me something important, so I turned the conversation to the flawless weather, the beautiful beaches, and Maui. I'd known from the time he said he thought we were a party of two that he was ready to fully commit, but I was still hesitant, even though we felt so right. I needed to get used to the idea. The moment passed.

Later that night, as we were settling back into our tent, Bill said, "I want to ask you something, though I thought we would have a more romantic setting." He paused. "Will you marry me?"

"Yes," I whispered.

Both of us had come a long way to end up in this tent, at this time, ready for this question. I had trusted the slender threads.

o o o

Bill and I were married on Keawakapu Beach in Wailea on October 21, 2004. As I held the gold band to put onto Bill's finger, I could just make out the inscription inside: "Party of Two."

Along with Sal, a close friend of Bill's, and David, Bill and I followed the ceremony with a gourmet dinner and a concert of Hawaiian-inspired music sung by Hapa at Mulligan's on the Blue. Barry Flanagan dedicated a song to us.

For the next eighteen months we lived the Hawaiian dream. We rented a small cottage in Kihei, searched for bamboo furniture to fill our space and Maui-themed pictures for the walls. Bill planted tiny palms in the adjacent garden beds while I cultivated orchids.

One night in our tiny home, as I lay safe at last in Bill's arms, one of my walls of silence broke down and thirty years of grief thundered out. For the first time I uttered to another person the whole horror of the assault I'd suffered at the hands of my first husband. I howled out the details of every punch, wailed out every whack as my head repeatedly hit the wall behind me, sputtered out my agony as the bone in my arm separated from the shoulder socket. I shuddered out my attempt at flight as Joe ran after me across the kitchen, shrieked my defeat as I fell and then knelt on the floor as he used my head as a punching bag, repeatedly hitting first one side of my head and then the other. I recalled my final scream at him to stop. Bill held me to him, trying to contain my tears and running nose, my red swollen face now soaking into the front of his shirt. He was shocked that what I revealed could have happened to the woman he loved.

In April 2005, we invited friends and family to come to Maui for a celebration of our marriage. That summer we honeymooned for a week on the Big Island.

But I was restless and homesick for Canada. I'd been away for over eleven years, first in England and now in the States. Also, though many people look on Maui as paradise, it was so hot that sometimes I felt as though I couldn't think. So in the summer of 2005, we flew to Arizona again, traded Bill's green van for an RV, and drove around the western states on our way north to Canada, exploring and trying to decide where we wanted to live. As we were soon to find out, our journey to happiness was not quite over.

We stopped in an out-of-the-way hippie campground at Mystic Hot Springs, Utah, run by a "Dead Head" who used to travel around the US following the Grateful Dead. The springs there have a continuous flow of hot water that fills green pools and bathtubs for individual soaks before it flows into the valley to form natural warm pools surrounded by green grass and waving trees. Bill and I soaked in this tranquil place, and then, while sitting on the edge of one of the hot pools, we argued about his ex-wife, Lorraine. He wanted to remain friends with her and still phoned her on a weekly basis.

Though Bill had told me they'd had an open relationship, we'd never discussed what that actually meant in detail. I'd known a married couple who'd had an open relationship for a short time. They'd been honest and respectful of each other's extra relationships and, after a year or so had decided it wasn't for them. They'd remained happily married.

But what Bill told me of the nature of his relationship with Lorraine disturbed me. They had discussed in detail all the sexual aspects of each other's lovers. They'd had threesomes with one of Lorraine's long-term lovers. Actively seeking other partners had been an everyday part of their relationship. When Bill had been successful in his pursuit of other women he'd felt momentarily worthwhile, alive, happy. When he hadn't been, he'd felt hurt, down, depressed, and empty.

Bill thought that if he were open and honest with me about all this it would bring us closer, but as I listened, I just felt more and more sick, as though I was in a strange land that I couldn't relate to, sinking into an abyss. The sexual activities Duncan and I had engaged in during the early part of our relationship came flooding back. When I'd gone into Bill and Lorraine's former home in Jemez Springs I'd felt as though I was being punched. Now I was finding out why. Perhaps I didn't really know him at all; had I made a mistake in marrying him?

During his third marriage—to Sue—he had reached a personal crisis and sat at the top of a hill near their home with a shotgun in his hands. He fought his way back from that cliff of despair, but remained unhappy, so he went to Santa Fe for nine months of intensive therapy. Initially he wanted to do this to save his marriage but while there, realized that he needed to know why he had tried to fill the empty emotional space in himself with physical love. He stuck with the therapy and at the end of the nine months reached a personal and spiritual sense of peace within himself. His marriage ended, but he had received the gift of healing—and had started his own journey toward wholeness. He'd met me on Little Beach two years into his single life.

All this fully explained Bill's initial hesitancy to get into another marriage, another committed relationship. But could I cope with his history? Even though I felt like a hypocrite, the pain within me wouldn't let go. Perhaps Bill's stories too accurately held a mirror up to me and forced me to look at my own solution to unhappiness—the obsessive pursuit of romantic relationships. Was he too much like me? But while he was open about his extra-marital relationships, I wanted to hide my sins behind a cloak of respectability.

Confused and hurting, I yelled at Bill all the way through Utah. Somewhere north of the Grand Canyon, I slept on the bed over the driver's seat in the RV while Bill slept on the couch. In the morning, I leaned over the edge of the bed and howled again. I would stop raising my voice for a while, then feel overwhelmed with emotion and start again.

On the way south to the Grand Canyon, Bill stopped the RV in the middle of nowhere. He walked to the back closet, took out a backpack, filled it with a few clothes, then brought out our stash of money and took half of it. He didn't talk, didn't look at me, just opened the door, stepped down from the RV, and stood there in the grass at the side of the road.

"That's it?" I said. "You tell me the sordid details of your life and then expect me just to accept it? With no time to make sense of any of this? You marry me and now you're leaving? Like that?"

"I'm afraid you'll never forget what I've told you and we'll never have a good relationship," he said quietly. "You won't ever let it go." Then he stood there in silence.

I felt the emptiness come crashing in on me. *Is this the end?*

But after a few minutes, Bill put his backpack back in the RV and agreed to stay. To see.

o o o

Perhaps I had forgotten that I wasn't the only one in the middle of trying to make my life work differently. Bill had wanted to reshape his life too—had left his wife, been to therapy, given up his work, his craft, and his home in New Mexico. And he'd also made the decision that he didn't do relationships very well. So he just shouldn't. But then he changed his mind for me.

Had I thought that I would solve all my own problems and then go out and find a perfect man, a man who had life all figured out?

The truth was, I didn't know yet what I could tolerate. But we were married now; I had made a commitment, and I had to see what would happen. He couldn't change his history any more than I could. Could I get past it?

I made many phone calls to Pam in the UK to discuss what was happening, without revealing too much of what Bill had told me about his life. I felt ashamed of him, and was afraid that I'd made a huge mistake and again fallen down the rabbit hole. She'd met him, had come to Maui for the wedding, had shared pub meals with us in England. Her advice was not to rush my decision, to wait and see. "You're right, his past life doesn't sound good, but he has so many good qualities," she said. "Don't panic. Give him a chance."

We traveled a few months more in the RV then went back to England at the end of 2005, so I could sell my house. While we were waiting on the house sale, we made some short trips to Greece and Rome. On one of those trips, as we flew over the Alps, I noticed that Bill was writing in his journal.

"What are you writing about?" I asked.

"Our relationship," he replied. "I see it as being about healing and travel."

"What about love? Don't you see it as being about love?" I was so quick to criticize. Healing and travel seemed so superficial to me, but I wasn't really paying attention to what he meant and what healing might mean for both of us. He listened to me—didn't yell, didn't bully, didn't punish. But every time I criticized, he looked defeated.

Sometimes we were fine together—exploring Venice, climbing over ruins on Rhodes—but then my doubts would come again in waves. When they hit the beach of my inner fears, I would sleep on the couch, feel worthless and betrayed, and, when back in England, go to see Dr. Z, my analyst.

"He lived a life of sexual indulgence, Karen, and he may slip again," Dr. Z said. "You may have to reconsider again and again until he is ready for a full relationship with full commitment. He really wasn't married before. Not in a true sense. This isn't just about someone accepting you; it is about you having the ability to accept another human being. Accept him for who he has been and who he is now."

Ironically, I was upset and embarrassed that Bill was being real with me, had told me the truth about himself, had revealed himself. Should he be judged for his past any more than I should? Was my challenge to realize that the things that had happened in his life, and mine, had all been steps along our journey to healing and a new life?

I'd followed the slender threads all the way from the book Duncan had left for me on our bookshelf in England to the opposite side of the globe, and Bill had appeared. He was my guru. The right man on the right nudist beach—kind, patient, and open to life. He'd lived on the island I'd felt an affinity for and, perhaps most importantly, had been in transition when I'd met him. Like me.

I'd spent my life judging myself and coming up short. I'd tried to appear perfect to the outside world, while bleeding on the inside— like my mother had—rather than being real. Now I could let all that go with a man who would be my partner, friend, lover, supporter, and companion.

Epilogue

I wanted to move back to Canada and Bill agreed as long as it was to a place that he felt an affinity for. We initially chose the interior of British Columbia—within driving distance of my sons in Calgary and in a very artistic, tolerant, laid back part of the world. But three years after moving back to Canada, and the arrival of two grandsons, we moved to Calgary to live close to them.

Today, Bill is "Grandpa" after never having been a father. He has a thriving Internet jewelry business and has expanded his designs to include ones we sell at highland games and music festivals, in addition to medieval reenactment events. He recently began acting as a background extra in a TV series. I, meanwhile, am involved with the jewelry business and spend time writing and volunteering in politics. Most recently I was asked to be on the board of an organization that provides peer support services to abused women.

I have learned that Bill is wiser than I knew, and he was right— our life *is* about healing and travel. We continue to make travel part of our lives. Since moving back to Canada, we've journeyed to Peru and Turkey, back to England, to the west coast of British Columbia, through the southern United States, and, of course, to our beloved Maui. We have both grown and healed in ways we could never have imagined when we first met, and have achieved an intimacy I could never allow myself with anyone before. I was too hurt, too frightened, too lacking in trust.

Faithfulness has never been a concern with Bill. When he said he wanted to commit to me, he meant it. We have been able to work through our differences with respect for each other's points of view, and rarely argue. In 2015, he and I will celebrate our eleventh anniversary. We truly are and plan to remain "a party of two."

In 1998 I went to my analyst to get my life back—but thank goodness I didn't. Instead, now I have a life I could never have imagined.

Acknowledgments

I want to thank the people who have made a difference in my life, who were there for me when I thought nothing would change or get better. My Jungian analyst, Dr. Z was a lifesaver, someone I could go to when the going got very rough. My husband Bill is my rock, my companion, my soul mate. My sons and stepson are strong, capable, and successful human beings. My mother and father did their best and loved me. My aunts and my grandmothers inspired me. Lastly, I can never be grateful enough to my friends Pam Francis, Nancy Anne, Peta Heskell, David Eirinberg, and the late Catherine Aymer for all their love and support.

About the Author

© William Guse

Karen E. Lee grew up in rural Southern Ontario, Canada, and is a retired clinical psychologist and management consultant. She has lived in Canada, England, and Hawaii. She received an undergraduate degree in 1970 in anthropology, worked in exploration geology in Toronto and Calgary, and in 1991 became a chartered psychologist in Alberta. She moved to England in 1995, where she lived and worked as an independent management consultant for ten years. Her consulting work and general interest have taken her to many different countries: the British Isles, France, Germany, Italy, the Netherlands, the Czech republic, Greece, Morocco, Egypt, Lebanon and Syria, Turkey, Peru, Nigeria, South Korea, Hong Kong, and Singapore. Today, she helps her husband, Bill, in his jewelry business, volunteers for political concerns, and is on the board of Peer Support Services for Abused Women (PSSAW). She and her husband live in Calgary, Alberta.

SELECTED TITLES FROM SHE WRITES PRESS

She Writes Press is an independent publishing company
founded to serve women writers everywhere.
Visit us at www.shewritespress.com.

Letting Go into Perfect Love: Discovering the Extraordinary After Abuse
by Gwendolyn M. Plano $16.95, 978-1-938314-74-2
After staying in an abusive marriage for twenty-five years, Gwen Plano
finally broke free—and started down the long road toward healing.

Loveyoubye: Holding Fast, Letting Go, And Then There's The Dog by
Rossandra White $16.95, 978-1-938314-50-6
A soul-searching memoir detailing the painful, but ultimately liberat-
ing, disintegration of a twenty-five-year marriage.

Insatiable: A Memoir of Love Addiction by Shary Hauer
$16.95, 978-1-63152-982-5
An intimate and illuminating account of corporate executive—and secret
love addict—Shary Hauer's migration from destructive to healthy love.

Uncovered: How I Left Hassidic Life and Finally Came Home by Leah Lax
$16.95, 978-1-63152-995-5
Drawn in their offers of refuge from her troubled family and promises
of eternal love, Leah Lax becomes a Hassidic Jew—but ultimately, as a
forty-something woman, comes to reject everything she has lived for
three decades in order to be who she truly is.

Where Have I Been All My Life? A Journey Toward Love and Wholeness
by Cheryl Rice $16.95, 978-1-63152-917-7
Rice's universally relatable story of how her mother's sudden death
launched her on a journey into the deepest parts of grief—and, ultimately, toward love and wholeness.

Seeing Red: A Woman's Quest for Truth, Power, and the Sacred by Lone Morch
$16.95, 978-1-938314-12-4
One woman's journey over inner and outer mountains—a quest that
takes her to the holy Mt. Kailas in Tibet, through a seven-year marriage,
and into the arms of the fierce goddess Kali, where she discovers her
powerful, feminine self.